In Defense of Judicial Elections

One of the most contentious issues in politics today is the propriety of electing judges. Should judges be independent of democratic processes in obtaining and retaining their seats, or should they be subject to the approval of the electorate and the processes that accompany popular control? While this debate is interesting and often quite heated, it usually occurs without reference to empirical facts—or at least accurate ones. Also, empirical scholars to date have refused to take a position on the normative issues surrounding the practice.

Bonneau and Hall offer a fresh new approach. Using almost two decades of data on state supreme court elections, Bonneau and Hall argue that opponents of judicial elections have made—and continue to make—erroneous empirical claims. The authors show that judicial elections are efficacious mechanisms that enhance the quality of democracy and create an inextricable link between citizens and the judiciary. In doing so, they pioneer the use of empirical data to shed light on these normative questions and offer a coherent defense of judicial elections. This provocative book is essential reading for anyone interested in the politics of judicial selection, law and politics, or the electoral process.

Chris W. Bonneau is Associate Professor of Political Science at the University of Pittsburgh.

Melinda Gann Hall is Distinguished Professor of Political Science at Michigan State University.

Controversies in Electoral Democracy and Representation
Matthew J. Streb, Series Editor

The Routledge series *Controversies in Electoral Democracy and Representation* presents cutting-edge scholarship and innovative thinking on a broad range of issues relating to democratic practice and theory. An electoral democracy, to be effective, must show a strong relationship between representation and a fair open election process. Designed to foster debate and challenge assumptions about how elections and democratic representation *should* work, titles in the series will present a strong but fair argument on topics related to elections, voting behavior, party and media involvement, representation, and democratic theory.

Titles in the series:

Rethinking American Electoral Democracy
Matthew J. Streb

Redistricting and Representation: Why competitive elections are bad for America
Thomas L. Brunell

Fault Lines: Why the Republicans lost Congress
Edited by Jeffery J. Mondak and Dona-Gene Mitchell

In Defense of Judicial Elections
Chris W. Bonneau and Melinda Gann Hall

Forthcoming:

Can Presidential Primaries Be Reformed?
Barbara Norrander

In Defense of Judicial Elections

Chris W. Bonneau
University of Pittsburgh

Melinda Gann Hall
Michigan State University

NEW YORK AND LONDON

First published 2009
by Routledge
270 Madison Ave, New York, NY 10016

Simultaneously published in the UK
by Routledge
2 Park Square, Milton Park, Abingdon, Oxon OX14 4RN

Routledge is an imprint of the Taylor & Francis Group, an informa business

© 2009 Taylor & Francis

Typeset in Gill Sans and Galliard by Prepress Projects Ltd, Perth, UK
Printed and bound in the United States of America on acid-free paper
by Walsworth Publishing Company, Marceline, MO

All rights reserved. No part of this book may be reprinted or reproduced or utilised in any form or by any electronic, mechanical, or other means, now known or hereafter invented, including photocopying and recording, or in any information storage or retrieval system, without permission in writing from the publishers.

Trademark Notice: Product or corporate names may be trademarks or registered trademarks, and are used only for identification and explanation without intent to infringe.

Library of Congress Cataloging in Publication Data
Bonneau, Chris W.
In defense of judicial elections/Chris W. Bonneau, Melinda Gann Hall.
p. cm.—(Controversies in electoral democracy and representation)
Includes bibliographical references and index.
KF8776.B66 2009
347.73'14—dc22
2009012360

ISBN10: 0-415-99132-3 (hbk)
ISBN10: 0-415-99133-1 (pbk)
ISBN10: 0-203-87699-7 (ebk)

ISBN13: 978-0-415-99132-2 (hbk)
ISBN13: 978-0-415-99133-9 (pbk)
ISBN13: 978-0-203-87699-2 (ebk)

To Heather Rice . . . my person.

Chris W. Bonneau

To Tony Duce . . . the love of my life.

Melinda Gann Hall

Contents

Figures

Tables

Acknowledgments

In the process of writing this book, we incurred many debts, both personal and intellectual. We (individually and collectively) would like to express our sincere thanks to the following individuals, without whom we could not have completed this project.

Chris Bonneau thanks the Department of Political Science at the University of Pittsburgh for providing a supportive, collegial environment as well as material support. He would also like to thank Traci Nelson, Brent Dupay, and Brandon Myers for their excellent research assistance. Robin Wolpert was a fantastic resource for chapter 5 on Wisconsin and Minnesota (as was State Representative Steve Simon). Chris also benefited from the helpful comments of Brent Boyea and Damon Cann at various stages of this project. Finally, Heather Rice, to whom Chris owes more than he could ever repay, allowed him to bounce ideas off her and showed incredible love and patience throughout this project. Her contributions, although difficult to quantify, were invaluable.

Melinda Gann Hall acknowledges the generous support of Michigan State University, particularly Richard Hula (Chair, Department of Political Science), Marietta Baba (Dean, College of Social Science), Kim Wilcox (Provost), and Lou Anna Simon (President). Also at MSU, she thanks Darren Davis for being a terrific colleague who discussed and encouraged this work. Melinda also benefited from the helpful comments of Tom Carsey, Herbert Kritzer, Laura Langer, and Ronald Weber at various stages of this project. Melinda is grateful to the members (especially Chris Mooney) of the State Politics and Policy Section of the American Political Science Association for outstanding conferences that contributed to this work and for providing an intellectually rich and highly collegial intellectual community. Melinda's career-long fascination with state judicial politics really began in 1983 when all of the justices of the Louisiana Supreme Court agreed to grant an earnest graduate student a series of personal interviews. For the few days of absorbing conversation and years of work inspired by those discussions, Melinda expresses sincere gratitude and abiding respect for Justices Fred A. Blanche, Pascal F. Calogero, James L. Dennis, John

A. Dixon, Harry T. Lemmon, Walter F. Marcus, and Jack Crozier Watson. On a much more personal level, she is deeply grateful to Anthony R. Duce (Tony) for his unwavering love, encouragement, and (especially) patience. Tony is the perfect partner in every possible way.

Together, we sincerely thank Matt Streb for encouraging us to write this book and for many exciting and productive conversations about the politics of judicial elections. Michael Kerns, our editor at Routledge, was incredibly helpful (as well as patient!) throughout this process, as was his editorial assistant Felisa Salvago-Keyes. We also thank the Richard D. and Mary Jane Edwards Endowed Publication Fund at the School of Arts & Sciences at the University of Pittsburgh for financial assistance in compiling the index to this book.

As an important matter, we must be very clear that, although many family, friends, and colleagues contributed to this project, we alone are responsible for the arguments presented throughout the chapters. In no way do we represent the views of others and, in fact, we think it a very safe bet that many would vigorously disagree with the arguments presented in this book.

We also want to be emphatically clear that the arguments we present in this book are about state courts only. We certainly are not suggesting that federal judges should be elected or subject to democratic processes. The differences in the roles of state and federal courts are both formally mandated and obvious in a federation.

Finally, although much in this book is new, earlier versions of portions of this book previously appeared in print or are forthcoming. Some of the basic arguments about the judicial reform movement and merits of electing judges will appear as an article by Hall, "The Controversy Over Electing Judges and Advocacy in Political Science" in the *Justice System Journal* (2009) and as a paper presented at the "What's Law Got to Do With It?" Conference at the Indiana University School of Law in March 2009, based on roundtable presentations at the 2008 Midwest and American Political Science Association meetings. A form of chapter 2 appeared as an article by Hall, "Voting in State Supreme Court Elections: Competition and Context as Democratic Incentives" in the *Journal of Politics* (November 2007); and Hall and Bonneau "Mobilizing Interest: The Effects of Money on Citizen Participation in State Supreme Court Elections" in the *American Journal of Political Science* (July 2008). Parts of chapter 3 first appeared as an article written by Bonneau, "What Price Justice(s)? Understanding Campaign Spending in State Supreme Court Elections" in *State Politics and Policy Quarterly* (Summer 2005). Earlier versions of portions of chapter 4 were published as Hall, "State Supreme Courts in American Democracy: Probing the Myths of Judicial Reform," *American Political Science Review* (June 2001); Hall and Bonneau, "Does Quality Matter? Challengers in State Supreme Court Elections," *American Journal of Political*

Science (January 2006); Bonneau, "The Effects of Campaign Spending in State Supreme Court Elections," *Political Research Quarterly* (September 2007); and Hall, "Competition as Accountability in State Supreme Court Elections," in Streb, ed., *Running for Judge* (2007). Finally, parts of chapter 6 appeared as an essay by Bonneau "Judicial Elections: Facts vs. Myths" in *The Rule of Law: Perspectives on Legal and Judicial Reform in West Virginia* (2009); and Hall, "The Controversy Over Electing Judges and Advocacy in Political Science," *Justice System Journal* (2009).

Because the chapters in this study draw from different time periods and analyze different subsets of elections, the numbers of cases will vary across chapters. For example, in chapter 2 we examine ballot roll-off, which causes us to exclude any elections that did not occur simultaneously with a presidential, senatorial, or gubernatorial election. In chapter 3, we examine campaign spending, looking at all elections regardless of when they were held. And in chapter 4 we examine incumbent–challenger races only, excluding open-seat contests. All of these choices are highly appropriate methodologically speaking but might cause some initial confusion for readers just looking at the tables. We have done our best to clarify exactly what is being examined in each chapter, and why. Along these lines and consistent with standard practice, we include odd-year elections with the previous even-year election cycle in the descriptive statistics.

This book is the culmination of over a decade of thinking and writing about judicial elections together. When we first started collaborating on this topic, there were few who thought judicial elections were worthy of scholarly attention. Now, judicial elections are occupying increasing amounts of time on the agendas of legislatures, the media, and academic journals and presses. This book represents the most comprehensive, systematic examination of state supreme court elections that we (or others) have ever undertaken. Although we started out agnostic about the merits of electing judges, the evidence we present here (and elsewhere) has convinced us that judicial elections certainly are as efficacious as elections to other political offices in the United States, and that any objections to electing judges cannot be made on empirical grounds. Of course, we hope that many other political scientists and legal scholars will begin to study judicial elections systematically as we do, and will bring much more evidence to the table for discussion of this critical and enduring issue.

Chapter 1

The Controversy over Electing Judges

In a recent op-ed piece in the *Wall Street Journal*, Sandra Day O'Connor, a retired Associate Justice of the United States Supreme Court, lamented the current state of affairs in American state judiciaries. Referring primarily to the rising costs of campaigns for the state court bench, Justice O'Connor wrote that interest groups "pouring money" into judicial elections "threaten the integrity of judicial selection and compromise public perceptions of judicial decisions."[1] Of course, Justice O'Connor is not alone in her concerns. The American Bar Association has produced a report entitled *Justice in Jeopardy*, which explicitly calls for the eradication of judicial elections. According to the American Bar Association, "[w]hatever its historic rationale there can no longer be justification for contested judicial elections accompanied by 'attack' media advertising that require infusions of substantial sums of money."[2] Joining Justice O'Connor and the American Bar Association are many of the nation's most influential court reform advocacy groups, including the National Center for State Courts, and a veritable throng of legal scholars in the nation's leading law schools. In short, there is an increasingly loud clamor in the United States to end the election of judges altogether.

With what appears to be a full-scale war being waged against judicial elections, especially partisan elections, there are few issues on the American political agenda more pressing today than the propriety of electing judges. Should judges be independent of democratic processes in obtaining and retaining their seats, or should they be subject to the approval of the electorate and the processes that accompany that control?

Many opponents of judicial elections rely primarily on arguments about the importance of judicial independence in American democracy to bolster their claims. These opponents start with the premise that judges are not like legislators or executives because judges are constrained by law and do not make overtly political judgments. From this perspective, the very nature of judging would dictate that judges be insulated from public pressures, including electoral politics. Critics of judicial elections also question whether citizens are capable of assessing judicial qualifications or are willing to participate in selection and retention processes. As Justice O'Connor asserts, "[v]oters generally don't express much interest in the election of judges." Part of the contention is that special interest activity and negative advertising will discourage voters from participating and will sway them against incumbents for arbitrary reasons, resulting in harmful consequences for judges or courts.

On the other side of the issue are proponents of electing judges, who rely primarily on arguments about the value of accountability and who recognize the inherently political nature of judicial decision making. Mostly a small handful of social scientists, these observers argue that, like other public officials, judges have considerable discretion and should be held accountable for their choices, at least at the state level where we would expect a close connection between public preferences and public policy, as well as significant variations in law across the states. They also challenge the negative portrait of judicial elections, citing evidence that indicates instead that judicial elections bear a striking resemblance to other types of elections and in some ways are the prototype for what elections should be in the United States. Moreover, elections generally are one of the most powerful legitimacy-conferring institutions in American democracy and should serve to balance if not counteract other negative features associated with campaigns.

Although this debate about independence and accountability is important and interesting, the public dialogue often is approached from a normative perspective without reference to facts, or at least accurate ones. For example, one of the leading attacks on judicial elections is the claim that voters know nothing about the candidates so that elections are decided by irrelevant, idiosyncratic factors such as candidates' names.[3] If true, this claim would strike at the heart of the argument favoring judicial elections and their ability to achieve any level of accountability in practice. After all, if voters have no idea what they are doing when selecting among candidates for state courts or are easily manipulated by campaign advertisements, then what is the point of having elections at all? The key *caveat*, though, is *if true*.

In this book we argue that, contrary to the claims of judges,[4] professional legal organizations,[5] interest groups,[6] and legal scholars,[7] judicial elections are democracy-enhancing institutions that operate efficaciously and serve to create a valuable nexus between citizens and the bench. We argue that, rather than being eradicated, judicial elections should be retained if not restored to their original form of partisan, competitive races, the situation that existed before modern reform advocates convinced the states to remove partisan labels and challengers from these contests. In making this argument, we rely on data on all state supreme court elections from 1990 through 2004. Overall, we find that many of the claims made by opponents of judicial elections are at best overstated and are at worst demonstrably false. In doing so, we briefly review the literature documenting the political nature of judicial choice and the naïveté of those who rely on normative, outmoded accounts of the judicial process.

This is a particularly timely topic for many different reasons, but perhaps most important is the changing nature of supreme court elections themselves in many states and the aggressive attacks from legal circles that these elections are drawing. As anyone knows who lives in a state where judges are elected, these races recently have become much more competitive and controversial,[8] although a number of states have experienced competitive supreme court elections for decades.[9] Even so, as these contests (particularly nonpartisan elections) have begun to look more like elections to other political offices in a growing number of states, fervor is rising from the legal community and advocacy organizations to eliminate them. In other words, judicial elections initially were opposed because challengers did not enter these races, incumbents rarely were defeated, and voters did not participate; now judicial elections are sharply criticized because the opposite is the case.[10]

In fact, judicial reform advocates have enjoyed two recent successes. In 2002, Arkansas stopped selecting judges in partisan elections and started choosing them in nonpartisan elections. Similarly, North Carolina abandoned partisan elections in 2004 for nonpartisan elections and initiated public financing to candidates who qualify. We will have much more to say about these states and their reforms in chapter 5. For now, it is worth noting that Arkansas and North Carolina have joined a sizable number of states that have modified judicial selection procedures over the past several decades in response to the dire prediction from judicial reformers that partisan elections will lead to the demise of state judiciaries. In total, thirteen states have abandoned partisan elections for nonpartisan elections (Arkansas, Georgia, Kentucky, Mississippi, North Carolina), the Missouri Plan (Colorado, Florida, Indiana, Iowa, Oklahoma, Tennessee, Utah), or gubernatorial appointment (New York), whereas New Mexico has adopted a hybrid plan of partisan elections for first-term candidates but retention elections for subsequent terms, much like the selection systems in Montana and Pennsylvania. Additionally, four states (Arizona, Nebraska, South Dakota, Wyoming) have switched from nonpartisan elections to the Missouri Plan, and Minnesota currently is considering following suit. If reform advocates are successful in Minnesota, then nineteen of the fifty states (38 percent) will have changed the way they elect judges, all in response to claims about the deleterious effects of partisan elections (and now nonpartisan elections) on American state judiciaries.[11]

As we will show, these changes in the ways judges are selected and retained have predictable consequences for the efficacy of elections in those states and the operations of the court systems themselves—consequences that those advocating reform of the electoral system may not have intended or anticipated. We also will show that many of the most pressing concerns about the ills of judicial elections are not grounded in empirical reality.

That is our task in this book. We will use extensive data on state supreme court elections to examine systematically and empirically a number of critical questions relevant to the judicial elections controversy. Are voters willing to participate in the selection of judges, and under what conditions are citizens best mobilized? Do challengers randomly target incumbents or are there systematic forces that draw challengers into the electoral arena? What is the role of money in these races? Do expensive campaigns alienate voters to the point that they will not participate, and can incumbents or challengers simply buy supreme court seats? And, perhaps most importantly, what do voters appear to know when casting ballots in elections to the state high court bench? Are elections simply games of chance or manipulation by interest groups and other big spenders in judicial elections, or can we understand the electoral performance of incumbents in systematic ways that are indicative of rational political choices by challengers and the electorate?

Electing Judges in Historical Perspective

Understanding the history of electing judges is a necessary first step in evaluating the current controversy and the overall record of the court reform movement. Without question, choosing judges through democratic processes is an almost uniquely American and, historically speaking, relatively modern phenomenon.[12]

Consider judicial selection methods operating at the beginning of the nation's history. At the nation's founding, the states selected their judges much like their former British rulers: judges were appointed for lifetime terms, although there often were provisions for impeachment.[13] In some states, legislatures made these appointments, and in other states governors did, but generally the selection of state court judges paralleled the selection of federal judges.[14]

Originally, judges were selected in this way because the judiciary was considered a weak institution without the power to reach important political judgments and thus was in no need of close public scrutiny. Moreover, courts were extremely deferential to legislatures because courts were heavily dependent on the other branches for appointment and, where lifetime terms were not granted, reappointment.[15]

Interestingly, selection schemes in which judges are appointed are being touted in today's political dialogue as promoting independence from the electorate and other political actors. As the argument goes, judges should be free to make decisions independent of as many constraints and political factors as possible. When the ability to serve is not conditioned on winning elections, judges should be free to rule in the cases before their courts using legal criteria (such as the facts of the case, the law, and precedent) rather than fear about how the public will react or other factors irrelevant to the actual cases.[16]

It is important to note that proponents of appointment schemes in the contemporary sense are not really arguing for complete independence from all political actors. After all, judges who are appointed and need to be reappointed can hardly be said to be independent from the appointing authority (legislature, governor, or both). Thus, the independence argument really is an argument for independence *from the electorate*. Indeed, states now providing lifetime tenure for judges are the rare exception (see Table 1.1), and judges who are dependent upon the governor or the legislature for reappointment are far from independent in the strictest sense. Arguably, appointed judges who make decisions that are contrary to the policy preferences of the actor (or actors) who has (have) the power to reappoint them could be subject to the same severe sanction (i.e., expulsion from the bench) as elected judges who make decisions contrary to the preferences of the electorate. In fact, this dependence on the legislature or governor (the *lack* of independence of judges) was one of the reasons to move *away* from the appointment of judges to elections in the first place.[17]

Contemporary evidence drawn from the abortion controversy confirms the concerns about the lack of independence from the other political institutions in appointive systems. Brace, Hall, and Langer established that systems in which elites control retention can inhibit the exercise of judicial review, at least in the context of abortion litigation.[18] Specifically, supreme court justices subject to retention by legislatures or governors are much less likely to docket constitutional challenges to restrictive abortion statutes, *ceteris paribus*. Broadly speaking, the willingness of courts to be active participants in the checks and balances system appears to be conditioned by judicial independence from the other branches of government.[19]

The appointment of judges was common until about 1830 and the rise of Jacksonian democracy (and demise of the Federalists). "Jacksonian democracy meant that the average citizen could not only use the extended franchise to pick his leaders, but he could share responsibility for governing."[20] In terms of courts, this philosophy led to reforms to elect judges and to provide incumbents with shorter terms of office.

There were three primary reasons why judicial elections gained popularity. First, there was the manner in which judicial review was being exercised. Because judges were invalidating laws enacted by legislatures and in the process were making some of the states' most important political decisions, it was argued that judges should be chosen by the electorate just like the legislature.[21] Second, the legal profession widely hailed the movement toward an elected judiciary as "an opportunity to provide the judiciary with its own separate constituency, thus ensuring it some

Table 1.1 Selection Systems for State Supreme Courts, 2007

Partisan	*Term*	*Nonpartisan*	*Term*	*Retention*	*Term*	*Appointment*	*Term*
Alabama	6	Arkansas	8	Alaska	10	Connecticut	8
Illinois*	10	Georgia	6	Arizona	6	Delaware	12
Louisiana	10	Idaho	6	California	12	Hawaii	10
New Mexico*	8	Kentucky	8	Colorado	10	Maine	7
Pennsylvania*	10	Michigan**	8	Florida	6	Massachusetts	Life
Texas	6	Minnesota	6	Indiana	10	New Hampshire	5
West Virginia	12	Mississippi	8	Iowa	8	New Jersey	Life
		Montana***	8	Kansas	6	New York	14
		Nevada	6	Maryland	10	Rhode Island	Life
		North Carolina	8	Missouri	12	South Carolina	10
		North Dakota	10	Nebraska	6	Vermont	6
		Ohio**	6	Oklahoma	6	Virginia	12
		Oregon	6	South Dakota	8		
		Washington	6	Tennessee	8		
		Wisconsin	10	Utah	10		
				Wyoming	8		

Source: Melinda Gann Hall, 2007b. "Courts and Judicial Politics in the American States." In *Politics in the American States: A Comparative Analysis*, ed. by Virginia Gray and Russell L. Hanson. Washington, DC: Congressional Quarterly Press. based on data reported by the American Judicature Society (2006).
* Initially selected in partisan elections but by retention elections for subsequent terms.
** Partisan affiliations not listed on general election ballots but partisan methods (partisan caucus, partisan primary) used to nominate candidates.
*** Retention election if the incumbent is unopposed.

measure of independence from the legislature."[22] It was believed that, as an independent branch of government, the judiciary should not be an agent of the legislature. Third, popular elections allowed for the removal of incompetent and arrogant judges. Although judges could be impeached under appointive schemes, impeachment was regarded as too drastic a punishment for most forms of judicial misconduct or incompetence and thus was used sparingly.[23] In this regard, the grounds for impeachment were quite limited.

Of course, the primary motivation for electing judges was the recognition that judges are important political actors and as such should derive their power from the people and not from a co-equal branch of government.[24] Indeed, the process of elections is the only process that can make judges completely independent from the legislature and governor. Further, competitive elections promote accountability: judges, like legislators, must answer to the electorate for their choices. Overall, we would expect judges chosen by democratic processes to reflect the political preferences of their states at the time they are chosen but also to be brought into line with the dominant coalition in the state by threat of electoral sanction.

An example relevant to today's debate is instructive. Thirty-eight states in the United States currently authorize the death penalty as a sanction for certain categories of murder, and the United States Supreme Court has held that the death penalty per se does not run afoul of federal constitutional protections. Generally, we would expect judges in those states to uphold death sentences in the cases before their courts except in the case of reversible error at trial. But what about a judge who refuses to uphold the death penalty because of her own political preferences opposing capital punishment? In this situation, the judge would be disregarding the rule of law and specific mandates enacted by representative institutions reflecting public will. Should this judge be allowed to continue in office? Whereas it would be difficult to remove this renegade judge in an appointive system (i.e., voting "wrong" is not an impeachable offense or misconduct in the usual sense), voters in elective states could do so in the next election.[25]

Critics of judicial elections make two central arguments. First, they claim that judges should not be subject to electoral sanction because judging is not an intrinsically political act like legislating.[26] Second, opponents of judicial elections argue that even if electing judges were not *de facto* inappropriate, judicial elections are ineffective in their current form. Specifically,

> [r]eformers argue that partisan elections, characterized by lackluster campaigns devoid of issue content, are disconnected from substantive evaluations of candidates or other meaningful considerations relevant to the judiciary, which renders them ineffective as a means of accountability.[27]

In other words, the debate over whether judges should, or should not, be independent from the electorate is irrelevant if elections fail to provide an efficacious means by which voters can engage in the judicial selection and retention process and make meaningful evaluations of candidates, including incumbent judges. The increasingly competitive and expensive nature of judicial elections only exacerbates these concerns.

In response to criticisms like these, judicial elections have undergone two significant transformations since the 1830s. The first was a transition from partisan to nonpartisan elections in a significant number of states. With partisan elections for judgeships, there were allegations of corruption and control of the bench by political machines.[28] Around 1900, Progressives began pushing for the removal of the partisan affiliations of the candidates from ballots for many political offices in the United States, including judicial elections. In nonpartisan elections, candidates run in competitive elections just like any other but ballots do not include the partisan affiliations of the candidates. Supporters of nonpartisan elections argue that they provide for electoral accountability while insulating judges from the vagaries and vicissitudes of partisan tides. Thus, in nonpartisan elections, voters have the formal power to remove judges from office, but these decisions will not be based on partisan ballot cues that might cause a judge to be ousted simply for belonging to the wrong political party. This reform also reduced the ability of political parties to control the selection of judges by not allowing political parties to nominate candidates. By removing the most overtly partisan features of elections, reform advocates hoped that more highly qualified jurists would be elected to the bench and that voters would make judgments based on the objective qualifications of the candidates instead of their partisan ties.[29]

The consequences of removing partisan labels from ballots in judicial elections were palpable: these races became much less competitive and citizen participation plummeted.[30] By taking a crucial piece of information away from voters, nonpartisan ballots dramatically reduced voter turnout and the presence of challengers, thereby strengthening the incumbency advantage. Thus, not only were judges in nonpartisan elections independent from the legislature (because they are elected), they were less accountable to the electorate (because of the strength of the incumbency advantage).

A second reform, first proposed around 1913 and also attracting the support of a number of states formerly using partisan elections, is the Missouri Plan, or "merit selection." This reform purports to combine the best features of appointed (independence) and elected (accountability) schemes. There are several variations of the Missouri Plan, but most commonly a judge initially is appointed by the governor from a list of candidates submitted by a nominating commission, and serves for a period of time (usually one or two years) before facing voters in a retention election.

On the ballot, voters are asked, "Should Judge X be retained?" If the judge receives more "yes" votes than "no" votes, the judge then begins a fixed term of office (six to twelve years, depending on the state) before facing the voters again to win another term. If the judge is defeated, the governor fills the vacancy just as she did originally and the election process begins anew. Like nonpartisan elections, the Missouri Plan was designed to ensure a more qualified bench and remove political considerations from selecting judges.

Of the various election schemes, the Missouri Plan is the system that gives the judges by far the maximum independence from the legislature and the electorate. Once appointed, judges are not dependent on the legislature (or governor) for reappointment. Further, because judges run unopposed for retention, they also are, according to all concrete indicators, independent from the electorate. For example, from 1980 through 2000, the average percentage of the vote to retain incumbents was 71.5 percent,[31] a striking proportion given that competitive elections generally are defined as those won with 55 to 60 percent of the vote or less. Moreover, judges in retention elections rarely lose, another notable contrast to other judicial and non-judicial statewide elections in the United States. Specifically, only 6 of 327 (1.8 percent) incumbents lost their bids for retention between 1980 and 2000.[32] Of course, one might be tempted to conclude that judges chosen by the Missouri Plan rarely are ousted because the system ensures that these judges are highly qualified and thus perform well. However, this is an implausible scenario. In fact, there are no measurable differences in qualifications between judges chosen by the Missouri Plan and other methods of judicial selection, including partisan elections.[33]

In sum, judicial reform advocacy has evolved over time from preferring that judges be independent from the electorate but highly dependent on the legislature and governor (appointive systems with fixed terms), to being accountable to the electorate and independent from the legislature and governor (partisan elections), to being independent from the legislature, the governor, and the electorate (the Missouri Plan and, to a lesser extent as we will discuss, nonpartisan elections).

Table 1.1 categorizes the states according to the methods in operation today for choosing supreme court justices. As the table indicates, partisan elections have become the rarity; only seven states use partisan elections today to select and retain the high court bench, compared with twenty states in 1960.[34] Instead, the Missouri Plan and nonpartisan elections dominate, and there is a continuing push toward appointive systems or the Missouri Plan in states where there is little likelihood that voters will completely relinquish their control over the selection process to political elites.

A Note on Institutional Variations in Election Systems across the States

In addition to the methods by which judges are selected and retained, the states vary considerably in the exact ways in which elections are conducted, constituencies are constituted, and terms of office are held. Table 1.2 displays several of these important features for the thirty-eight states using some form of elections to select their supreme courts. As the table indicates, terms of office for state supreme courts range from six to twelve years. Similarly, most supreme court justices are elected from statewide constituencies but a small handful of states (Illinois, Kentucky, Louisiana, Maryland, Mississippi, Nebraska) prefer district-based constituencies. Likewise, the large majority of geographic constituencies are single member, but three states (Michigan, Pennsylvania, West Virginia) hold multimember elections for at least some seats. Finally, most states hold supreme court elections during the normal national election cycle, but six states (Arkansas, Idaho, Kentucky, Louisiana, Pennsylvania, Wisconsin) time their supreme court elections to be either in off years or in the same year as the national election cycle but earlier than November.

These variations in the ways in which elections are conducted and constituencies are structured are important for two reasons. First, these institutional arrangements play a major role in influencing the behavior of judges in significant and measurable ways.[35] Second, these institutional arrangements affect the way judicial elections actually operate in practice and the extent to which accountability can or cannot be achieved.[36] We discuss both of these topics in considerable detail in the chapters to follow.

The Current Landscape of Judicial Elections

Without question, judicial elections in recent years have become much more interesting and now attract challengers, big money, and the attention of voters. In fact, in many ways judicial elections can be understood in much the same way as elections to other branches of government.[37] This was not always the case; for decades judicial elections in many states were low-information, low-salience affairs that went largely unnoticed by both the public and by scholars.[38]

However, those days are long gone. Today's supreme court elections in most states involve strong challengers, narrower margins of victory, and expensive campaigns. For instance, three of every four incumbents seeking reelection in partisan and nonpartisan elections were challenged from 1996 through 2000, but the rate is over 90 percent in partisan elections.[39] Similarly, incumbents are winning by narrower margins. From 1980 through 1990, the average percentage of the vote received by incumbents in nonpartisan elections was 82.4 percent but dropped to 72.3 percent from 1992 through 2000. Similarly, incumbents in partisan elections averaged 73.3 percent of the vote from 1980 through 1990 but only 61.8 percent from 1992 through 2000.[40] At the same time, campaign spending has increased steadily,[41] whether one measures spending in actual or constant dollars, and whether one looks at all races, partisan races, or nonpartisan races. For instance, the average contested supreme court election in 1990 cost $364,348 but in 2004 cost $711,867 (in constant dollars). The days of low-key, uninteresting, and anonymous races are over, at least for most partisan and nonpartisan elections to the states' highest courts.

This has not gone unnoticed by opponents of elections, state legislatures, and the public at large. Both the American Bar Association[42] and the National Center for State Courts[43] released reports calling for the eradication of judicial elections; minimally, they suggest radical overhauls in the conduct of these elections. As mentioned, these efforts have had some successes. Arkansas and North Carolina recently switched from partisan to nonpartisan elections. North Carolina also implemented a full public financing plan, with twenty of twenty-eight candidates (71 percent) for the Supreme Court or Court of Appeals qualifying for the program in the 2004 and 2006 elections.[44] Minnesota currently is considering the Quie Commission's recommendation that nonpartisan elections be scrapped for retention elections.[45] Finally, Wisconsin recently held a special legislative session to consider a call from the Wisconsin Supreme Court for meaningful public financing of all judicial elections in the state.[46]

These examples illustrate well that the debate about judicial elections and their possible eradication is more than an academic exercise. Rather, electing judges is a topic occupying significant space on the political agendas of several states, and the rather remarkable concern is that judicial elections finally are operating like elections instead of the sleepy manifestation of the incumbency advantage of prior decades. In this discussion, the stakes for democratic control of the state court bench are very high.

On the Nature of Judicial Choice

Two fundamental propositions grounded solidly in the empirical literature on courts underlie the arguments in this book: (1) that judges in courts of last resort are important political actors with considerable discretion to shape judicial decisions to their personal preferences and (2) that judges are constrained in their ability to pursue their own agendas by various strategic contingencies that provide rewards and sanctions for individual conduct. Both of these principles are essential tenets of modern judicial politics scholarship and have been documented extensively.

Starting with the strong foundations provided by the legal realists and path-breaking political scientists like C. Herman Pritchett and Glendon Schubert, scholars have challenged the validity of traditional, normative

Table 1.2 State Supreme Court Election Features, 2007

State	*Election Type*	*Term of Office*	*Electoral Constituency*	*Seat Structure*	*Odd Time*
Alabama	Partisan	6	Statewide	Single-member	No
Alaska	Retention	10	Statewide	Single-member	No
Arizona	Retention	6	Statewide	Single-member	No
Arkansas	Nonpartisan	8	Statewide	Single-member	Yes^
California	Retention	12	Statewide	Single-member	No
Colorado	Retention	10	Statewide	Single-member	No
Florida	Retention	6	Statewide	Single-member	No
Georgia	Nonpartisan	6	Statewide	Single-member	No
Idaho	Nonpartisan	6	Statewide	Single-member	Yes
Illinois	Partisan/retention*	10	District	Single-member	No
Indiana	Retention	10	Statewide	Single-member	No
Iowa	Retention	8	Statewide	Single-member	No
Kansas	Retention	6	Statewide	Single-member	No
Kentucky	Nonpartisan	8	District	Single-member	Yes
Louisiana	Partisan	10	District	Single-member	Yes
Maryland	Retention	10	District	Single-member	No
Michigan	Nonpartisan**	8	Statewide	Multimember	No
Minnesota	Nonpartisan	6	Statewide	Single-member	No
Mississippi	Nonpartisan	8	District	Single-member	No

Missouri	Retention	12	Statewide	Single-member	No
Montana	Nonpartisan/ retention***	8	Statewide	Single-member	No
Nebraska	Retention	6	District	Single-member	No
Nevada	Nonpartisan	6	Statewide	Single-member	No
New Mexico	Partisan/retention*	8	Statewide	Single-member	No
N. Carolina	Nonpartisan	8	Statewide	Single-member	No
N. Dakota	Nonpartisan	10	Statewide	Single-member	No
Ohio	Nonpartisan**	6	Statewide	Single-member	No
Oklahoma	Retention	6	Statewide	Single-member	No
Oregon	Nonpartisan	6	Statewide	Single-member	No
Pennsylvania	Partisan/retention*	10	Statewide	Multimember	Yes
S. Dakota	Retention	8	Statewide	Single-member	No
Tennessee	Retention	8	Statewide	Single-member	No
Texas	Partisan	6	Statewide	Single-member	No
Utah	Retention	10	Statewide	Single-member	No
Washington	Nonpartisan	6	Statewide	Single-member	No
W.Virginia	Partisan	12	Statewide	Multimember	No
Wisconsin	Nonpartisan	10	Statewide	Single-member	Yes
Wyoming	Retention	8	Statewide	Single-member	No

*Initially selected in partisan elections; retention elections for subsequent terms.
**Nominated in partisan primaries/caucuses.
***Retention election if the incumbent is unopposed.
^Judges selected in nonpartisan elections at the same time as partisan primaries; if more than two candidates, top two vote-getters advance to run-off held at the same time as the general election.

accounts that portray judges as impartial actors closely bound by law when rendering judgments. Using empirical research techniques, several generations of scholars have established the primacy of the judges' personal preferences on judicial choice.

In studies of the United States Supreme Court, most recent in this long line of work is Segal and Spaeth's *The Supreme Court and the Attitudinal Model Revisited*.[47] Although there are critics who assert that Segal and Spaeth's arguments are overdrawn about the ability of the justices to forward their preferences without constraint (including the constraint of law), the fact remains that the body of evidence is overwhelming that "private attitudes . . . become public law"[48] in the nation's highest court. Moreover, these various works attribute the ability of the justices to engage in such behavior to several institutional arrangements defining the Court: lifetime tenure, the lack of progressive ambition, and the impossibility of reversal by a higher court.[49]

State supreme courts are quite different, institutionally speaking. In the states, various institutional arrangements and other contextual features constrain the ability of the justices simply to vote their preferences. Particularly important among these are selection method and, to a lesser extent, length of term. Justices who are elected (especially from unsafe seats) and who must face voters regularly to retain their seats (particularly where terms of office are short) have a strong incentive to consider constituency preferences on those few issues that are publicly salient and politically visible. Indeed, a substantial body of work has established that justices vote strategically on some of the most important issues decided in state supreme courts, including the death penalty,[50] abortion regulations,[51] and tort litigation involving power asymmetric litigants.[52] The story consistently revealed in this work is one of strategic choice and striking differences between elected and appointed justices in their approach to the most politically divisive and controversial issues of the day.

These empirical studies confirm what practicing attorneys and appointing Presidents already know intuitively. Skilled attorneys understand quite well that *which* judge sits will affect the likelihood of winning. Likewise, Presidents know that the judges they appoint to the federal courts, particularly the United States Supreme Court, will have an ideologically predictable impact on public policy long after the President leaves office. Although it is the modern equivalent of declaring that the emperor has no clothes to say so, politically astute observers fully recognize that the basic political preferences of judges influence their votes. Systematic research merely confirms this basic truth.

Of course, the first reaction to the proposition that state supreme court justices might act as representatives on important state constitutional and other important legal questions might be shock and dismay: justices should be bound by law and precedent when deciding the cases before their courts rather than represent voters or, for that matter, their own political predilections. We argue that this simply is not possible in many types of disputes. In state supreme courts, many issues embodied in the cases are hardly simple or the solutions obvious, and a strong argument can be made that if the law offered a definitive guide there would be no need for high court resolution in the first place. Particularly in politically volatile and highly divisive disputes, justices must draw upon their personal beliefs, values, and experiences in making decisions because the law is not a sufficient guide, particularly in matters of common law.

We also suggest that, at the state level, law should represent public preferences and political culture, as long as the mandates of the United States Constitution and other federal law is observed. We think it far better for justices to draw upon public perceptions and the prevailing state political climate when resolving difficult disputes than to engage in the unfettered pursuit of their own personal preferences. In fact, strategic contingencies created by democratic processes should bring justices into line with the rule of law rather than negate it.[53]

Plan for the Chapters

In this book, we will address a number of issues central to the judicial elections controversy by testing hypotheses derived from the broader debate using econometrics applied to data on state supreme court elections from 1990 through 2004. We begin this enterprise in chapter 2 by evaluating one of the primary arguments used to attack judicial elections: that citizens do not care enough about them to vote. Contrary to the highly negative characterizations of voters in the popular press and judicial reform literature, we show that under certain conditions the electorate participates in these elections at very high rates. Thus, public disengagement is not an inevitable characteristic of these elections. We also document that low voter turnout in some supreme court elections largely is the consequence of the judicial reform movement. By removing partisan labels and challengers in the transition to nonpartisan and retention elections, citizen lack of interest became a "self fulfilling prophecy."[54]

In this same regard, we assess whether expensive campaigns alienate voters and reduce their willingness to participate in judicial elections. We demonstrate, contrary to conventional wisdom, that highly spirited and expensive campaigns strongly increase the propensity to vote. Indeed, campaign spending is one of the best mobilization agents in state supreme court elections. Thus, any claims about the deleterious effects of money on citizen participation in judicial elections are sharply overdrawn.

We take up the controversial issue of campaign spending in chapter 3. In this chapter, we demonstrate that high-cost races are not random events in which incumbents are targeted idiosyncratically, nor do expensive campaigns occur in all races or in all states. However, we can predict the conditions under which these types of high-stakes campaigns will occur. Of critical importance is whether partisan labels are on the ballot. Contrary to conventional wisdom, we show that partisan elections decrease the costs of campaigns whereas nonpartisan elections increase the costs. Rather than relieving the pressures on judges to solicit campaign contributions and generate large campaign war chests, nonpartisan elections do the opposite. In fact, the very reform of removing partisan labels from ballots has intensified the need to elicit funds and exacerbates any problems of the seeming impropriety of doing so.

In chapter 4, we examine electoral competition from the perspective of the willingness of challengers to enter supreme court elections and the judgments of the electorate about incumbents once challenged. Opponents of judicial elections allege that these races are devoid of meaningful choice, wherein voters are incapable of making candidate-based evaluations beyond incumbency. In fact, this is one the most compelling arguments used to condemn judicial elections, both historically and in the current debate. Our analysis of supreme court election results demonstrates that this serious accusation is false. When casting votes for supreme court candidates, the electorate distinguishes between challengers who have experience on the bench from challengers who lack it and thus are less suitable alternatives to incumbents. Moreover, voters have the capacity to go beyond the simple dichotomy of the presence or absence of experience by differentiating among types of judicial service (trial court or appellate court service). In essence, the popular negative stereotype of voters is inaccurate.

Also in chapter 4, we show that challengers in state supreme court elections strategically target incumbents, just as challengers do in elections to non-judicial offices. Essentially challengers take on incumbents when they have the chance to win, because of the electoral vulnerability of the incumbent or other favorable contingencies in the state political environment. In brief, challengers and voters make smart political choices.

Regarding vulnerability, incumbents most susceptible to challenge are those who are unpopular with voters in the first place, evidenced by narrow vote margins of victory in the previous election bid, or who were appointed by governors to fill unexpired terms and are facing the electorate for the first time. With respect to favorable contingencies, among the most important are partisan elections. As with citizen participation in the election process, partisan elections promote the entry of challengers, which in turn generates interesting and hard-fought campaigns that stimulate citizen interest and mobilize the electorate to vote. Indeed, partisan elections appear to be excellent agents of democracy.

Finally in chapter 4, we investigate the notion that state supreme court justices are at the mercy of special interests and other financial high rollers when their electoral fates are being determined. Overall, we show that money is important in supreme court campaigns as in reelection campaigns for other important offices in the United States. However, money is but one of the many important factors that affect how well incumbents will do with voters on election day. Also, the real concern should be not with total spending per se but rather with the differentials in spending between the candidates. On average, campaign spending strongly favors incumbents. Thus, it would take incredibly well-financed challengers and unpopular incumbents who could not raise money to tip the balance away from the status quo.

In chapter 5, we discuss five states that recently have altered the judicial selection process or are contemplating specific proposals to do so. Among other things, we examine changes in electoral competition, voter participation, and other relevant factors in the states recently enacting reforms. In states currently considering major changes, we discuss the specific proposals on the agenda and their likely consequences for the efficacy of judicial elections and the state judiciary generally. We find that these structural revisions have had or will have consequences beyond those suggested or anticipated, but that these consequences are easily predicted by the current base of knowledge about the politics of state supreme court elections and elections to other important offices in the United States.

Finally, we summarize our findings and offer conclusions about the judicial elections controversy in chapter 6. We include in this discussion the latest research on the controversial subject of whether judges chosen in partisan elections are less qualified than judges chosen by other methods, as judicial reformers have asserted. Overall, evidence indicates that the best supreme court justices in America are the product of democratic politics, especially partisan elections. Not only are justices chosen in partisan elections far from unqualified for office, they actually are *better* on several objective indicators than justices chosen by other methods, including appointment schemes.

More broadly, we consider the alternative to judicial elections: appointment schemes. In doing so, we examine the contention that appointment schemes improve selection by taking politics out of the process while better promoting the rule of law. Among other things, we argue that appointment systems merely relocate politics from the electorate to political elites while promoting judicial decisions that better resemble the personal preferences of the judges. Appointment schemes simply are not the miracle cure for any ills of judicial elections.

In sum, we show in the following chapters that state supreme court elections are far from being institutional failures. Instead, judicial elections are powerful legitimacy-conferring institutions that enhance the quality of democracy and create an inextricable link between citizens and the judiciary. On just about every empirical point of contention, the evidence strongly suggests that critics of judicial elections simply are wrong.

At a minimum, the evidence presented in this book should help to alleviate the fears of those concerned with recent developments in judicial elections and should promote a more informed discussion of how best to select and retain judges in the American states. The strength of the evidence we present also should encourage healthy skepticism about the claims of judicial reform advocates generally. After all, judicial elections critics are not just assaulting a method for choosing judges but also are waging war on the democratic process. We should demand very high standards of proof and concrete evidence supporting their contentions before acquiescing to their agenda.

From our perspective, partisan elections are a highly effective means for promoting citizen control of government and should be reconsidered. Indeed, democratic politics in the form of state supreme court elections is flourishing and should be fostered rather than impaired.

Questions beyond the Scope of this Study

A few words are in order about what we are not going to do. First, our focus is on state supreme courts because these institutions are the most important politically in state judicial hierarchies. We also limit our focus to state supreme courts because obtaining systematic data on lower court elections over any substantial period is a nearly impossible task. That being said, we will reference the few empirical studies of lower courts conducted to date and discuss those findings where appropriate.

Second, we speak only to those aspects of judicial elections that can be addressed scientifically. Basically, we reduce the major assertions of the court reform movement to testable hypotheses and examine these hypotheses systematically by applying objective social science techniques to empirical data. Of course, we realize that objective evidence alone will not convince anyone who simply does not like judicial elections or opposes them on normative grounds. Nonetheless, we hope that facts will inform the debate and promote more reasoned opinions.

In this manner, we do not have scientifically valid survey data disaggregated to the state level that would allow us to assess whether competitive elections and expensive campaigns harm public perceptions of the integrity or independence of courts. Instead, we search for evidence of behavioral manifestations of such alienation: a failure to participate in judicial elections when conditions would predict otherwise or a tendency to vote against incumbents randomly regardless of other considerations. We also do not want to walk through the quagmire of sorting out what really influences citizens' perceptions of courts and whether citizens must perceive state court judges as being above politics in order to view courts as legitimate institutions. While we suspect that such views are "ivory tower myths,"[55] particularly in states that have experienced competitive judicial elections for decades, we leave that discussion to future research. We merely point out that in the American state context there is no evidence suggesting that variations in public perceptions of courts have any direct, measurable, or lasting impact on citizen behavior or the operations of courts themselves, nor have we seen any "crises" in states that historically have seen highly competitive and expensive judicial elections campaigns.

Chapter 2

Mobilizing Citizens to Vote

Since the 1960s, eighteen states have endorsed the agenda of the modern court reform movement by abandoning partisan elections for nonpartisan elections or the Missouri Plan, which combines initial appointment with subsequent retention elections.[1] Among other concerns, reform advocates consistently have asserted that partisan elections fail to achieve their primary goal of accountability, evidenced in one important aspect by the widespread lack of voting. The conventional wisdom, based largely on anecdotal evidence,[2] is that voters "know nothing and care less,"[3] are plagued by "ignorance, apathy, and incapacity,"[4] are "only slightly affected" by close contests,[5] and attach "limited importance to the work of the judicial branch of government" and thus decline to vote.[6]

More recently, reform advocates have sharpened their criticisms by alleging that vigorous competition and expensive campaigns have deleterious effects on courts. As the story goes, challengers increasingly are seeking to oust incumbents in judicial elections, thereby intensifying campaigns and other aspects of democratic politics. Additionally, organized interests and other political players are seeking to forward their agendas by injecting big money into campaigns, thereby exacerbating the problems already caused by aggressive challengers. As a consequence of the rigors of electoral politics not befitting judges or courts, voters now are being deterred from the polls and are developing negative perceptions of judges that threaten the legitimacy of courts. Stated differently, citizens first were criticized because they purportedly did not pay any attention to judicial elections, and now they are being criticized because they do.[7]

In this chapter, we address two sets of questions vitally important to these claims and the controversy over electing judges: (1) to what extent do voters participate in judicial elections, and (2) to what extent do hard-fought, expensive campaigns alienate voters and thus diminish citizen participation in the democratic process? Voters simply remaining indifferent to the judicial recruitment process would severely undermine the basic premise upon which elections are held, thus rendering elections irrelevant, ineffective, and obsolete. Indeed, Dubois cites non-voting as "the leading indicator" that the electorate is "unwilling and incapable of holding its judiciary accountable through elections."[8] Similarly, rough-and-tumble campaigns and big-money politics producing observable consequences, such as voters refusing to go to the polls, would serve as convincing evidence that the wisdom of electing judges should be reevaluated.

Contrary to the claims of judicial reform advocates and conventional wisdom, we show that voters in state supreme court elections are drawn into the electoral arena by the same factors that stimulate voting for elections to non-judicial offices, including strongly contested races and well-financed campaigns. In fact, rather than being alienated by competitive elections and costly campaigns, citizens in supreme court elections embrace highly spirited expensive races by voting in much greater proportions than in more mundane contests.

In the same manner, we demonstrate that the reform agenda of removing partisan labels from ballots and precluding challengers, both of which stimulate voting in American elections for legislative and executive offices, has had the consequence of significantly inhibiting voting, thus making criticisms about low citizen participation in judicial elections a "self-fulfilling prophecy."[9]

The Democratic Imperative

The American electorate's ambivalence toward elections is pronounced. For offices at all levels of government, large proportions of the eligible electorate simply do not bother to vote, causing scholars and other political observers to ponder the likely effects of such behavior on the operations of the popularly elected institutions and to recommend solutions to enhance citizen participation. As even the most casual observer of politics understands, the foundations of representative democracy rest squarely on the willingness of citizens to go to the polls. Stated succinctly by Hajnal and Trounstine, "[a]t its core, democracy rests on the vote."[10]

Moreover, this problem of voter apathy seems particularly acute when those who actually do make it to the polls fail to complete their ballots. In fact, the phenomenon of ballot roll-off, whereby voters cast votes only for a selective set of offices, raises serious issues about legitimacy and accountability and thus has received considerable attention from scholars of electoral politics. By examining ballot roll-off in elections to the United States House of Representatives,[11] state legislatures,[12] a variety of local offices,[13] and on ballot propositions,[14] scholars have determined that ballot roll-off, like voter turnout, varies significantly across elections and largely is the product of factors specific to each election, the external political environment, and institutional arrangements governing the conduct of elections. Especially important among these for enhancing voter activity is electoral competition. In essence, at least in non-judicial elections, ballot roll-off does not reflect a sort of indifference that necessarily poses a threat to the democratic process or to the accountability function so essential to democracy.

But are judicial elections simply different? At first glance, it seems that at least some state supreme court elections diverge from the stereotype of being "uniquely different"[15] or of incumbents being "rarely challenged and infrequently defeated."[16] As recent research demonstrates,[17] for example, defeat rates in state supreme courts are higher on average than in the United States House of Representatives, United States Senate, and statehouses.

In order to determine whether judicial elections diverge from elections to other political offices in the ways that citizens are mobilized, and whether vigorous competition and costly campaigns alienate voters, we analyze 264 state supreme court elections held from 1990 through 2004 in the eighteen states using partisan or nonpartisan elections to staff the high court bench.[18] By comparing these elections systematically over time and across states, we can evaluate which specific forces influence the propensities of the American electorate to vote. Thus, we can determine quite readily whether, and to what degree, voters respond to contextual incentives that should facilitate voting, including heated contests and well-financed campaigns.

We also display descriptive data on 210 retention elections from 1990 though 2004, contrasting overall levels of participation in partisan, nonpartisan, and retention elections over a fourteen-year period. We do not include retention elections in the more complex models because our primary focus is on the impact of challengers and big money politics on the propensity to vote. As we know, retention elections preclude challengers and rarely involve campaign spending.

Measuring Citizen Participation as Ballot Roll-Off

The concept of ballot roll-off is very important for thinking about citizen participation in less visible elections below the top of the ballot.[19] Also, when generating empirical models there is a key analytical advantage to using ballot roll-off instead of voter turnout to measure citizen participation: ballot roll-off provides an efficient and practical means to address the complicated specification and data issues that arise when modeling a process affected by elections not being evaluated and not easily included.

Studies of judicial elections,[20] elections to the House of Representatives,[21] and sub-gubernatorial elections[22] have recognized that it is unlikely that turnout is determined by lower-level races when a presidential, senatorial, or gubernatorial contest is on the ballot. Thus, generating models that maintain parsimony while controlling for the variety of factors affecting the electoral climate in general, and turnout for the most salient races in particular, is daunting. Further, there is the ongoing debate over how best to measure voter turnout. Examining roll-off, although not a perfect solution, helps to alleviate these problems by treating turnout for the most important offices as a baseline and then gauging interest in other elections relative to the top draw on the ballot.

Thus, our measure of citizen participation is ballot roll-off rather than voter turnout. In defining roll-off, we follow the well-beaten path established in earlier elections studies by defining ballot roll-off as the percentage of the electorate casting votes for the major office on the ballot who do *not* vote in each supreme court race. Also consistent with previous work, we define the major office as "the presidential, gubernatorial, or U.S. senatorial contest attracting the most voters in each election."[23] Thus, higher values of roll-off indicate lower levels of participation in supreme court races.[24]

The Nature of Roll-Off in Modern Supreme Court Elections

To begin an examination of roll-off and to provide an important basis for understanding the nature of citizen participation in supreme court elections, Table 2.1 displays average roll-off rates for the states from 1990 through 2004. First and foremost, it is understandable why many would criticize voters in state supreme court elections. Overall, these elections have a roll-off rate that averages 22.9 percent, or a pattern wherein one of every four or five voters already at the polls declines to vote in supreme court races. However, Table 2.1 reveals a fairly complex reality. Overall, the states, and elections within states, differ markedly, and there are reasons to criticize judicial elections while viewing them as an excellent means for assessing the factors that promote mass political participation.

Specifically, ballot roll-off ranges from 1.6 percent to 65.1 percent across elections, and averages from 12.5 percent (Alabama) to 59.2 percent (Wisconsin) across states.[25] These differences of 47 to 64 percentage points across elections and states are dramatic reflections of the extent to which voters can, and cannot, be motivated to participate in supreme court elections. Similarly, elections within states can be quite similar or differ substantially. For example, compare Indiana, Missouri, and Oklahoma, which have relatively minor fluctuations across elections, with Colorado, Missouri, and North Carolina, which can see differences of over 42 percentage points. Clearly, the extraordinary variations that occur in citizen participation both across and within states do not speak to a consistently apathetic electorate and simply beg scientific explanation.[26]

For a different perspective, Table 2.2 displays average roll-off rates in state supreme court elections from 1990 through 2004 by election year and selection system, and also distinguishes between contested and

Table 2.1 Average Roll-Off (in Percentages) in State Supreme Court Elections, 1990–2004

State	*Election Type*	*Mean*	*Standard deviation*	*Minimum*	*Maximum*	*n*
Alabama	Partisan	12.52	12.29	3.67	42.48	22
Alaska	Retention	16.61	4.39	11.26	22.45	7
Arizona	Retention	31.40	4.56	22.05	36.55	15
Arkansas[a]	Partisan to nonpartisan	16.25	7.17	6.44	25.19	5
California	Retention	33.33	3.46	26.47	37.45	15
Colorado	Retention	30.77	16.17	19.59	61.75	10
Florida	Retention	20.30	3.38	13.38	24.69	17
Georgia[b]	Partisan to nonpartisan	48.15	6.17	38.35	57.50	15
Idaho	Nonpartisan	14.50	0	14.50	14.50	1
Illinois	Partisan or retention	15.01	10.85	1.58	30.72	10
Indiana	Retention	39.27	1.29	36.99	40.14	5
Iowa	Retention	41.31	3.67	37.97	47.09	12
Kansas	Retention	25.16	2.44	19.14	30.69	19
Kentucky	Nonpartisan	37.50	17.61	17.71	65.13	6
Louisiana	Partisan	14.03	0	14.03	14.03	1
Maryland	Retention	36.09	12.10	21.00	52.35	8
Michigan	Nonpartisan	30.17	4.02	24.04	36.78	18
Minnesota	Nonpartisan	24.00	6.89	13.57	54.00	18
Mississippi[c]	Partisan to nonpartisan	26.35	10.59	10.65	39.74	5
Missouri	Retention	20.80	1.48	19.47	23.54	8

Montana[d]	Nonpartisan or retention	17.77	13.04	2.42	46.69	14
Nebraska	Retention	28.60	11.79	18.00	53.80	11
Nevada	Nonpartisan	15.04	7.14	2.70	32.28	19
New Mexico	Partisan	15.37	12.03	4.77	38.77	12
North Carolina[e]	Partisan to nonpartisan	14.09	13.51	3.85	46.08	16
North Dakota	Nonpartisan	13.02	6.75	3.35	21.17	8
Ohio	Nonpartisan	20.21	6.12	7.52	38.27	20
Oklahoma	Retention	18.50	1.43	15.29	21.29	40
Oregon	Nonpartisan	36.75	8.80	24.77	45.68	5
South Dakota	Retention	17.58	2.27	12.32	19.68	8
Tennessee[f]	Partisan to retention	50.11	2.52	46.05	52.41	5
Texas	Partisan	12.95	9.89	4.34	39.60	53
Utah[g]	Nonpartisan to retention	23.01	3.09	19.99	27.63	8
Washington	Nonpartisan	29.00	8.20	16.93	40.96	19
West Virginia	Partisan	23.82	11.41	3.85	38.43	7
Wisconsin	Nonpartisan	59.22	0	59.22	59.22	1
Wyoming	Retention	15.17	2.35	9.20	18.83	11
All states		22.89	12.53	1.58	65.13	474

Notes

a Arkansas changed from partisan elections to nonpartisan elections in 2002.

b Georgia changed from partisan elections to nonpartisan elections in 1984.

c Mississippi changed from partisan elections to nonpartisan elections in 1994.

d Montana uses nonpartisan elections in contested races, and retention elections otherwise.

e North Carolina changed from partisan elections to nonpartisan elections in 2004.

f Tennessee changed from partisan elections to retention elections in 1994.

g Utah changed from nonpartisan elections to retention elections in 1982.

uncontested partisan and nonpartisan races. As Table 2.2 documents, ballot roll-off in partisan elections is considerably less on average than roll-off in nonpartisan and retention elections. During the eight election cycles from 1990 through 2004, average roll-off in partisan elections was 14 percent, compared with 27 percent in nonpartisan elections and 26 percent in retention elections. However, when we consider contested elections only, roll-off falls to 22 percent in nonpartisan elections and 11 percent in partisan elections. Overall, roll-off rates are lowest in every election cycle in partisan elections.

Figure 2.1 displays these data graphically to illustrate better the various system differences and temporal trends. Immediately apparent are the differences in civic engagement between partisan elections and the other two types of election systems. In the eight election cycles, partisan elections draw more citizens into state supreme court races than any other system. Indeed, the effects of partisan elections are pronounced. Only in 1992 do contested nonpartisan elections outperform partisan elections generally, but contested partisan elections significantly outperform contested nonpartisan elections in every cycle, including 1992.

In head-to-head competition with nonpartisan and partisan elections, retention elections do not fare well. In four of eight election cycles (1992, 1998, 2002, 2004), retention elections attract the fewest voters of all three selection systems, and in the other four cycles (1990, 1994, 1996, 2000) retention elections outperform nonpartisan elections only. However, in 1990 and 1994, contested nonpartisan elections do better than retention elections in retaining voters already at the polls for other elections, and the differences in 2000 between retention elections and contested nonpartisan elections are negligible.

Looking at roll-off rates over time, we see a downward trend in ballot roll-off in nonpartisan elections and, to a lesser extent, in partisan elections. However, there are no dramatic shifts over time for either nonpartisan or partisan elections. Alternatively, retention elections show no discernable temporal trends, which likely is because of the absence of challengers and the meager amounts of campaign spending that consistently occur in these races.

Retention Elections as Democratic Disincentives

Recent research has evaluated the comparative effects of the three types of elections used to recruit and retain state supreme court justices on the willingness of citizens to participate in these contests. Overall, the verdict on nonpartisan and retention elections is not good. Using data on all 654 elections from 1980 through 2000, Hall generated models of ballot roll-off that systematically assessed the comprehensive range of factors that affect citizen participation in supreme court elections, including the

Table 2.2 Average Ballot Roll-Off (in Percentages) in State Supreme Court Elections, 1990–2004, by Type of Election System

Year	*Nonpartisan elections*		*Partisan elections*		*Retention elections*	*All elections*	
	All races	*Contested races*	*All races*	*Contested races*	*All races*	*All races*	*Contested races*
1990	29.77	20.84	13.76	10.58	25.61	23.42	14.00
1992	25.58	18.25	19.95	12.66	29.23	24.91	15.45
1994	28.80	21.94	13.92	10.75	22.86	22.97	16.01
1996	31.13	27.25	11.63	11.63	23.54	22.75	18.57
1998	22.59	20.43	7.65	7.65	29.72	23.09	13.91
2000	28.39	25.36	17.69	17.69	24.20	24.08	21.52
2002	19.06	19.60	5.42	5.42	23.47	17.94	9.89
2004	23.24	20.08	15.25	10.41	25.62	22.56	16.36
Total	26.52	21.77	13.75	11.08	25.68	22.89	16.08
n	143	94	121	109	210	474	203

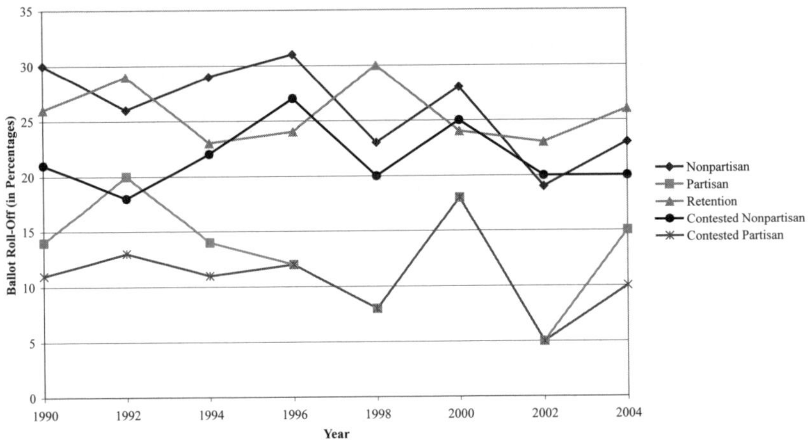

Figure 2.1 Average Ballot Roll-Off in State Supreme Court Elections.

presence of challengers, strong competition, the type of selection system, the nature of the constituency (district versus statewide), and incumbency.[27] The results are dramatic.

Controlling for the wide range of contingencies that affect whether citizens vote in supreme court elections relative to the top draws on the ballot, Hall documented that under the conditions most conducive to voting (including competitive state electoral environments and closely contested seats), retention elections cannot outperform nonpartisan elections, and that retention and nonpartisan elections cannot do better than partisan elections, *ceteris paribus*.[28] In other words, retention elections do not have the same capacity as nonpartisan elections and partisan elections for promoting citizen control of the bench through democratic processes, though retention elections may do about as well as nonpartisan and partisan elections in the most low-key races. However, because these are a rarity in partisan elections and are not typical in nonpartisan elections, retention elections overall are not effective agents of voter mobilization.

Critiques of Money in Supreme Court Politics

One of the most pressing issues on the American political agenda is the influence of private dollars in public institutions. Whether viewed from the perspective of the powerful impact of special interests in the political process or the skyrocketing cost of election campaigns, the issue of money and its potentially corrosive effects on democracy is at the forefront of contemporary political discourse.

Particularly interesting among these considerations is the impact of money on the politics of the judiciary, not only with respect to recruitment and retention processes but also on the operations of courts themselves. As we have mentioned, considerable momentum is beginning to build among those scholars, practitioners, and organizations concerned with judicial reform to challenge the wisdom of electing judges in light of the current trends toward escalating campaign costs. Almost universally, the charge is that raising and spending money in heated campaigns will have deleterious effects on courts.[29]

Consider, for example, recent claims by the National Center for State Courts, one of the nation's most important advocacy groups for the judiciary. According to the National Center for State Courts, "[j]udicial election campaigns pose a substantial threat to judicial independence . . . and undermine public trust in the judicial system."[30] Sharing these perceptions is the American Bar Association, which cites the rise of heated campaigns and fundraising activities as evidence of the "excessive politicization of state courts."[31] As the American Bar Association reports:

> [m]oney is the elephant in the room on judicial selection. It raises serious questions, such as how much money is required for judicial election, from whom does it come, what is the public perception, and so on.[32]

Precisely because of these concerns, the National Center for State Courts now recommends that partisan elections be replaced by nonpartisan elections, in an effort to reduce competition and "the need for large campaign contributions."[33] Taking a more extreme position, the American Bar Association advocates that the election of judges be abandoned altogether in favor of commission-based appointive systems.

Scholars are beginning to echo these cries. Recent work describes the seeming impropriety of judges accepting campaign contributions from law firms regularly appearing in court, as well as possible influences of these contributions on the decisions of judges.[34] Of course, this work is in its infancy but does voice the fear that competitive and expensive elections may impair public confidence and bias judicial decisions. To date, however, there is no systematic evidence of these hypothesized effects.

In this chapter, we suggest that campaign spending actually might have a positive effect on the democratic process by increasing citizen participation in the recruitment and retention of judges. Specifically, by using a research design and modeling strategy that allows us to separate the effects of the presence of challengers from the effects of money, we can assess systematically whether relatively expensive campaigns improve the chances that citizens will vote. Our particular focus will be on 264 state supreme court elections held from 1990 through 2004 in the eighteen states using partisan or nonpartisan elections to staff the high court bench.

Generally, we argue that by stimulating mass participation and giving voters greater ownership in the outcomes of these races, expensive campaigns strengthen the critical linkage between citizens and the bench and enhance the quality of democracy. In fact, this heightened electoral connection might be a powerful antidote to some of the negative consequences of spirited and costly judicial elections, thereby complicating the conventional wisdom that money and judges should not mix.

Spending in Supreme Court Elections

Over the decade of the 1990s, state supreme court races have become more contested,[35] competitive,[36] and expensive.[37] Although there have been few systematic explanations for these trends, we might surmise that this seeming sea change in judicial elections is related to several developments in the overall political context, summarized well in *Justice in Jeopardy*.[38] Among other things, supreme court dockets have experienced a proliferation of controversial cases with broad policy implications, perhaps because of rising lower court caseloads and the power of discretionary review now held by most state high courts. Second, the national government has demonstrated a pronounced tendency to devolve power to the states. This devolution has enhanced the power of the states' highest courts in an overall sense but also has produced a "new judicial federalism" in which the protection of individual rights in some states is now being based more on state constitutions rather than the United States Constitution. Third, many states have seen the demise of one-party dominance and now experience lively two-party competition. Finally, interest groups have emerged as major players in electoral politics, including elections to the state high court bench. These groups may find it easier and more effective to attempt to win some public policy battles by controlling who sits on the bench rather than lobbying the legislature or working to elect its majority.

Regardless of the exact causes, however, these well-documented changes in the competitiveness and cost of judicial elections have significant consequences. Among other things, big spending by incumbents relative to their challengers increases incumbents' electoral margins and reduces the likelihood of defeat.[39] Likewise, substantial spending by challengers can diminish the advantages of incumbency.[40] As the literature suggests,[41] campaign spending is an effective way for candidates to publicize themselves and their views on relevant issues, which in turn mobilizes voters and influences their choices.

This is highly relevant for understanding ballot roll-off because one of the most fundamental reasons voters choose not to participate in elections is the lack of information about the candidates.[42] Whatever one's views of the propriety of judges (and candidates) campaigning and spending money in order to obtain (and retain) their seats, one cannot deny that competitive, vigorous campaigns reduce information costs to voters and provide them with facts about the candidates, both of which increase the likelihood of voting. Thus, campaign spending is a key component to understanding the nature of participation in elections, including those to the state high court bench.

It is most instructive to consider the exact nature of campaign spending in recent state supreme court elections. Table 2.3 displays data from 1990 though 2004 by election cycle, using two different measures for each race: (1) total spending in dollars and (2) dollars spent per capita (calculated as total spending in dollars divided by the voting age population of the state—or district for those states which elect justices in a district—reported in *The Statistical Abstract* annually by state year). To render both measures comparable over time by controlling for inflation, we convert dollars to 1990 dollars.

As Table 2.3 documents, the average amount spent in each election from 1990 through 2004 was $581,807 overall, or $502.78 per capita. These figures reflect a starting point in 1990 of $364,348 and $139.25, respectively, and an end point in 2004 of $711,867 and $2,209.61. Thus, we clearly can see the increasingly expensive nature of these races over the fourteen-year period being examined.

However, two *caveats* are in order. First, the extraordinary per capita costs in 2004 may be somewhat of an anomaly in that several races in small constituencies were incredibly and unusually expensive. Specifically, the Karmeier–Maag race in Illinois (which utilizes district-based elections) and the Benjamin–McGraw race in West Virginia (which has a relatively

Table 2.3 Average Spending (in 1990 Dollars) in State Supreme Court Elections, 1990–2004, by Year

Year	*Total spending (number of elections)*	*Total spending per capita (number of elections)*
1990	$364,348 (30)	$139.25 (30)
1992	$525,809 (34)	$251.78 (34)
1994	$645,161 (31)	$226.10 (31)
1996	$516,512 (36)	$397.38 (36)
1998	$636,725 (31)	$218.89 (31)
2000	$635,865 (42)	$311.13 (42)
2002	$603,792 (25)	$196.25 (25)
2004	$711,867 (33)	$2,209.61 (33)
Average	$581,807 (262)	$502.78 (262)

small population) were among the most expensive supreme court races in the nation's history. Second, the increases in spending have not been monotonic. Obviously much is at play here that needs further explanation. Nonetheless, we expect these variations to have a considerable impact on the willingness of citizens to participate in state supreme court elections.

For a different look at money in supreme court elections, Table 2.4 displays campaign expenditures by state. Again, we see significant variation across the states in the cost of judicial elections, whether measured as total spending or on a per capita basis. Least costly in total dollars are elections in Minnesota, where the average campaign costs only about $86,887. Compare this with Alabama, Illinois, and Pennsylvania, where the average campaign exceeds $1,000,000. We see different rankings on a per capita basis. Minnesota remains the least expensive state with respect

Table 2.4 Average Spending (in 1990 Dollars) in State Supreme Court Elections, 1990–2004, by State

State	*Total spending (number of elections)*	*Total spending per capita*
Alabama	$1,123,084 (21)	$346.55
Arkansas	$241,290 (8)	$132.33
Georgia	$248,179 (7)	$45.01
Idaho	$119,790 (4)	$136.56
Illinois	$1,012,167 (11)	$6,110.94
Kentucky	$350,056 (10)	$844.03
Louisiana	$957,851 (8)	$1,920.99
Michigan	$780,451 (15)	$108.09
Minnesota	$86,887 (10)	$25.29
Mississippi	$448,893 (16)	$657.19
Montana	$296,897 (6)	$469.08
Nevada	$493,796 (10)	$402.99
New Mexico	$190,044 (2)	$147.51
North Carolina	$280,224 (16)	$49.53
Ohio	$976,823 (19)	$117.56
Oregon	$159,312 (6)	$63.46
Pennsylvania	$1,779,438 (6)	$194.69
Texas	$551,439 (52)	$41.77
Washington	$167,380 (21)	$40.79
West Virginia	$664,891 (7)	$474.58
Wisconsin	$575,387 (7)	$149.77

to campaign expenditures whereas Illinois emerges as the most expensive, followed by Louisiana. But again, the figures in Illinois are inflated by grossly disproportionate spending in 2004.

We do not know if this will continue. After having unprecedented spending in 2004, Illinois and West Virginia did not have any supreme court elections in 2006, making it impossible to know whether excessive spending will continue in these states. However, in fifteen states with elections in 2004 and 2006, fundraising decreased in eight states, stayed the same in one state, and increased in six states.[43] At the same time, a small handful of elections were very costly, setting records in their states. Thus, high-priced elections for some may be here to stay.

Modeling Citizen Participation in State Supreme Court Elections

Although our primary question is whether campaign spending can serve to enhance citizen participation in state supreme court elections (or, from the critics' perspective, whether campaign spending inhibits voting), we focus more broadly on the general conditions promoting voting in these contests. To do so, we draw on three recent lines of work on the politics of state supreme court elections: Hall's[44] analyses of ballot roll-off and electoral competition, Bonneau's[45] work on campaign spending, and Bonneau and Hall's collaborative work[46] on the emergence and effects of challengers. Using the cumulative knowledge in these previous studies, all of which are grounded in the theoretical and methodological insights gained from studies of elections to nonjudicial offices, we generate a two-stage model of voter participation in supreme court elections by estimating: (1) the conditions under which challengers enter these races, and (2) the correlates of voter participation in elections once contested, including the total amount of campaign spending for each seat.

Our basic research strategy is to capitalize on the significant analytical advantages of comparative state analysis, which in this case will include both temporal and cross-sectional variation, to examine the wide array of institutional and other contextual forces influencing the propensity to vote, as well as election-specific factors such as campaign spending. And as mentioned, we follow the example in judicial politics scholarship[47] and in studies of other less visible political offices[48] of examining ballot roll-off rather than voter turnout. Thus, our basic research question more precisely can be formulated as asking why many citizens who actually go to the polls for the most visible races simply choose not to participate in elections to the state high court bench. To assess the effects of campaign expenditures on the willingness of voters to participate in these elections, we employ the Heckman two-stage modeling strategy to take into account the conditions under which elections draw challengers and the conditions under which voters participate in these elections once contested.

We have both theoretical and practical reasons for using the Heckman procedure. Theoretically, we must distinguish between the conditions that promote competition and those that cause voters to participate in general elections, including campaign expenditures. Essentially, because contested elections constitute a censored sample, failure to control for these effects would present a serious threat to valid inference. Stated succinctly, voters have little reason to participate in uncontested elections simply because the candidate listed on the ballot will win with or without their votes. Similarly, we seek to disentangle the effects of the presence or absence of challengers from the effects of the actual amounts spent by candidates in their campaigns.

Practically speaking, either the states do not consistently report spending data for uncontested elections or the amounts are so small that they would seriously distort any empirical analysis by giving disproportionate weight to the uncontested cases. Thus, we treat the uncontested races as missing on the dependent variable and then estimate a two-stage Heckman model controlling for the likelihood that the race is contested. Although the dependent variable is not missing in the traditional sense, because of the stark differences between contested and uncontested elections, and because many uncontested races are missing information on our key independent variable, analyzing the data this way is appropriate and will produce unbiased estimates and robust conclusions.

Stage One: Challengers in State Supreme Court Elections

The dependent variable in the first-stage of our model of ballot roll-off in state supreme court elections is whether there are at least two candidates in the general election (Contested). In specifying the independent variables, we merely replicate Bonneau and Hall,[49] except that we add one theoretically important variable to capture the effects of a landmark supreme court decision that occurred after our initial study. We also adjust the measure of the incumbency advantage to capitalize on the added variation of open-seat elections.

In general, we expect challengers to run when incumbents are electorally vulnerable, supreme court seats are attractive, a sizable candidate pool exists, and the political and institutional context promotes competition.

Electoral Vulnerability

Both the legislative and judicial selection literatures have found that one of the key determinants of contestation is the vulnerability of the incumbent.[50] Candidates who win by narrow margins are more likely to be challenged in their next elections. Thus, we predict that candidates winning with less than 60 percent of the vote (Competitive Seat) will be more likely to draw challengers than their more electorally popular counterparts. The

60 percent cutoff is the standard measure used in most leading studies of marginality in congressional elections[51] and in state legislative elections.[52]

Another important indicator of vulnerability has to do with the incumbency advantage, which is complicated in state supreme courts by the fact that a sizable portion of incumbents initially are appointed to fill unexpired terms. Generally, because of the extraordinary benefits that accrue to incumbents by virtue of holding office and running successful campaigns, we expect justices who have won elections (Elected Incumbent) to be less likely to face challengers than their novice counterparts, whether candidates for open seats or justices appointed but not yet elected. However, we also expect some advantages to accrue to those initially appointed, though the magnitude of the effect should be less than for their more seasoned colleagues. Thus, we include a second variable (Appointed Incumbent) to capture these effects. Overall, we expect open-seat races (the omitted baseline category) to be more competitive.[53]

Attractiveness of the Seat

The attractiveness of the seat also should affect the likelihood of contestation. Studies of both the United States House of Representatives[54] and the federal courts[55] have documented that financial incentives affect retirements. It is reasonable then to expect salary considerations to affect the likelihood of a contested race, with seats that are more desirable (higher paying) more likely to be contested. Thus, we hypothesize that higher salaries (Salary) increase the likelihood that supreme court elections will be contested.

Along the same lines, the length of the term of office (Term) should influence the willingness of challengers to enter supreme court contests.[56] Longer terms of office provide better job security to officeholders while reducing the incentives to be mindful of constituency preferences. Thus, we expect contested elections to be more prevalent in states with longer terms of office.

Political and Institutional Context

There is little doubt that the context of an election matters a great deal.[57] Of particular importance is a state's partisan climate. In general, states characterized by higher levels of partisan competition[58] have more competitive elections. Therefore, we include a measure of partisan competition, defined as whether the legislative and executive branches are controlled by the same political party at the time of each election (Unified Government).

One of the fundamental differences between state supreme court elections and elections for many other statewide offices is that most judicial elections are not partisan in format. Indeed, the effects of removing partisan labels from ballots are a central focus of this chapter. Overall, studies have demonstrated that challengers are more common in partisan elections than in nonpartisan elections.[59] Thus, we include a variable that indicates whether or not the candidates' political party affiliations are listed on the ballot (Partisan), and expect that there will be a greater likelihood of contestation in partisan elections than in nonpartisan races.

Another key institutional difference is that some state supreme court races are held statewide whereas others occur in districts. We expect electoral competition to vary between district-based and statewide constituencies, and that this relationship will be conditioned by election system. Election studies have established that smaller constituencies are less competitive.[60] Thus, we expect challengers to run less frequently in districts than in statewide races. However, Bonneau and Hall[61] have demonstrated that this effect is reversed in states using nonpartisan ballots. Among other things, without partisan labels on the ballot, the minority party has an incentive to field candidates where their effect might be greater in smaller constituencies, particularly when the minority party is concentrated geographically. Therefore, we include an interaction term (Partisan x District) to distinguish the effects of district-based elections in partisan election states from district-based elections in nonpartisan states (District).

In a departure from Bonneau and Hall,[62] we include one additional variable that takes into account the changing nature of constitutional law governing judicial elections. As we have mentioned, whereas many judicial elections in the past appeared to be low-key events,[63] recent increases in both contestation and campaign spending have raised the profile of judicial elections.[64] One factor alleged to be contributing to this trend is the United States Supreme Court's June 2002 decision in *Republican Party of Minnesota* v. *White*. In this landmark case, the Court effectively eliminated the "announce" restrictions preventing candidates from expressing their views on political issues likely to come before their courts. This change purportedly leaves incumbent judges open to the same sorts of policy-based and politically motivated attacks as their legislative and executive counterparts and thus may have radically altered the nature of these contests.

If *White* has heightened the competitiveness of judicial elections as some have suggested,[65] then we should notice more races being contested after *White* (Post-*White*) than before *White*. Thus, we include a variable to test for this effect.

Candidate Pool

Finally, for challengers to emerge, there must be a pool of candidates from which to draw. For judges, this pool consists of licensed attorneys. More attorneys should translate into larger numbers of challengers. Thus, we include the number of attorneys in each state at the time of each election (Lawyers).

For convenience, Table 2.5 describes all of the variables in the selection model, as well as their measurement.

Table 2.5 Variable Descriptions for a Model of Challengers in State Supreme Court Elections

Variable	*Variable description*
Dependent Variable	
Contested	1 if a challenger entered the supreme court race 0 otherwise
Electoral Vulnerability	
Competitive Seat	1 if the incumbent supreme court justice won previously by a margin less than 60% 0 otherwise
Elected Incumbent	1 if the election involves an incumbent who has previously won election 0 otherwise
Appointed Incumbent	1 if the election involves an incumbent who was initially appointed and has never won election 0 otherwise
Attractiveness of Seat	
Salary	Supreme court base salary/state per capita disposable income, in dollars
Term	Length of the term of office for state supreme court, in years
Political and Institutional Context	
Unified Government	1 if the legislative and executive branches of state government are controlled by the same political party 0 otherwise
Partisan	1 if the election is a partisan election 0 otherwise
District	1 if the seat represents a district rather than the state 0 otherwise
Post-*White*	1 if the election occurred after the *White* decision in 2002 0 otherwise
Candidate Pool	
Lawyers	Number of lawyers in each state at the time of each election

Stage Two: Ballot Roll-Off in State Supreme Court Elections

As mentioned, we measure ballot roll-off (Roll-Off) as the percentage of voters who *did not* vote in the state supreme court race but who *did* vote for the highest office on the ballot. In specifying this model, we rely on the literature on judicial elections and court reform to identify the factors that should encourage or inhibit citizen participation.

Campaign Spending

One of the primary determinants of ballot roll-off should be campaign spending. Simply put, the more money candidates spend, the more information they can provide to the voters; and the more information the voters have, the more likely they are to participate. Thus, we expect that higher amounts of total campaign spending by all candidates in the race (Total Spending) will lead to lower amounts of ballot roll-off. Given the critical importance of this variable to our analysis, however, we also estimate the models using an alternative measure of spending that adjusts expenditures by the voting age population of the state (Per Capita Spending). Thus, we can have greater confidence that our results are robust with regard to measurement. To make these figures comparable over time and to be consistent with studies of elections to other offices, we recalculate both spending measures in 1990 dollars.[66] We also adjust the measure in district-based elections (described below) by the size of the voting age population for each district.

State and Electoral Context

It also is important to distinguish between two types of elections based on the candidates' experience with supreme court electoral politics: (1) elections involving sitting justices who successfully have organized campaigns and won elections to the state high court and (2) elections in which the candidates lack such critical experience, either because they are running for open seats or because they initially were appointed and are facing voters for the first time. Overall, open-seat races and elections involving newly appointed justices are more expensive[67] and more competitive than elections in which established incumbents are seeking reelection. Given this, we expect open-seat races and those involving newly appointed justices (New SC Candidate) to have less roll-off on average than other incumbent–challenger contests.

Presidential elections are another important general contextual factor affecting the propensity to vote. Studies have established that turnout[68] and ballot roll-off[69] are higher in presidential election years than in midterm elections. In essence, highly visible presidential elections motivate large proportions of the electorate to vote, but a significant number of these voters have no information about, or interest in, other races on the ballot, including judicial elections. Therefore, we expect significant differences in ballot roll-off between presidential election years (Presidential Election) and midterm election years.

The final state contextual factor that should influence roll-off is the education level of the state citizenry. Scholars have found a relationship between education and turnout[70] as well as roll-off.[71] In general, educated people should have a greater capacity to receive and process the information provided by candidates and make informed choices. Thus, we hypothesize that higher education levels (Education Level) will produce lower levels of ballot roll-off.

Institutional Arrangements

Concerning ballot type, that institutions affect the behavior of the American electorate has been demonstrated time and again, and voter participation is no exception. Other things being equal, voters participate in elections when they have readily accessible information. Of the sources of possible information about candidates, there is perhaps no more useful cue than partisan affiliation. Thus, voters should participate in higher numbers in states using partisan ballots (Partisan) to select their high court justices compared to nonpartisan ballots.[72]

Similarly, some elections take place statewide whereas others occur in districts. Generally, we would expect less roll-off in district elections (District) than in statewide elections,[73] but we also predict that this relationship will be conditioned by whether or not partisan labels are on the ballot.[74] As mentioned, without partisan labels in smaller constituencies, the minority party has a greater incentive to field candidates. Under these conditions, voters are more likely to be contacted by a candidate or a candidate's campaign, which in turn should lead to more voters participating in the election.[75] Alternatively, in partisan elections, there are fewer challengers and a reduced probability of active campaigning.[76] Thus, we include an interaction term (Partisan x District) to capture these effects. In districts, which simply are aggregations of counties (or in the case of Louisiana, parishes), we use county-level (or parish-level) presidential, senatorial, and gubernatorial election results to generate roll-off figures.

Temporal Variables

To control for any temporal effects in the model,[77] we include dummy variables based on when the election occurred: Period 1 covers elections from 1990 through 1992 (which we omit to prevent perfect collinearity among variables), Period 2 is 1994–1996, Period 3 is 1998–2000, and Period 4 is 2002–2004. Note that Period 4 covers the same time period as Post-*White* in the first stage of our selection model. Thus, we will be able to ascertain the influence of the *White* case on ballot roll-off as well as contestation. We hypothesize that "new style"[78] campaigns should be better able to capture voters' attention, provide voters with information, and increase their willingness to vote in judicial elections.

For convenience, Table 2.6 summarizes the variables used in our model of ballot roll-off as well as their measurement.

Table 2.6 Variable Descriptions for a Model of Ballot Roll-Off in State Supreme Court Elections

Variable	*Variable Description*
Dependent Variable	
Ballot Roll-off	Percentage of ballot roll-off in the election
Campaign Spending	
Total Spending	Natural log of the total amount of campaign spending in the election by all candidates in 1990 dollars
Per Capita Spending	Natural log of the total amount of campaign spending in the election by all candidates in 1990 dollars divided by voting age population (1000s)
State and Electoral Context	
New SC Candidate	1 if the election is for an open seat or an incumbent initially appointed and facing first election 0 otherwise
Presidential Election	1 if the election occurs in a presidential election year 0 otherwise
Education Level	Percentage of the state population 25 years of age or older with a high school diploma
Institutional Arrangements	
Partisan	1 if the election is a partisan election 0 otherwise
District	1 if the election occurs in a district 0 otherwise
Temporal Variables	
Period 2	1 if the election was held from 1994–1996 0 otherwise
Period 3	1 if the election was held from 1998–2000 0 otherwise
Period 4	1 if the election was held from 2002–2004 0 otherwise

Estimation Technique

As mentioned, we use a Heckman two-stage procedure to estimate our model. Additionally, we use robust variance estimators clustered on state, which are robust to assumptions about within-group (i.e., state) correlation.

Results

The results of estimating our two-stage model of ballot roll-off in state supreme court elections are shown in Tables 2.7 and 2.8. Table 2.7 contains the results using total spending in dollars as our measure of campaign expenditures, whereas Table 2.8 presents the results using our per capita spending measure. To begin, please note that in both tables the result for the Wald test of independent equations is significant, confirming that there are systematic differences between contested and uncontested elections and thus that a two-stage procedure is appropriate.

Looking more closely at Table 2.7, the results in stage one of our model almost precisely echo those of Hall and Bonneau[79] though the time frames of our studies differ. As expected, candidates who won their last elections by narrow margins are more likely to attract challengers in their next reelection bids. Also as hypothesized, electorally experienced incumbents are less likely to be challenged than candidates seeking open seats. Interestingly, this incumbency advantage does not extend to those initially appointed and facing voters for the first time. Instead, these novices do not differ statistically from candidates for open seats in their tendency to draw challengers.

Although neither larger salaries nor longer terms of office affect the likelihood of a challenge (consistent with Hall and Bonneau[80]), the institutional variables are highly significant. Challengers are less likely in states with partisan homogeneity (Unified Government) and also in district-based partisan elections. On the other hand, partisan statewide elections and nonpartisan district elections are more likely to see electoral competition. Also as predicted, the pool of available candidates (lawyers) increases the likelihood of competition. However, the effects are substantively small.

Finally, the *White* variable is not statistically significant, indicating that races are not more likely to be contested after the *White* decision. Contrary to the rhetoric of some, it appears that this decision did not have the dramatic impact predicted, at least from the perspective of the propensity of challengers to take on incumbents. Of course, it may be too soon to see such an effect. However, other studies[81] document a rise in contestation well before *White*, leading us to conclude that *White* is not responsible for this trend.

Table 2.7 Ballot Roll-Off in State Supreme Court Elections, 1990–2004 (using Total Spending)

Stage 1: Challengers in State Supreme Court Elections, 1990–2004

	Coefficient	*Robust SE*	z	P > |z|
Competitive Seat	0.543	0.159	3.42	0.001
Elected Incumbent	–0.901	0.214	–4.21	0.000
Appointed Incumbent	–0.348	0.284	–1.23	0.220
Salary	0.154	0.222	0.69	0.488
Term	0.001	0.104	0.01	0.990
Unified Government	–0.513	0.166	–3.09	0.002
Partisan	0.652	0.362	1.80	0.072
District	1.102	0.502	2.19	0.028
Partisan x District	–2.717	0.506	–5.37	0.000
Post-*White*	0.106	0.228	0.46	0.642
Lawyers	0.000	0.000	3.71	0.000
Constant	–0.452	1.473	–0.31	0.759

Dependent variable: contested.

Stage 2: Ballot Roll-Off in State Supreme Court Elections, 1990–2004

	Coefficient	*Robust SE*	z	P > |z|
Total Spending	–1.762	0.551	–3.20	0.001
New SC Candidate	–0.631	1.024	–0.62	0.538
Presidential Election	4.787	0.770	6.22	0.000
Education Level	–0.586	0.297	–1.97	0.049
Partisan	–15.077	2.634	–5.72	0.000
District	–13.038	4.043	–3.22	0.001
Partisan x District	15.071	3.527	4.27	0.000
Period 2	2.402	1.674	1.43	0.151
Period 3	3.428	2.089	1.64	0.101
Period 4	0.735	2.208	0.33	0.739
Constant	90.376	22.245	4.06	0.000

Dependent variable: percentage of ballot roll-off
Mean of dependent variable = 14.16
Number of observations = 260; censored = 69, uncensored = 191
Log likelihood = –764.466
Test of independent equations: χ^2 (1) = 26.74; Prob > χ^2 = 0.000

Table 2.8 Ballot Roll-Off in State Supreme Court Elections, 1990–2004 (using Per Capita Spending)

Stage 1: Challengers in State Supreme Court Elections, 1990–2004

	Coefficient	*Robust SE*	*z*	*P > |z|*
Competitive Seat	0.572	0.183	3.12	0.002
Elected Incumbent	–0.913	0.225	– 4.05	0.000
Appointed Incumbent	–0.359	0.294	–1.22	0.222
Salary	0.120	0.229	0.53	0.599
Term	0.005	0.109	0.04	0.965
Unified Government	–0.519	0.170	–3.05	0.002
Partisan	0.721	0.368	1.96	0.050
District	1.062	0.519	2.05	0.041
Partisan x District	–2.655	0.510	–5.21	0.000
Post-*White*	0.120	0.230	0.52	0.601
Lawyers	0.000	0.000	3.20	0.001
Constant	–0.239	1.513	–0.16	0.875

Dependent variable: contested.

Stage 2: Ballot Roll-Off in State Supreme Court Elections, 1990–2004

	Coefficient	*Robust SE*	*z*	*P > |z|*
Per Capita Spending	–1.729	0.451	–3.83	0.000
New SC Candidate	–0.145	0.996	–0.15	0.884
Presidential Election	4.919	0.780	6.31	0.000
Education Level	–0.585	0.298	–1.96	0.050
Partisan	–15.773	2.566	–6.15	0.000
District	–9.633	4.441	–2.17	0.030
Partisan x District	14.203	4.019	3.53	0.000
Period 2	2.150	1.606	1.34	0.181
Period 3	3.353	2.111	1.59	0.112
Period 4	0.769	2.065	0.37	0.709
Constant	74.771	23.267	3.21	0.001

Dependent variable: percentage of ballot roll-off
Mean of dependent variable = 14.16
Number of observations = 260; censored = 69, uncensored = 191
Log likelihood = –761.197
Test of independent equations: χ^2 (1) = 10.62; Prob > χ^2 = 0.001

Turning now to the second stage of our model, our results largely confirm our predictions. Most importantly, campaign spending exerts a statistically significant impact on the willingness of voters to participate in supreme court elections once these voters are already at the polls.

As Table 2.7 illustrates, higher amounts of campaign spending produce significantly lower levels of roll-off. In fact, a 1 percent increase in spending yields a 0.018 percent decrease in ballot roll-off. Although at first blush this may seem like a small substantive change, a look at predicted values of roll-off suggests otherwise. For example, if all variables are held at their means in our model, predicted roll-off is 18.2 percent. However, when spending is increased by one standard deviation, predicted roll-off drops to 15.8 percent. Considering that 19 percent of the incumbents in nonpartisan and partisan elections from 1990 through 2004 won by 55 percent of the vote or less, even small changes produced by better-than-average spending could mean the difference between winning and losing for a sizable number of justices. Even more dramatic are the changes that take place at the extremes. In our model, holding all other variables at their means, we would predict roll-off at 22.1 percent when spending is reduced by two standard deviations. However, when spending is increased two standard deviations, predicted roll-off is 12.7 percent. Again, money matters in these races. Contrary to critics of judicial elections who claim that competitive and expensive campaigns alienate voters, the empirical evidence suggests otherwise.

In terms of electoral factors, races in which candidates lack electoral experience, either because the seats are open or involve newly appointed incumbents seeking their first election victory, are not important in motivating citizens to participate in contested supreme court elections. As Table 2.7 indicates, there are similar levels of roll-off in open-seat and appointed incumbent races to those in incumbent–challenger races when both of these types of elections include challengers. Thus, the effects of open seats and appointed incumbents are largely in their ability to attract challengers in the first place.

However, as expected and consistent with the dominant finding in the literature, ballot roll-off is somewhat higher in presidential election years than otherwise, by almost 5 percent. Presidential elections encourage "casual" voters to participate, and these people are not likely to vote for "insignificant" races, such as state supreme court.

Also important is the average education of the electorate. Generally, well-educated electorates vote in higher proportions than less educated electorates. This further strengthens our findings regarding campaign spending: when voters are more knowledgeable and better informed, they are more likely to participate.

Looking at institutional factors, there is less roll-off in partisan statewide races and nonpartisan district races relative to our baseline category of nonpartisan statewide races. However, partisan district races have higher roll-off. Clearly, institutions can either encourage or discourage participation in these elections, an important finding for those seeking to improve voting in judicial elections. In fact, voter participation can be influenced considerably simply by modifying the rules under which the elections take place.

From the perspective of judicial reform, statewide partisan elections and, to a lesser extent, district-based nonpartisan elections, are excellent agents of democracy. Both significantly reduce voter defection in state supreme court elections in a particularly strong way. These findings make eminent sense when we consider the critical information provided by partisan ballots, as well as the incentive structure for the minority party to field candidates in district-based constituencies and their increased odds of winning relative to statewide races.

Although none of the temporal variables is significant, particularly noteworthy is the result for Period 4. Recall that this represents the post-*White* period. All things being equal, it does not appear that the *White* case has had much of an effect on either contestation or voter participation in state supreme court elections. Although it is too early to draw any definitive conclusions, early evidence suggests that *White* may not have had the impact expected or widely believed to have occurred. Judicial reform advocates appear to have sounded the alarm in error, at least from the perspective of challengers and citizen participation in state supreme court elections.

Table 2.8 presents the results of estimating our two-stage model of ballot roll-off using per capita spending instead of total spending. As Table 2.8 illustrates, the differences produced by changing the spending measure are negligible with respect to any substantive conclusions we would reach from the analysis.[82] Whether measured as the total level of spending or as dollars spent per voter, campaign spending increases voter participation significantly, other things considered. In fact, the remarkable stability of our results across different measures of spending speaks strongly to the robustness of our analysis and the strength of our inferences.

Graphical depictions of the relationship between spending and roll-off, with other variables in the model controlled, illustrate these points well. As we can easily observe in Figures 2.2 and 2.3, spending (total or per capita) increases predicted voting in a straightforward linear fashion. These same patterns are evident in graphs (not shown) of the bivariate relationships between roll-off and our spending measures (with or without conversion to a logarithmic function). No matter how we measure spending or model the relationship, money significantly reduces roll-off in state supreme court elections.

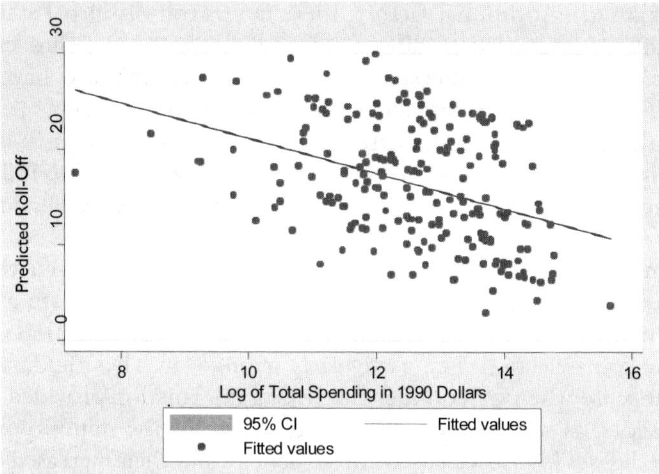

Figure 2.2 Total Spending and Ballot Roll-Off.

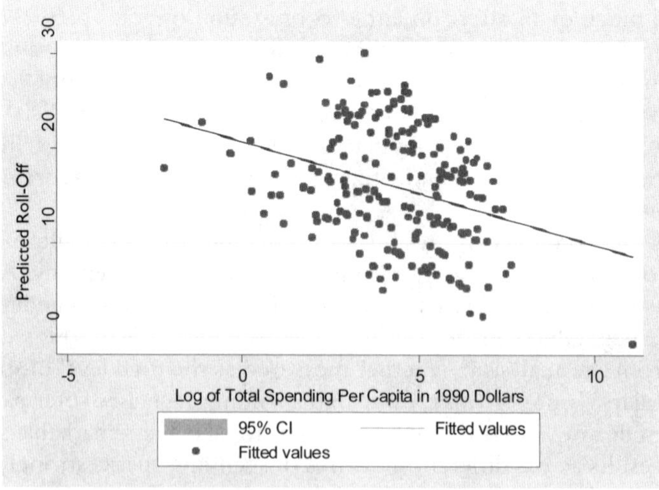

Figure 2.3 Total Spending per Capita and Ballot Roll-Off.

Conclusion

We have just established that increased spending in elections to state supreme courts has the effect of substantially enhancing citizen participation in these races. Whether measured as the overall spending in each election or in per capita terms, the fact remains that expensive campaigns serve to encourage participation in elections for the state high court bench once those voters already have gone to the polls to cast ballots for other important elections. In short, money means voters in supreme court elections.

The implications of these findings for linkages between citizens and the bench, and for democratic pressures on state supreme courts, are significant. Of course, we cannot speak directly to the issue of whether citizen participation enhances positive short-term and long-term perceptions of courts, or whether the positive effects of aggressive spending in judicial campaigns can outweigh any negative consequences of contested elections and heated campaigns. Nonetheless, it certainly seems reasonable to postulate that by stimulating mass participation and giving voters greater ownership in the outcomes of these races, expensive campaigns strengthen the critical linkage between citizens and courts and enhance the quality of democracy. In fact, conventional wisdom about the deleterious effects of money in judicial elections is overdrawn. At a minimum, we know that there are no observable negative behavioral consequences for voters of vigorous competition and costly campaigns.

Recently, several scholars have observed lower levels of confidence in courts[83] and diffuse support for courts[84] in states using partisan judicial elections, and have attributed these differences largely to the presumed negative effects of vigorous electoral competition. However, this chapter failed to detect any negative consequences for voters of hotly contested elections. Instead, as we have documented, the more expensive and contentious the race, especially in statewide partisan elections, the more likely it is that voters will participate. Moreover, voters in these states consistently have rejected proposals to replace partisan elections with other methods for selecting judges. Thus, we suggest that lower levels of confidence and diffuse support for courts in partisan states might be less related to judicial elections and more closely connected to factors in the broader political environment that prompt states to choose competitive judicial elections in the first place. Rather than judicial elections creating negative feelings about courts, it seems just as likely that voters in some states start out being more negative toward government and, as a consequence, choose to elect judges rather than surrender this important power to political elites. Thus, partisan elections might well be the effect of negative feelings toward government rather than the cause.

From the perspective of selection systems, we know from previous studies[85] that retention and nonpartisan elections are quite limited in their ability to engage voters in state supreme court elections and that partisan elections perform quite well on this dimension. However, we now have even better evidence that statewide partisan elections, the most common form of partisan elections, have a decided impact on voter participation when the effects of money and challengers are taken into account. Statewide partisan elections attract challengers and significantly reduce roll-off, *ceteris paribus.* With regard to voter mobilization, judicial reform advocates are wrong about the effects of big spending and are wrong about the performance of partisan elections.

From a different perspective, the decisions of challengers to enter supreme court elections, and decisions of voters to participate in these races once they already are mobilized for other contests, are quite predictable and are determined by similar factors governing elections for nonjudicial offices. Contrary to prevailing opinion, judicial elections are neither unpredictable nor unique.

Chapter 3

Explaining Campaign Spending

Rising campaign costs and the use of television airtime to advertise in state supreme court elections are widely regarded by judicial reform advocates as among the most serious and pressing threats to the integrity and legitimacy of American state judiciaries. Consider, for example, the following statement from the Justice at Stake Campaign about the 2004 supreme court elections:

> Television advertisements are the canary in the coalmine of judicial elections: when they appear, the nasty and costly new politics of judicial elections are not far behind. In the space of four short years, television advertising in state supreme court races has migrated from a handful of battleground states to four of every five states with contested high court races.[1]

Indeed, television advertisements and their corresponding price tags are at the heart of the controversy over electing judges, particularly in partisan elections. The basic contention is that judicial elections are getting "noisier, nastier, and costlier,"[2] and that these features of highly competitive elections will diminish citizens' positive perceptions of judges and courts.[3]

In this chapter, we seek to understand why some candidates spend considerably more than others. Our fundamental point is that campaign costs are not rising uniformly for all candidates or all states. Instead, campaign spending in supreme court elections reflects the types of considerations present in elections to other offices in the United States: the closeness of the race, the value of the seat, the institutional arrangements that define the election (especially whether partisan labels are on the ballot), and the overall political context (including the size of the tort docket and its draw on the particular set of interests concerned with the outcomes of those cases). Very important among these is the nonpartisan ballot, which was a reform vigorously advocated over partisan elections. Not only do nonpartisan elections inhibit citizen participation in state supreme court elections (as we documented in chapter 2), nonpartisan elections significantly raise the costs of seeking office.

We begin our discussion of this issue by noting that detailed systematic information has yet to be provided about the nature of campaign spending in state supreme court elections, including who is spending, when they are spending, and exactly on what.[4] For instance, according to *The New Politics of Judicial Elections, 2004* (Deborah Goldberg, Sarah Samis, Edwin Bender, and Rachel Weiss, 2005, Washington, DC: Justice at Stake Campaign), only about $1 of every $4 raised by candidates is spent on the costs of airtime, yet the report does not list or classify where the remaining 75 percent goes.[5]

Moreover, television campaign spots in state supreme court elections were quite unusual until recently, despite the fact that these elections consistently were drawing challengers and were being decided by increasingly narrow margins at least by 1990 (and much earlier in some states). In 2000, for example, television advertising was used in less than one of every four states with contested supreme court elections, in less than two of three states in 2002, and in four of five states in 2004.[6] Unquestionably the use of television in supreme court campaigns has increased dramatically in a short time, but these increases considerably lag behind electoral competition overall (as we will discuss in chapter 4). Moreover, television advertising still failed to appear in 20 percent of the states with *contested* supreme court elections by 2004.

Consider these figures in relation to the wide array of statewide races that take place simultaneously with supreme court elections. It simply is unimaginable that a *contested* race for the United States Senate, Governor, or even Secretary of State would exclude television ads as an essential part of the campaign.

More importantly, there is little scientific evidence that advertising (including the small proportion of negative messages contained therein) diminishes citizen perceptions of judges or courts,[7] nor is there any real-world evidence of what kinds of impacts any variations in confidence would have in any practical way. However, we have documented (as in chapter 2) that there are significant positive consequences to expensive campaigns. Aggressive spending energizes the electorate and promotes voting. Also (as we will demonstrate in chapter 4), campaign spending is but one factor that determines how well candidates perform in state supreme court elections. Candidates do not simply "buy" supreme court seats, conventional wisdom notwithstanding.[8]

Consider the presence of television in state supreme court campaigns from the perspective of political scientists concerned with democratic politics and processes. State supreme courts are vitally important institutions, with the incredible power to resolve some of the nation's most significant controversies. State supreme courts are the final arbiters of state law and in many cases federal law, particularly given the shrinking docket of the United States Supreme Court. We also know that the justices' political preferences are a strong predictor of their decisions on the bench.

Despite these facts, there was a complete lack of television advertising in the large majority of states with *contested* supreme court races in 2000, and in 20 percent of the states in 2004. In elections as important as the states' highest courts, anybody with the slightest interest in politics should be asking what took so long for candidates to use television in their campaigns, and why have so many states with judicial elections remained immune to important democratic processes.

These are the questions we seek to answer in this chapter. We look systematically at campaign spending in state supreme court elections from 1990 through 2004 and identify the most important factors that give rise to costly campaigns. In doing so, we discuss the importance of campaign activity for citizen education and mobilization in modern democracies. As we will show, highly competitive races and the expensive campaigns that accompany them do not occur in all states or in all races within single states. However, the amounts of money spent in these races are quite predictable. By knowing fundamental features of the states' electoral systems, candidate incumbency, and the political context, we can explain campaign spending in state supreme court races much in the same way as elections to non-judicial office.

In response, reform advocates would assert that any similarities between judicial elections and elections for legislative or executive offices prove their point. That is, reformers assert that judges simply are different because the judicial function is different: judges interpret and apply law created by other political actors. Thus, judges should not engage in the unseemly game of electoral politics, including television advertising. Indeed, it would appear that the real concern of judicial reform advocates is not campaigning or television *per se* but the increasingly competitive nature of state supreme court elections.

We argue that judges are not different politically speaking, particularly when seeking to retain office through the electoral process. Judges should defend their discretionary political choices that have been demonstrated to reflect their underlying personal preferences, and should pursue strategies to retain office, including advertising. Moreover, there is little reason to think that such actions will harm the integrity of courts.[9] On the contrary, lively well-financed campaigns help to inform voters and motivate them to go to the polls. This act of voting in turn enhances political trust and efficacy, and legitimizes judicial power.

Spending in State Supreme Court Elections

Those who live in states where judges (particularly supreme court justices) are elected have been bombarded by criticisms of these elections in the press. Harsh commentary about the impropriety of electing judges comes not only from the media[10] but also from the judges themselves.[11] Indeed, condemnation of judicial elections has increased in recent years as elections to the state high court bench have become more interesting, competitive, and well financed.[12]

In chapter 2, we documented that spending in state supreme court elections has increased since 1990, and we illustrated the considerable variation across the states in average dollars spent, both overall and on a per capita basis. We also wish to demonstrate the significant spending differences that occur between partisan and nonpartisan elections. These data are presented in tabular form in Table 3.1 and in graphical form in Figure 3.1.[13]

As Table 3.1 and Figure 3.1 clearly illustrate, supreme court elections in 2004 were significantly more expensive on average than those in 1990, whether partisan or nonpartisan. However, partisan elections were more expensive in 1994 than in any other election cycle except 2004. Similarly, nonpartisan elections cost more in 1994 than those in three subsequent election cycles. Thus, the overall increase in spending over time in state supreme courts clearly has not been monotonic. Additionally, partisan races always were more expensive on average than nonpartisan races, with the exception of 2002 (where they were about equal). However, we want to be careful about using descriptive data to draw the inference that partisan elections increase campaign spending. In the multivariate analysis below, we demonstrate that these descriptive patterns are the result of factors other than ballot type.

In other work, Bonneau found that open-seat races were more expensive on average than incumbent–challenger races.[14] We also demonstrated in chapter 2 that the states themselves differ considerably in the average costs of campaigns. Thus, campaign spending seems to be related to the type of race (partisan versus nonpartisan, incumbent versus open seat), as

Table 3.1 Average Total Spending (in 1990 Dollars) in State Supreme Court Elections, 1990–2004, by Election Type

Year	*Partisan (Number of Elections)*	*Nonpartisan (Number of Elections)*
1990	$404,937 (18)	$303,464 (12)
1992	$571,631 (18)	$474,259 (16)
1994	$958,840 (16)	$310,570 (15)
1996	$662,670 (17)	$385,739 (19)
1998	$833,872 (15)	$451,900 (16)
2000	$713,229 (21)	$558,501 (21)
2002	$593,459 (13)	$614,986 (12)
2004	$1,097,978 (12)	$491,232 (21)
Average	$712,013 (130)	$452,575 (132)

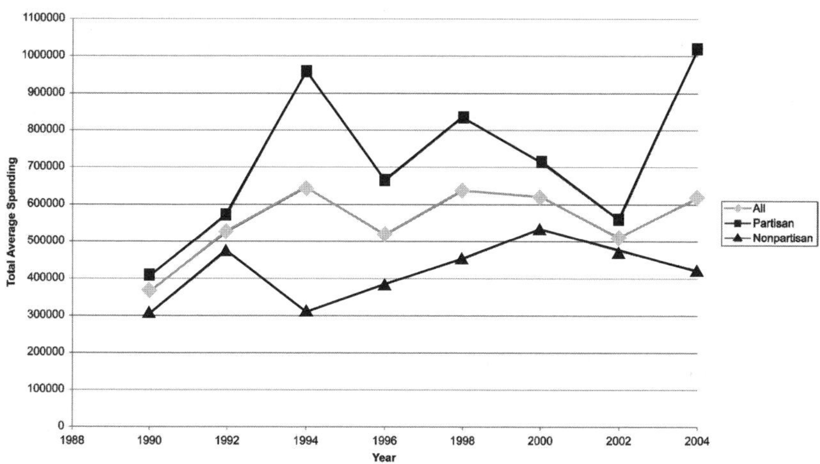

Figure 3.1 Total Average Spending by Year in 1990 Dollars, Contested General Elections, 1990–2005.

well as when and where the election occurs. We examine these relationships more systematically in the models below.

What explains intrastate and interstate variations in the amounts of money spent in supreme court races? Do the various contingencies that drive campaign spending in legislative and executive elections also drive the campaign dynamic in judicial elections?[15] There are strong reasons to think that judicial elections are just like other elections in the United States. In the most fundamental way, candidates for all public office must campaign and spend money to win electoral support. However, current scholarship points to less obvious similarities between judicial elections and their legislative and executive counterparts. Empirical studies document that the same basic forces that determine incumbent defeats,[16] contestation by challengers,[17] and the electoral margins of incumbents[18] in judicial elections are those operating in a wide array of legislative and executive offices.

Despite important similarities, judicial races differ from their legislative and executive counterparts on three primary dimensions. First, judges do not have a direct representative function. Whereas legislators, for example, are expected to attend to the needs of their constituents, judges are charged with interpreting and applying the law in an impartial manner, without reference to the desires of the public or, for that matter, their own personal preferences.[19]

Second, judicial candidates historically have been prohibited from discussing their positions on public policy issues, particularly any subjects that might reasonably come before their courts. Whereas legislative and executive candidates can debate the relative merits of tax cuts, the death penalty, or any other hot-button issue, judicial candidates effectively could talk only about their qualifications for office until *Republican Party of Minnesota* v. *White* (2002).

Third, and perhaps most importantly, state supreme court elections occur in a variety of institutional contexts. Some states elect their judges on partisan ballots, whereas other states use nonpartisan ballots. State supreme court elections also can occur statewide or in districts, for one seat or multiple seats. Additionally, terms of office range significantly, from six to twelve years.

In sum, state supreme court elections vary in a number of ways (institutional and otherwise) from elections for many other types of political offices, and these variations might have an important impact on candidate spending. Indeed, evaluating the importance of formal institutional design on campaign politics is the essence of evaluating the efficacy of recent reforms on judicial campaign politics. We know that institutional arrangements matter, from studies of the judiciary,[20] legislatures,[21] and bureaucracies.[22] With campaign spending, the question is how, and with what consequence.

The Importance of Campaign Spending

Campaign spending is very important for candidates, particularly in low-information, low-salience elections below the top of the ballot.[23] Simply put, candidates must spend money to identify themselves to voters. Indeed, studies of legislative elections[24] and state supreme court elections[25] have documented the critical link between spending and candidate name recognition. Although such exposure does not guarantee that voters will choose the best-known candidates, voters are more likely to vote for candidates with whom they are familiar.[26] Thus, being known is a necessary but not sufficient condition for obtaining electoral support.

In the same manner, campaign spending is highly beneficial for voters. Well-financed campaigns increase the knowledge base of the electorate and improve their chances of voting. Examining elections to the United States House of Representatives in 1994 and 1996, Coleman and Manna conclude that:

> [c]ampaign spending neither decreases political trust, efficacy, or interest in and attention to campaigns. Spending does contribute to knowledge and affect. Accurate perceptions of the incumbent's record are generally improved by incumbent spending and reduced by challenger spending, in practice typically producing a net result of more accuracy and more competitiveness.[27]

In presidential elections, Alvarez finds that "uncertainty [about the candidates] generally diminishes across the course of a presidential campaign in response to issue and substantive information."[28] In state supreme court elections, Hall and Bonneau determine that high levels of campaign spending increase voter participation (as reported in chapter 2).[29] Thus, evidence from studies of a wide array of elections consistently indicates that voters benefit from campaigns by learning about the candidates and their records and by being mobilized to vote. At the same time, candidates benefit by improving their chances of winning.

Modeling Campaign Spending in State Supreme Court Elections

Our primary goal in this chapter is to identify the determinants of campaign spending in partisan and nonpartisan state supreme court elections from 1990 through 2004.[30] More specifically, we assess whether partisan elections reduce or increase campaign costs (and the associated need to raise money from contributors) relative to nonpartisan elections. In doing so, we specify a model consisting of variables hypothesized to affect spending based on what we know about other offices and the unique institutional features of state supreme court elections.

As with our model of ballot roll-off in chapter 2, we use the Heckman two-stage modeling strategy to take into account the conditions under which elections draw challengers and the conditions under which candidates spend money in these elections once contested. Theoretically, we must distinguish between the conditions that promote competition and those that cause candidates to spend money in their campaigns. Essentially, because contested elections constitute a censored sample, failure to control for these effects would present a serious threat to valid inference. Stated succinctly, candidates have little incentive to spend money in uncontested elections simply because the candidates listed on the ballot will win with or without spending. Similarly, we must disentangle the effects of the presence or absence of challengers from the effects of the actual amounts spent by candidates in their campaigns.

Practically speaking, either the states do not consistently report spending data for uncontested elections or the amounts are so small that they would seriously distort any empirical analysis by giving disproportionate weight to the uncontested races. Thus, we estimate a two-stage Heckman model controlling for the likelihood that the race is contested. Stage one of our model estimates the likelihood of contestation using a selection of variables that explain contestation but do not explain campaign spending. We then use the results from the first stage of the model to generate unbiased estimates of candidate spending in contested elections. This procedure provides consistent, asymptotically efficient estimates for all the parameters in both stages of the model and promotes robust substantive conclusions.[31]

The dependent variable of interest is the total amount of campaign spending (in 1990 dollars) in the election. Because this variable is continuous, we use ordinary least squares regression (OLS) to estimate the models. Additionally, we estimate Huber/White/Sandwich robust standard errors clustered on state for the regression coefficients, set to recognize the panel structure of the data.

Stage One: Challengers in State Supreme Court Elections

Stage one of our model seeks to explain why state supreme court elections draw challengers. This model of contestation is the same model we used in chapter 2.[32] Here, as in chapter 2, the dependent variable is whether there are at least two candidates in the general election (Contested).

Also recall the independent variables in this model: electoral vulnerability (measured as competitive seats and various conditions of the incumbency advantage), attractiveness of the seat (salaries and term length), the political and institutional context (unified government, partisan elections, district-based constituencies, including a dummy variable for the period after *Republican Party of Minnesota* v. *White* (2002)), and candidate pool (lawyers).

In general, we expect challengers to run when incumbents are electorally vulnerable, supreme court seats are attractive, a sizable candidate pool exists, and the political and institutional context promotes competition.[33] For convenience, Table 3.2 lists these variables and their exact measurement.

Stage Two: Campaign Spending in State Supreme Court Elections

The dependent variable in the second stage of our analysis is the total amount of money spent in each race by all candidates, measured as the natural log of total spending (Log of Total Spending).[34] To make these figures comparable over time and to be consistent with studies of elections to other offices, we recalculate spending for all years in 1990 dollars.[35] We use the total amount of spending because we are interested in understanding what factors affect the overall costs of a given seat and not the individual strategies pursued by incumbents or challengers.[36] Using existing literature on legislative and judicial elections, we hypothesize that three broad categories of factors will influence the costs of campaigns in state supreme court elections: characteristics of the race, institutional arrangements, and the state and electoral context. For convenience, these variables and their measurement are reported in Table 3.3.

Table 3.2 Variable Descriptions for a Model of Challengers in State Supreme Court Elections

Variable	*Variable description*
Dependent Variable	
Contested	1 if a challenger entered the supreme court race 0 otherwise
Electoral Vulnerability	
Competitive Seat	1 if the incumbent supreme court justice won previously by a margin less than 60% 0 otherwise
Elected Incumbent	1 if the election involves an incumbent who has previously won election 0 otherwise
Appointed Incumbent	1 if the election involves an incumbent who was initially appointed and has never won election 0 otherwise
Attractiveness of Seat	
Salary	Supreme court base salary/state per capita disposable income, in dollars
Term	Length of the term of office for state supreme court, in years
Political and Institutional Context	
Unified Government	1 if the legislative and executive branches of state government are controlled by the same political party 0 otherwise
Partisan	1 if the election is a partisan election 0 otherwise
District	1 if the seat represents a district rather than the state 0 otherwise
Post-*White*	1 if the election occurred after the *White* decision in 2002 0 otherwise
Candidate Pool	
Lawyers	Number of lawyers in each state at the time of each election

Characteristics of the Race

First and foremost, elections for open seats (Open Seat) should be more costly than other contingencies of incumbency, *ceteris paribus*. Open-seat races should involve significant spending because both candidates must

Table 3.3 Variable Descriptions for a Model of Campaign Spending in State Supreme Court Elections

Variable	*Variable Description*
Dependent Variable	
Log of Total Spending	Log of total campaign spending (constant dollars) by all candidates in a race
Characteristics of the Race	
Open Seat	1 if the race was for an open seat 0 otherwise
Incumbent Elected	1 if the incumbent has previously won election to the court (as opposed to being appointed to the seat) 0 otherwise
Margin of Victory	Margin of victory (%) for the winner
Control of Court	1 if partisan control of the court was at stake 0 otherwise
Number of Seats	Number of available state supreme court seats in the state that year
Institutional Arrangements	
Partisan	1 if the election was a partisan election 0 otherwise
District	1 if the election was held in a district (i.e., not statewide) 0 otherwise
Multimember	1 if the election was held in a multimember district 0 otherwise
Term	Length (in years) of the term of office
Electoral and Supreme Court Context	
Voting Age Population	Voting age population of the state/district (1000s)
Prior Close Race	1 if the most recent judicial election in that jurisdiction was decided by 55% of the vote or less 0 otherwise
Tort Docket	Proportion of the supreme court docket (1995) involving tort cases
Control Variables	
Period 1	1 if the election occurred in 1990 or 1992
Period 2	1 if the election occurred in 1994 or 1996
Period 3	1 if the election occurred in 1998 or 2000

become known to the electorate as appropriate contenders for the state high court bench, though some candidates may already be serving in the lower courts. Furthermore, it should be easier for candidates for open seats to raise (and thus spend) money than challengers seeking to unseat incumbents, because incumbents generally are likely to be reelected.[37] Open-seat races raise the stakes for both candidates and donors, and spending should rise with the uncertainty of electoral outcomes. Indeed, both Sorauf[38] and Hogan[39] found that open-seat races are more expensive in the state legislative context, and Bonneau[40] found the same pattern in state supreme court races.

These findings illustrate well the powerful force of incumbency. Generally speaking, incumbents have a strategic advantage relative to their less experienced counterparts, not only in deterring challengers but also in doing better with voters. Incumbents already have been legitimized by voters and have gained name recognition in previous campaigns. All things considered, incumbents should be able to spend less money and still perform well electorally. Thus, we hypothesize that there will be less spending in races where the incumbent gained his or her seat through election (Incumbent Elected) than appointment or open-seat contests. In assessing the impact of open seats and electorally experienced incumbents, our baseline category for comparison are those justices initially appointed to fill vacancies created mid-term (usually by the retirement of a sitting justice). In fact, about 32 percent of supreme court justices seeking reelection from 1990 through 2004 were facing voters for the first time. Appointed incumbents may not receive all the benefits of incumbency.[41] For example, appointed incumbents are more likely to be ousted from office, other things being equal, than their previously elected counterparts.[42] In this way, appointed incumbents should spend more like candidates running in open-seat races than like previously elected incumbents.

Another critical factor in campaign spending should be the closeness of the race. As with open-seat contests, uncertainty should promote spending, other things being equal. As we know, candidate viability is an important key to fundraising.[43] Candidates who are performing well raise more money and thus have more money to spend.[44] Unfortunately, valid and reliable a priori measures of candidates' and donors' expectations of closeness have not been developed.[45] As a practical alternative, we use the standard second-best measure: the actual margin of victory.[46] We hypothesize that lower margins of victory (Margin of Victory) lead to correspondingly higher expenditures in state supreme court elections.

From a different perspective, partisan control of a collegial court is a valuable political commodity, and we would expect significant sums of money to be paid for such influence.[47] Indeed, elections that could tip the balance of the court from conservative to liberal or vice versa significantly raise the political stakes. Thus, those campaigns in which the partisan control of the court is up for grabs (Control of Court) should be significantly more costly, other things being equal.

Finally regarding factors characteristic of individual races, the amount of money spent in any supreme court race may depend on how many other seats are up on the same court simultaneously. Unlike legislative and gubernatorial elections, the number of available supreme court seats in any given election cycle varies by state and by year, and can range from none to five (at least during the time period in this study).

Because of this unique feature of judicial elections, we are unsure of the exact manner in which these variations in available seats might influence campaign spending. Theoretically, we might predict that the more seats are contested at any given time, the more money candidates should need to spend to gain the attention of voters in a very crowded field.[48] Alternatively, we might reasonably posit that individual campaigns occurring simultaneously for the same court might reduce campaign spending, because each candidate benefits from the mobilization effects of the other candidates. Given the absence of strong theory either way, we hypothesize that the number of seats being contested will influence campaign expenditures, but we do not offer a prediction about the direction of that impact (Number of Seats).

Institutional Arrangements

One of the fundamental tenets of political science scholarship is that institutions matter. Institutions structure the rewards and sanctions for actors, as well as the range of feasible alternatives.[49] In the context of elections, institutions influence the manner in which information is presented to voters, the extent to which citizens are likely to participate, and a host of other processes in democratic politics.

With regard to campaign expenditures in state supreme court elections, the most fundamental institutional difference is that between partisan and nonpartisan elections. In Table 3.1 and Figure 3.1, we saw that nonpartisan races, on average, are much less costly than partisan elections. However, these simple descriptive statistics did not take into account the wide range of factors that might influence such a result, such as the tendency for partisan elections to be competitive at higher rates. Multivariate models, which control for the major influences on campaign spending, might reveal a different result.

In fact, that is precisely what we predict. Other things considered, partisan elections should be significantly cheaper than nonpartisan elections, resulting in far less need by the candidates to engage in fundraising activities that grab the attention and condemnation of judicial reform advocates.

Partisan judicial races bring a powerful organizational actor—the political party—directly into campaigns. Political parties have considerable experience in generating funds and have a greater stake in the success of judicial candidates running under their label. Similarly, candidates directly affiliated with a political party should find it easier to raise (and thus spend) money because there are groups of contributors who regularly support the party. From a different perspective, candidates who are members of the majority party in their states will benefit from having that all-important voting cue next to their names and will be able to garner votes on that basis. Alternatively, candidates in nonpartisan elections, which exclude partisan labels from ballots, must work to educate and mobilize voters to their particular candidacies. Although political parties are highly involved in these elections also, overcoming the information deficit is formidable. Thus, we hypothesize that partisan elections for state supreme courts (Partisan) will be much cheaper than nonpartisan elections.

States also differ in the manner in which geographic constituencies are constructed. Most states elect their supreme court justices statewide, but a select number of states divide the state into geographic districts for election purposes only. By definition, district-based constituencies are smaller and more geographically compact that statewide races. Furthermore, districts are more likely to be homogenous because of their smaller size, at least to some degree. Therefore, the cost of a campaign in a district-based constituency (District) should be less than a statewide campaign, other things being equal.[50]

Another institutional difference among the states is whether supreme court justices are elected in single-member or multimember elections. In state legislative races, multimember districts generate higher campaign spending than their single-member counterparts because candidates will be less well known and will be in greater competition for voter attention. Thus, candidates in multimember legislative races need to spend more money. However, we do not know if this same dynamic will be in play in judicial races. As with the number of available seats on a court in any given election cycle, we have no strong theoretical grounds upon which to offer predictions about the direction of this influence. Thus, we hypothesize that multimember state supreme court elections (Multimember) will affect campaign spending, but we offer no predictions about direction.

Finally regarding institutional arrangements, states provide varying term lengths for the high court bench, ranging from six to twelve years. Seats on the bench in states with longer terms of office are more valuable because of increased job security for the officeholder and fewer opportunities for accession.[51] Since valuable seats are more sought after, we hypothesize that there will be more campaign spending when a longer term of office is at stake (Term).

Electoral and Supreme Court Context

The final set of independent variables in our model assesses the impact of the state and electoral context on campaign spending. First is the size of the voting age population. Campaigns are all about disseminating information to voters, and as the number of voters increases so should the costs.[52] Indeed, Hogan and Hamm[53] and Hogan[54] found that the size of the voting age population is an important determinant of state legislative campaign spending. Therefore, we hypothesize that the larger the voting age population is (Voting Age Population), the more money will be spent on state supreme court campaigns.

Second, the states vary widely in the extent to which the supreme court electoral climate is competitive. Particularly important would be signals from the previous election cycle. Candidates observing narrowly decided races in the most recent election should fear for their own electoral fates and begin to raise and spend money earlier and more aggressively in anticipation of another close call.[55] Therefore we hypothesize that narrowly decided elections (in which the winner received 55 percent of the vote or less) in the most recent supreme court election in the state (Prior Close Race) will produce higher spending in the current race, other things being equal.

Finally, the composition of supreme court dockets may affect campaign spending. The kinds of cases dominating the dockets of state supreme courts vary considerably.[56] Some courts deal primarily with criminal or governmental regulation cases, whereas other courts decide a large proportion of tort disputes. Of course, the battle over tort reform is intense, pitting trial lawyers against corporations and other business interests. These fierce political battles have involved significant sums of money, as each side competes to elect justices sympathetic to their particular point of view.[57]

This can be seen very clearly by looking at the two courts of last resort in Texas, where the amount of money spent for the Texas Supreme Court (which handles civil cases only) greatly surpasses the Texas Court of Criminal Appeals (which has jurisdiction over criminal cases only). For example, in incumbent–challenger races from 1990 through 2004, campaign expenditures for the Texas Supreme Court averaged $1,017,228, compared with an average of $93,534 for the Texas Court of Criminal Appeals. The same pattern held true for open seats, with an average of $958,865 per race for the Texas Supreme Court, compared with $111,683 for the Texas Court of Criminal Appeals.[58]

Therefore, we hypothesize that races for state supreme courts with larger proportions of tort cases on their dockets (Tort Docket) will be considerably more expensive than campaigns in states that do not litigate torts extensively.

Temporal Variables

To control for any temporal effects in the model, we include dummy variables for when the election occurred.[59] Period 1 covers elections from 1990 through 1992, Period 2 is 1994 through 1996, Period 3 is 1998 through 2000, and Period 4 (which we omit to prevent perfect collinearity among the variables) is 2002 through 2004. Note that Period 4 (the omitted category) corresponds to the period after *Republican Party of Minnesota* v. *White* (2002), in which the United States Supreme Court held that states could not prohibit candidates for judicial office from taking positions on issues. Given this fundamental change in constitutional law and the electoral environment, we expect much higher levels of spending after the *White* case. Indeed, this is a fundamental contention of the judicial reform movement—that *White* politicized the electoral climate for judges. If true, the signs of the coefficients for Period 1, Period 2, and Period 3 all should be negative and statistically significant in the model.

Results: Explaining State Supreme Court Campaign Spending

Table 3.4 displays the results of estimating our model of state supreme court campaign spending estimated using Heckman's two-step correction for selection bias. Note that although the chi-square test of independent equations is just barely outside the bounds of conventional statistical significance (by a mere 0.004), the fact is that it is incredibly close and our strong theoretical rationale for using a selection model indicates that failing to correct for the selection bias could lead to biased coefficients and erroneous conclusions.[60]

Stage One: Contestation

The results for stage one of our model estimating the propensities for challengers to enter state supreme court races are similar to those reported in chapter 2, with some important exceptions that are easily explained by differences in the numbers and types of elections being analyzed. In chapter 2, we examined only those elections held simultaneously with presidential, senatorial, or gubernatorial elections, and we also excluded multimember races because of the difficulty of coding several of the independent variables. Those cases are reintroduced here. Thus, we increased the number of elections from 260 in chapter 2 to 361 here, which introduced more variability.

As the results in the top half of Table 3.4 indicate, justices who won their previous elections by narrow margins are more likely to be challenged in their next election. Also as expected, elected incumbents are less

Table 3.4 Campaign Spending in State Supreme Court Elections, 1990–2004

Stage 1: Challengers in State Supreme Court Elections, 1990–2004

	Coefficient	*Robust SE*	*Z*	*P > |z|*
Competitive Seat	0.809	0.319	2.53	0.011
Elected Incumbent	–0.776	0.165	–4.69	0.000
Appointed Incumbent	–0.279	0.119	–2.34	0.020
Salary	0.000	0.000	2.43	0.015
Term	0.032	0.046	0.70	0.486
Unified Government	–0.150	0.179	–0.84	0.400
Partisan	0.580	0.192	3.02	0.003
District	0.753	0.328	2.29	0.022
Partisan x District	–1.144	0.497	–2.30	0.021
Post-*White*	–0.238	0.350	–0.68	0.496
Lawyers	0.000	0.000	2.18	0.029
Constant	–1.563	0.877	–1.78	0.075

Dependent variable: contested

Stage 2: Campaign Spending in State Supreme Court Elections, 1990–2004

	Coefficient	*Robust SE*	*Z*	*P > |z|*
Open Seat	0.169	0.139	1.21	0.225
Elected Incumbent	0.230	0.194	1.18	0.238
Margin of Victory	–0.027	0.004	–7.57	0.000
Control of Court	0.022	0.144	0.15	0.877
Number of Seats	–0.168	0.057	–2.96	0.003
Partisan	–0.570	0.261	–2.18	0.029
District	0.067	0.358	0.19	0.852
Multimember	–0.767	0.343	–2.24	0.025
Term	0.214	0.067	3.20	0.001
Voting Age Population	0.000	0.000	0.55	0.583
Prior Close Race	0.284	0.185	1.53	0.125
Tort Docket	0.051	0.006	8.18	0.000
Period 1	–0.296	0.325	–0.91	0.363
Period 2	–0.153	0.269	–0.29	0.770
Period 3	–0.065	0.221	–0.29	0.770
Constant	11.225	0.783	14.34	0.000

Dependent variable: log of total campaign spending (constant dollars)
Number of observations = 361; censored = 101, uncensored = 260
Log pseudo-likelihood = –486.111
Test of independent equations: χ^2 (1) = 3.70; Prob > χ^2 = 0.054.

likely to face challengers than are candidates for open-seat races, as are appointed incumbents (contrary to the findings in chapter 2 and the previous work of Hall and Bonneau, which detected no incumbency advantage for newly appointed justices).[61]

Regarding the attractiveness of supreme court seats, higher salaries increase the likelihood that races will be contested. This result diverges from Hall and Bonneau (as well as chapter 2), for the reasons just discussed.[62] However, consistent with Hall and Bonneau and chapter 2, the term of office is not statistically significant.[63]

In terms of the political and institutional context, the presence of unified government is not a statistically significant influence on the presence of challengers in supreme court elections. However, as predicted, district-based partisan elections reduce the likelihood of challengers, whereas partisan statewide elections and nonpartisan district elections increase the odds of challengers. Also as posited, the larger pools of available candidates enhance the chances for challengers, although the effects are substantively small.

Finally, the *White* variable is not statistically significant, indicating that races are not more likely to be contested after the *White* decision. Contrary to the rhetoric of some, it appears that this decision did not have the dramatic impact purported, at least from the perspective of the propensity of challengers to take on incumbents.[64]

Stage Two: the Determinants of Campaign Spending

The results of estimating our model of campaign spending are very interesting and, in some cases, surprising. First, consider the unexpected results. Contrary to our expectations, races involving open seats and established incumbents are not statistically different from races involving appointed incumbents, *ceteris paribus.* The nature of incumbency simply does not affect the amount of money spent in supreme court elections once these races have drawn challengers. Similarly, campaign spending is not affected by whether partisan control of the court is at stake, whether the election occurred in a district or statewide, the size of the voting age population, or close races in the previous election cycle. These unexpected findings are themselves not very unexpected, since we are just beginning to understand campaign politics systematically in state supreme court elections. Obviously much remains to be explained and explored.

Even so, our model reveals some fascinating results. With the two variables about which we found little theoretical guidance in the literature for predicting the direction of impact (i.e., the number of available seats and multimember races), we see that both are statistically significant and negative in effect. First, larger numbers of available seats on the court in any given election cycle reduce campaign spending. Other things being equal, several seats up for grabs in an election cycle lower costs, whereas fewer seats translate into higher costs. In fact, one fewer seat leads to an increase in total spending of about 16.8 percent. One possible explanation is that contributors tend to be the same actors regardless of the candidates, and the presence of more seats means that contributions for each individual seat are less. Metaphorically, the pie is sliced into more (and smaller) pieces when multiple seats are up for grabs, and fewer contributions means lower expenditures. Also, when multiple seats are contested, the value of any particular seat declines. Finally, each set of candidates may benefit from the mobilization efforts of candidates vying to win the other seats, thus reducing campaign costs.

Multimember races also attract less spending than single-member elections. We suspect that the same causes that make multiple-seat elections cheaper than single vacancies are the same that reduce the costs of multimember elections. That is, the candidates for each vacancy may benefit from the mobilization efforts of the other candidates, whether the elections are decided in separate multiple races or only in one election in which multiple candidates win.

Otherwise, as Table 3.4 indicates, declining margins increase campaign spending in a statistically significant way. Substantively, a decrease of 1 percent in the margin of victory leads to an increase of about 2.7 percent in total spending. Indeed, competitiveness (or expected competitiveness) is one of the key factors driving campaign spending in judicial races.

Similarly, partisan elections are very important determinants of campaign spending in supreme court elections. Other things being equal, partisan elections are significantly cheaper than nonpartisan elections Clearly, the bivariate results in Figure 3.1 do not hold once other relevant variables are included in the model. Indeed, this goes to the very heart of one of the arguments about partisan elections. Rather than increasing the demands on judges to solicit campaign contributions and generate large campaign chests, partisan elections actually reduce them. More than partisan elections, nonpartisan elections are the problem.

Terms of office are another important institutional feature influencing the costs of campaigns. Longer terms of office provide better job security and also afford fewer opportunities to attain the high court bench, thus increasing the value of these seats and raising the costs of seeking them. Substantively, the size of this coefficient is large. A two-year increase in term increases spending by over 42 percent.

Looking at the electoral and supreme court context, tort cases as a significant percentage of the high court docket increase campaign costs considerably. This is further confirmation of the adage that larger stakes will attract bigger money. Indeed, given the financial implications of supreme court decisions on tort liability, it is not surprising that courts devoting larger proportions of their dockets to these cases will incur higher costs for seeking and retaining office, other things being equal. Substantively, a 1 percent increase in the proportion of tort cases leads to a 5.1 percent increase in total spending. Clearly, candidates are more easily able to raise (and thus spend) money in states where tort cases are prevalent and where contributors affected by this litigation will be motivated to try to shape the outcomes of these cases by influencing who hears them in the first place.

Finally, as can be seen in the statistical performance of the temporal variables, there are no observable differences in the time periods in this study. Apparently, the controversial *White* decision did not have any effect on the costs of contested campaigns just after the decision in 2002 and 2004. In other words, some of the dire predictions about the purported consequences of *White* were exaggerated or incorrect.

Spending in Lower Court Elections

Our analysis focuses only on state supreme court elections, and we have consistently shown that supreme court elections are similar to other statewide elected offices in some very important ways. However, others have attempted to extend our results to lower courts, with mixed results.

Recently, Streb and Frederick examined campaign costs in contested intermediate appellate court (IAC) elections and found that spending is not increasing in the same way at the intermediate appellate court level as the supreme court level.[65] This is not terribly surprising. Although IACs are important, the large majority of their dockets consist of routine appeals devoid of important questions of law or policy. Thus, other than the fact that closely contested IAC races make campaigns much more expensive, there are few similarities between our results (as well as those of Bonneau)[66] and the findings of Streb and Frederick. For example, whereas we failed to detect any differences by incumbency in campaign spending, Streb and Frederick established that open-seat races for IACs are cheaper than incumbent–challenger races. Also, whereas Streb and Frederick observe that spending increases as the number of seats increases, we find the opposite.[67]

Clearly judicial elections are not monolithic. State supreme court elections are more similar to elections for other statewide offices, whereas IAC elections are more typical of other down-ballot elections. This makes a great deal of sense given the power asymmetries between the two sets of institutions. However, research on lower court elections is in its infancy, and we need much more work on these important institutions before any definitive conclusions can be reached. Actually, the same applies to campaign financing in supreme court elections, as just mentioned.

Spending in State Legislative Elections

State supreme court elections differ in important respects from state legislative races also. As mentioned, Hogan and Hamm found that larger electoral constituencies increased the costs of campaigns.[68] We found no such effect in state supreme courts, not only in the differences between statewide and district-based constituencies but also with voting age populations. Second, there are no statistically observable differences between open seat races and incumbent–challenger races in state supreme courts, but studies of legislative elections find important incumbency effects.[69]

But in a general sense, we should not expect state supreme courts to resemble state legislative races, just as we would not expect supreme court elections to resemble those to IACs. State supreme courts are powerful institutions with statewide authority and often are the culmination of political ambition within the judiciary. On the other hand, IAC judgeships and positions like state legislator are far less powerful and prestigious, and state legislative office usually is considered the launching point for careers in politics rather than the culmination. Thus, while studies of other institutions might guide our initial explorations, finding disparities in the ways these institutions function is not surprising. An important task will be sorting out how various institutions function and how these functions are shaped by the rules and structures defining the institutions and their contexts.

Conclusion

Why do some state supreme court elections cost a fortune compared with others? Other things being equal, contested races for the state high court bench will be expensive if the race is closely contested, if only one seat is up for grabs, if the ballot is nonpartisan, if the race is single-member, if the term of office is longer, and if the court decides a relatively high number of tort cases. Factors that do not appear to affect state supreme court campaign spending are open seats, established incumbents, partisan control of the court at stake, close races in the previous election cycle, district-based constituencies, and the size of the voting age population.

These results have important implications for the current debate about judicial election reform and the basic assertion that the process of electing judges should end. In our analysis of campaign spending in state supreme court elections, we find that that various institutional arrangements play a definitive role in how much will be spent in campaigns. Most important from the perspective of this chapter are the differences between partisan and nonpartisan elections. Partisan elections reduce the costs of campaigning and provide critical cues to voters selecting between competing candidates for judicial office. Alternatively, nonpartisan elections increase information costs to voters, reduce the likelihood that voters will cast ballots in supreme court elections even when voters already are at the polls to vote for other important offices, and raise the costs for candidates seeking office. This increased spending characteristic of nonpartisan elections intensifies the efforts that candidates must make to elicit funds and exacerbates the problems of the seeming impropriety of doing so. Through the lens of campaign spending, nonpartisan elections are not the best choice. In fact, the very reforms proposed to improve electoral politics have had the opposite effect for those who consider the rising costs of campaigns to be a serious problem.

These results also speak directly to those who lament high campaign costs as an inevitable feature of state supreme court elections. The results here clearly show that this criticism is misguided. Rather, expensive elections are predictable based on several easy-to-identify factors, some of which are under the control of the states and the candidates, and some of which are not. Because of the crucial role played by institutions in the campaign finance game, it is possible that the high costs of campaigns can be reduced simply by changing the rules of the game. Partisan elections with shorter terms of office would be an effective start.

From a different perspective, competitive, well-financed campaigns substantially improve the willingness of citizens to participate in elections. Given this fact, we are not entirely sure why we should be concerned about amounts of money spent in supreme court campaigns, absent a showing of adverse effects on candidate entry, quality recruitment, or other important aspects of the political process like citizens' perceptions of courts and their observable consequences. If judicial elections are to be efficacious mechanisms of democratic control, then it is imperative that voters participate in them after being sufficiently educated about the candidates. In a healthy democracy where citizens garner knowledge about candidates and are mobilized to vote through election campaigns, we should be open to the fact that lively well-financed campaigns actually might be *preferable* to lackluster and poorly financed campaigns that fail to serve voters.

Chapter 4

Quality Challengers, Money, and the Choices of Voters

In this chapter, we examine the strategies of challengers and the choices of voters to answer two vitally important questions about elections to the states' highest courts: (1) does the *quality* of challengers have a significant impact on the electoral performance of incumbents, and (2) does money dictate electoral outcomes? With the first question, we seek to understand whether voters appear to have the capacity to distinguish challengers who have experience on the bench from challengers who lack it and thus are less suitable alternatives to incumbents. Stated differently, we evaluate whether the electorate seemingly has the ability to make candidate-based evaluations. With the second question, we address the highly controversial issue of big-money politics and whether state supreme court seats appear to be "for sale." With both questions, we focus on factors that determine the electoral performance of incumbents seeking reelection to state supreme courts.

These intriguing though straightforward issues about the importance of candidate quality and the role of money have significant theoretical import for illuminating the complex relationship between democratic processes and political institutions. As studies of elections to various types of offices have established, electoral competition forges observable linkages between citizens and government, enhancing the accountability function. Among other things, tighter margins of victory increase the likelihood of future electoral challenge and possible electoral defeat, thus promoting another cycle of competition to enhance the incumbent–constituency connection.[1] Similarly, some challengers actually do win, and the resulting turnover can serve to bring the institution more in line with public preferences generally. Therefore, understanding electoral competition, and specifically whether challenger quality and big spending decrease the electoral safety of incumbents, is directly relevant for delineating the precise mechanisms through which democratic processes allow citizens to control the composition of the bench and promote political outcomes consistent with citizen preferences.

On the specific question about the ability of voters to distinguish quality versus non-quality challengers, numerous studies, which we discuss in detail below, have evaluated the effects of candidate quality on the electoral fortunes of incumbents. Studies of the United States House of Representatives, United States Senate, and state legislatures all have established that quality matters. Candidates with previous electoral experience exert a significant impact on the votes garnered by incumbents, including incumbents' ability to retain their seats.

The question of whether the electoral fates of judges are affected by the quality of their challengers is a relatively new inquiry for judicial politics scholars, despite the fact that judicial elections are quite competitive. Consider, for example, reelection rates for the United States House of Representatives, United States Senate, Statehouses, and state supreme courts. From 1990 through 2004, reelection rates were, respectively, 94.9 percent, 90.0 percent, 81.1 percent, and 91.3 percent.[2] Thus, the likelihood of electoral defeat in state supreme courts is on average at least equivalent to, if not higher than, the electoral threat for other important offices. Moreover, seats in the House of Representatives, the quintessential representative institution, are safer on average than state supreme court seats.

In this chapter, we assess the impact of challenger quality while simultaneously controlling for other important forces affecting elections to the state high court bench, including campaign expenditures. Our test is simple: if experienced challengers relative to their novice counterparts significantly lessen the electoral security of incumbents, we will need to rethink traditional notions that the electorate is incapable of responding to candidate stimuli beyond incumbency and that judicial elections inherently are an ineffective means for securing popular control over the bench. Similarly, we will need to think more systematically than currently is the case in the debate over judicial selection about the manner in which institutional arrangements, including selection and retention mechanisms that promote competition, structure the politics of courts.

Similar arguments can be offered about campaign spending. We ask whether state supreme court incumbents simply are at the mercy of special interests and other high rollers when their electoral fates are being determined, as many accounts in the judicial reform literature suggest. Stated well by the American Bar Association, concerns about single-interest groups and other political contributors are "most acute" in campaigns in which incumbents are seeking reelection.[3] Generally, we consider, and find empirical support for, the proposition that money is but one of many important factors that affect electoral margins in competitive elections, just as in elections to other political offices. Also, on average, spending in incumbent–challenger races strongly favors incumbents. In this regard, we argue (as we did in chapters 2 and 3) that money is a necessary condition for educating and mobilizing voters and for publicizing the candidacies of challengers, so that the mere presence of money in an election is not reasonably a cause for alarm. In fact, it is difficult to imagine any serious run against an incumbent that would not include significant spending. Without advertising and other forms of political information dissemination, challengers are incapable of discussing their credentials with voters and because of the incumbency advantage are highly likely to lose, regardless of the merits of the candidates.

Social Science Versus Judicial Reform

Our central focus in this inquiry is the controversy over judicial reform in the American states and the serious contradictions about the nature of judicial elections that have emerged between the scholarly and judicial reform literatures. Whereas scientific work has documented the vital importance of challenger quality on the electoral performance of incumbents in a variety of elected institutions, the court reform literature, which dominates today's thinking about designing courts, predicts the opposite for judicial elections. In fact, because of grave doubts about the ability of the electorate to make meaningful choices, reformers have long advocated that judicial elections be abandoned in favor of either executive appointment or the Missouri Plan.

Advocacy groups and individuals interested in court design have proffered numerous criticisms of competitive judicial elections, but one of the most fundamental and consistent assertions is that the electorate is incapable of distinguishing between qualified and unqualified candidates. Summarized effectively by Dubois, the classic reform literature describes voters as "ignorant about competing candidates"[4] and as "voting blindly."[5] In fact, this assertion readily became one of the cornerstones upon which judicial elections were, and are still being, attacked.

Recent examples are not hard to find. The American Bar Association, which now recommends that state court judges be appointed, reported:

> [u]ninformed about the candidates' positions on relevant issues, uncertain about the candidates' qualifications or training, and unfamiliar with the candidates' job performance, voters are often unable to cast an informed ballot.[6]

Similarly, the Citizens for Independent Courts Task Force asserts that "[v]oter awareness of candidates' qualifications has been limited . . . Winning elections often turns on factors irrelevant to candidates' credentials."[7] As a final example, Rottman and Schotland argue that "as long as forty-five years ago, exit polls and other polls have shown a startling lack of voter awareness of even names of the candidates."[8]

However, there is a serious conflict between reform advocates and political scientists over the ability of the electorate to distinguish candidates in judicial elections. At least with respect to state supreme courts, several path-breaking studies have documented that the electorate does make informed choices and that these elections by many measures bear a striking resemblance to elections to other political offices.[9] Rather than being unpredictable, competition in judicial races varies systematically with assessments of the candidates, evaluations of issues, and contextual forces generally operating in elections.

We enter this debate by asking whether one of the primary arguments used to oppose judicial elections has any merit. Specifically, we evaluate whether the electorate as a whole is responsive to challengers who in some way represent qualified alternatives to incumbents. If the general thrust of the critics' arguments is correct, candidate-specific forces unrelated to incumbency should not affect competition in judicial elections. Alternatively, if judicial elections are like other elections, the opposite should occur. Thus, we add to a growing body of work[10] that considers whether recommendations for particular institutional designs are premised on sound assumptions.

Challenger Quality in American Elections

A substantial body of research examines the effects of challenger quality in non-judicial institutions. As Van Dunk summarizes, "[r]esearch at the congressional level has demonstrated that the quality of a challenger is one of the most important determinants of competition."[11] More recently, the importance of quality challengers has been documented in state legislative elections. We highlight these findings.

Challenger Quality in Congressional Elections

An extensive literature on the United States House of Representatives and Senate assesses the effects of candidate quality on the electoral success of incumbents, and also evaluates the conditions under which incumbents attract quality challengers. Although it is difficult to reduce such a large and complex body of work to a few simple propositions, especially given ongoing controversies in the literature, several patterns are apparent.

First, many House elections and some Senate races are low-key affairs that do not attract the attention of quality challengers, the media, or voters.[12] Second, a variety of forces serve to determine whether quality challengers take on incumbents, including the incumbent's performance in the previous election, strategic behavior by the incumbent, and other short-term and long-term forces in the political environment.[13] Third, in both House and Senate elections, quality challengers fare substantially better with voters than their weaker counterparts.[14] Further, this pattern is present even when the effects of a host of other variables related to the candidates and trends in national and state politics are controlled.

Interestingly, these substantive results are robust across studies that use alternative measures of challenger quality. Whether measured as a dichotomy of whether the challenger has held elective office,[15] as separate dichotomies or ordinal scales based on challengers' personal characteristics or political experience,[16] or using challengers' campaign expenditures,[17] the consistent conclusion is that quality matters.

Challenger Quality in State Legislative Elections

As state politics scholars are keenly aware, attention to state legislative elections is scant. Nonetheless, a growing body of work is beginning to answer vital questions about state races, including the nature of the incumbency advantage.[18]

Most relevant for this inquiry, Van Dunk examined all races for ten state legislatures from 1988 through 1992 and established that quality challengers (i.e., those who have been elected to any office) fare significantly better, both with respect to vote shares and winning seats, than their novice counterparts.[19] Although the evidence is limited and now somewhat dated, it does appear that challenger quality is also important at the state level.

Challenger Quality in Judicial Elections

As discussed throughout the previous chapters, a considerable literature has been generated on the politics of judicial selection, replete with all sorts of claims about the purported advantages and disadvantages of the various selection schemes. With notable exceptions,[20] however, judicial elections have not received much scholarly attention. Also somewhat surprising is the fact that the only two studies evaluating, though indirectly, the effects of candidate quality in state supreme court elections produce opposite results.

Dubois established that ballot information about the candidates' occupations in California nonpartisan trial court elections, which by their very nature do not list the candidates' partisan affiliations, significantly increases competition by providing an advantage to incumbents and inferior court judges (i.e., those candidates we would consider quality candidates).[21] In contrast, Klein and Baum documented through a series of experiments that information about incumbency in Ohio Supreme Court elections, which also are nonpartisan, would not affect voter turnout.[22] Of course, voter turnout is not equivalent to the electoral security of incumbents, but the Klein and Baum study challenges the notion that career information in judicial elections is important.

Despite this contradictory evidence, there are convincing reasons to think that candidate quality might matter even more in judicial elections than in other types of elections. Given formal qualifications for the state court bench—qualifications that are not placed on other offices—and the clearly hierarchical nature of the judiciary, voters reasonably might view lower court experience as a prerequisite for the state high court bench.[23] Thus, candidates who have served in the lower courts become more attractive by representing qualified alternatives to incumbents, whereas challengers who have never been judges might be viewed as failing to meet the basic job requirements.

The Costs of Judicial Campaigns

Judicial reform advocates consistently have argued that judicial elections fail to fulfill their goal of electoral accountability. The "old school" argument was that these elections rarely draw challengers, oust incumbents, or attract the attention of voters. The "new school" contention is that judicial elections have become "noisier, nastier, and costlier," which threatens not only the accountability function but independence as well. Particularly related to the purported "new style" campaign is the concern that organized interests and other high rollers are hijacking the democratic process by buying seats.[24] Underlying both sets of arguments is the premise that judicial elections are not fulfilling their fundamental role of promoting democratic control of the bench. From reformers' initial concerns that citizens consistently refuse to participate in state supreme court elections and vote idiosyncratically when they do, to the latest concerns that voters are being duped to vote for the "wrong" candidates (i.e., challengers rather than incumbents) by false and negative advertising bought by special interests and other powerful political actors, the problem is the same: the lack of meaningful participation in the judicial selection process by the American electorate. Indeed, scholars widely recognize that the alleged failure of judicial elections to achieve any measure of accountability is "the most fundamental and damning of the criticisms leveled against popular judicial elections."[25]

Given the alarm being loudly and vigorously expressed over the rising costs of campaigns and television advertising by such groups as the Brennan Center for Justice, the Justice At Stake Campaign, the American Judicature Society, and the American Bar Association, we offer empirical examinations of several of the most widely articulated contentions. First, we ascertain whether decisions of voters are consistent with meaningful substantive evaluations of the candidates. Second, we assess systematically whether money controls the election returns.

Consider the current political landscape. In December 2000, the Chief Justices of fifteen states, as well as a variety of the nation's most prominent legal scholars and attorneys, held a summit in Chicago to discuss issues purportedly plaguing the conduct of judicial elections. This meeting, which culminated in a Call to Action, was primarily designed to address the "growing concerns about the million dollar war chests, attack advertising and even outright distortion of an opponent's record that seems to have become more widespread."[26] The summit came on the heels of two *60 Minutes* stories (1987, 1998), a *Frontline* investigation (1999), and countless law review articles and other reports in the popular media, all of which assume a strong, direct link between campaign expenditures and election outcomes.[27] Even former governors have jumped onto the bandwagon[28] by proposing that judicial elections be replaced with gubernatorial appointments (which is not a particularly surprising position for former governors to take).

Money and Competition in Non-Judicial Offices in the United States

Given the centrality of elections to democratic government, studying the causes and consequences of electoral competition has been a mainstay of political science scholarship for decades. A voluminous literature systematically has examined elections to a wide array of political offices in the United States, including the United States Congress,[29] state legislatures,[30] and executives.[31] Generally, these studies indicate that electoral competition is determined by a variety of factors related to the candidates, the issues, and the political context, including campaign expenditures. However, candidates are not just buying seats. Instead, various contingencies in the races themselves and the overall political environment influence how well candidates fare at election time. In other words, money is a necessary but insufficient condition for electoral success.

With few exceptions,[32] electoral competition in judicial elections has escaped systematic inquiry by political scientists. This is almost unbelievable given the ongoing outcry from the court reform movement about the impropriety of electing judges and the extraordinary lack of empirical support for many of their contentions. Many scholars, attorneys, and court observers have argued that judges should never stand for election because raising campaign funds creates the appearance of impropriety that undermines public trust and confidence in judges and courts.[33] These advocates for appointive and noncompetitive election systems also argue that big spenders in judicial election campaigns effectively buy election outcomes, unfairly unseating qualified incumbents. Of course, there are those on the other side of the debate who view judges as public officials having considerable discretion to influence important policy matters and thus consider that they should be required to answer to the electorate for their decisions at the state level, where public policies are supposed to vary.[34] From this perspective, money is an essential part of running for office.

Unquestionably, the electorates of the large majority of states are on the side of accountability rather than the side of judicial reform advocates working to eliminate the democratic process altogether. Voters consistently have been hesitant about replacing elections with appointive schemes and continue to reject recent efforts to move in that direction.[35]

Why is money so important in elections? Simply put, money buys access to voters. As we discussed in chapter 3, although candidate exposure does not necessarily mean that voters are more likely to choose those candidates, voters are more likely to select candidates with whom they are familiar.[36] In this regard, campaign spending benefits those candidates with whom the electorate is least familiar (generally, challengers).

Stated differently, money allows candidates to publicize their candidacies and educate voters about their credentials. This may be even more important in elections to state supreme courts because, unlike elections for statehouses or Congress, candidates for the high court bench do not receive much "free" publicity that comes from such activities as announcing new policy initiatives, having many of their regular duties described and evaluated by the media, or performing constituency service.[37] Further, most state supreme court races have to compete for the voters' attention with a wide variety of elections for other important state and federal offices. This makes publicizing one's candidacy essential to success—and it makes such publicity expensive.

Before proceeding to a more rigorous analysis, it is useful to consider spending differences between incumbents and challengers in state supreme court elections, and also between winners and losers of open seat races. Table 4.1 reports these figures.

As Table 4.1 indicates, incumbents on average outspent challengers in every election cycle from 1990 through 2004. In a number of years, incumbents outspent challengers by an almost two-to-one ratio. This makes eminent sense, since the very essence of the incumbency advantage is the ability to attract greater electoral support, including support in the form of campaign contributions. However, in elections for open seats, we do not see a consistent pattern. In 1990, 1994, 1996, 1998, 2000, and 2004, winners of open seats spent more on average than challengers campaigning for those seats, but in 1992 and 2002 the losers outspent the winners. From a different perspective, and looking at the eight-cycle averages, we see much greater inequities in spending between candidates in incumbent–challenger races than in open seat races, where average spending is closer among contenders.

Table 4.1 Average Spending (in 1990 Dollars) in State Supreme Court Elections, 1990–2004, by Incumbency Status

Year	*Incumbent*	*Challenger*	*Winner of Open Seat*	*Loser of Open Seat*
1990	$276,787	$74,811	$294,688	$91,372
1992	$261,330	$175,107	$291,994	$329,102
1994	$407,184	$155,768	$428,226	$304,431
1996	$301,247	$202,322	$275,487	$215,011
1998	$422,706	$201,007	$347,196	$312,226
2000	$355,926	$266,512	$295,143	$275,923
2002	$269,735	$188,498	$374,883	$410,125
2004	$286,814	$128,077	$747,016	$529,147
Total	$322,572	$177,805	$378,494	$302,977

Electoral Competition as Accountability in Practice

Inherent in this inquiry is the fundamental premise that accountability is "a product of electoral competition, produced by the willingness of challengers to enter the electoral arena and the propensity of the electorate not to give their full support to incumbents."[38] Indeed there is perhaps no better device for forging linkages between citizens and government. Electoral competition enhances the ability of voters to voice disapproval of incumbents and remove unsatisfactory ones, thereby bringing the judiciary better into line with citizen preferences.

To begin this exploration of competition and accountability, we provide descriptive data about state supreme court elections from 1990 through 2004 in which incumbents were seeking reelection. We exclude open seat races because our theoretical focus is on accountability and particularly how challengers and voters respond to incumbents. In doing so, we examine the three leading indicators of electoral competition: the presence of challengers, the narrowness of vote margins, and electoral defeats.[39]

How might challengers and electoral margins serve as tools of democratic accountability? Without challengers in nonpartisan and partisan elections, incumbents cannot be defeated. Thus, the symbolic ideal of citizen control over the bench cannot be realized in its most basic form under these conditions, regardless of the extent to which the electorate disapproves of the incumbent. Similarly, even when incumbents win, voters in the absence of challengers cannot signal incumbents that there are preferred alternatives for sizable proportions of the electorate or that these voters are in some way dissatisfied. Instead, even the most unworthy incumbents are reelected with 100 percent of the vote.

Moreover, heated campaigns between opponents stimulate voter interest, provide information about candidate qualifications, and mobilize the electorate to vote.[40] Without the excitement generated by hard-fought campaigns, information upon which to cast votes is poor, and voters remain uninterested and unmotivated to participate. Finally, slim margins of victory produced by close races between candidates increase the likelihood of future electoral challenge, setting into motion another cycle to enhance the accountability function.[41] Thus, the presence of challengers, which is necessary to produce narrow vote margins for incumbents and electoral defeats, becomes an important mechanism for promoting accountability.

Retention elections always preclude challengers, but there is a functional equivalent: the ever-present ballot option not to retain. In effect, retention elections always provide choice, which in turn at least in theory has the potential to produce the same tight margins and defeats as nonpartisan and partisan elections. In this context, campaigns are directed exclusively at the incumbent rather than on the relative merits of any challengers and the incumbent. The obvious disadvantage is that without challengers forcing a public dialogue, and with no identifiable alternative to the incumbent, retention election campaigns are stunted and uninteresting, democratically speaking.

Electoral defeats are the most extreme form of voter disapproval, and the connection to accountability is clear. In these cases, the electorate has made a judgment to replace the incumbent with a successful challenger, presumably bringing the seat better in line with the prevailing climate. However, electoral defeats are not necessary to forge a close connection between citizens and the bench. As mentioned, challengers and close races also promote accountability.

Examining descriptive data from 1990 though 2004 allows us to assess whether contemporary state supreme court elections appear to have any of the qualities necessary to promote accountability. Consider first the entry of challengers into these races, displayed in Table 4.2 as contestation rates by election cycle and ballot type. Retention elections are excluded from the table because these elections preclude challengers by design.

As Table 4.2 indicates, challengers have entered state supreme court contests at increasing rates since 1990, with the most dramatic changes occurring in nonpartisan elections. In 1990, only about one of every three justices seeking reelection was likely to be challenged, but by 2004 almost three of every four faced the possibility of being ousted from office. Indeed, the changes in nonpartisan elections are pronounced. These elections have evolved from sleepy contests with an incredible incumbency advantage to elections that better resemble those to other important offices in the United States. Actually, considering that a significant proportion of these seats initially are filled with *ad interim* appointments, it is fair to say that nonpartisan elections essentially have been transformed from *de facto*

Table 4.2 State Supreme Court Incumbents Challenged for Reelection, 1990–2004, by Type of Election System

Year	*Nonpartisan Elections*		*Partisan Elections*		*All Elections*	
	Running n	*Challenged % (n)*	*Running n*	*Challenged % (n)*	*Running n*	*Challenged % (n)*
1990	24	37.5 (9)	17	70.6 (12)	41	51.2 (21)
1992	22	54.5 (12)	20	65.0 (13)	42	59.5 (25)
1994	17	52.9 (9)	11	81.8 (9)	28	64.3 (18)
1996	23	65.2 (15)	11	100.0 (11)	34	76.5 (26)
1998	17	70.6 (12)	12	91.7 (11)	29	79.3 (23)
2000	26	65.4 (17)	11	90.9 (10)	37	73.0 (27)
2002	18	61.1 (11)	10	90.0 (9)	28	71.4 (20)
2004	25	72.0 (18)	10	90.0 (9)	35	77.1 (27)
Total	172	59.9 (103)	102	82.4 (84)	274	68.2 (187)

appointive systems into actual electoral systems. Even so, in 2004 fully 28 percent of all incumbents seeking to retain their seats in nonpartisan elections still had no possibility of losing because they were not challenged in the first place.

Partisan elections also have become more competitive by this standard, starting with contestation rates between 65 and 71 percent in 1990 and ending with a contestation rate of 90 percent in 2004. Interestingly, partisan elections started out in 1990 being about as competitive as nonpartisan elections are now. In today's partisan supreme court elections, challengers are a near certainty. This is precisely what we should expect for statewide offices as important as these.

Figure 4.1 illustrates these trends quite well by providing a graphical depiction of contestation over time and by selection system. In Figure 4.1, the increases over time in rates of contestation are obvious for nonpartisan and partisan elections. Moreover, Figure 4.1 clearly documents the considerable differences over time between partisan and nonpartisan elections. From 1990 through 2004, partisan elections always are more competitive by this standard than nonpartisan elections, although the differences in 1992 are the least pronounced.

In Table 4.3 we provide information about the electoral performance of incumbents from the perspective of the average percentage of the vote received, calculated for all elections and for contested races only. With retention elections, we see that electoral support for incumbents has increased, with incumbents receiving about 75 percent "yes" votes in 2004 compared with 67 percent in 1990. This finding is inconsistent

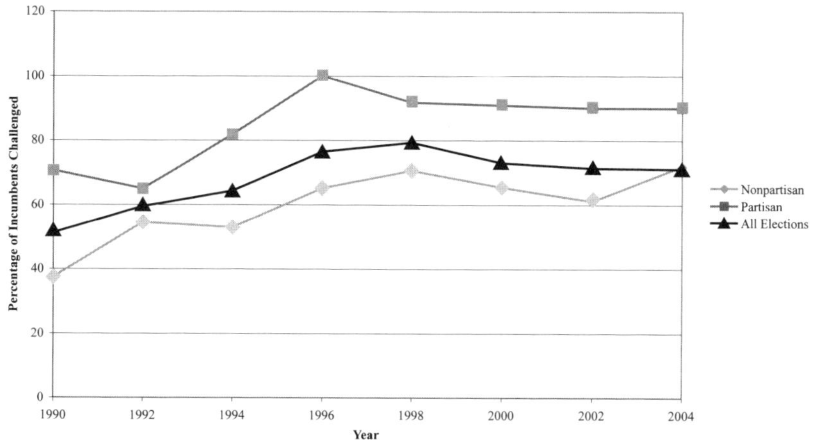

Figure 4.1 State Supreme Court Incumbents Challenged for Reelection.

with any notion of electoral accountability. Generally speaking, competitive elections are defined as those having been won by 60 percent (or in some studies, 55 percent) of the vote or less, and it is easily apparent that retention elections on average fall short of this standard. In fact, modern retention elections are landslides and are becoming even more so.

Table 4.3 also indicates that nonpartisan elections are strikingly similar to retention elections when all races are considered. The average percentage of the vote received by incumbents in nonpartisan elections is 73 percent, compared to 71 percent in retention elections. Overall, partisan elections are the most competitive, averaging about a 63 percent vote share for incumbents. However, when we consider contested elections only, the differences between retention elections and nonpartisan elections become pronounced, and the similarities between partisan and nonpartisan contests emerge. When elections are contested, incumbents do about as well on average in partisan elections as nonpartisan elections. In fact, in the 1992 and 2000 election cycles, contested nonpartisan elections were more competitive than contested partisan elections, on average. Generally, when challengers decide to enter the electoral arena, partisan and nonpartisan elections become quite competitive and relatively indistinguishable by this standard.

Figure 4.2 graphs these figures over time, revealing a fair degree of stability in the electoral margins of incumbents in contested partisan and nonpartisan elections, as well as the increases in electoral security in retention elections. Of course, the electoral performance of incumbents in partisan and nonpartisan elections has declined as contestation rates have risen, and this trend is particularly apparent in nonpartisan elections. Further, partisan elections are more inconsistent over time, with significant

Table 4.3 Average Vote (in Percentages) for Incumbents in State Supreme Court Elections, 1990–2004, by Type of Election System

Year	Retention Elections	Nonpartisan Elections		Partisan Elections		All Elections	
	All Races	*All races*	*Contested races*	*All races*	*Contested races*	*All races*	*Contested races*
1990	67.1	80.5	59.5	66.8	53.5	71.5	56.4
1992	69.2	73.7	54.0	71.1	55.5	71.3	54.8
1994	66.3	70.8	55.8	61.4	52.8	66.7	54.3
1996	67.8	70.6	55.0	54.4	54.4	66.4	54.7
1998	74.6	72.7	63.6	57.6	53.8	71.2	58.9
2000	72.0	69.3	55.9	64.6	61.0	69.8	57.8
2002	74.6	74.0	57.6	58.6	54.0	71.6	56.0
2004	75.3	72.1	61.4	64.8	60.9	72.2	61.2
Total	71.0	73.0	57.9	63.3	55.7	70.2	56.9
n	231	172	103	99	82	502	185

Note: 3 cases lost because of missing data for district based elections; 2 contested, 1 not.

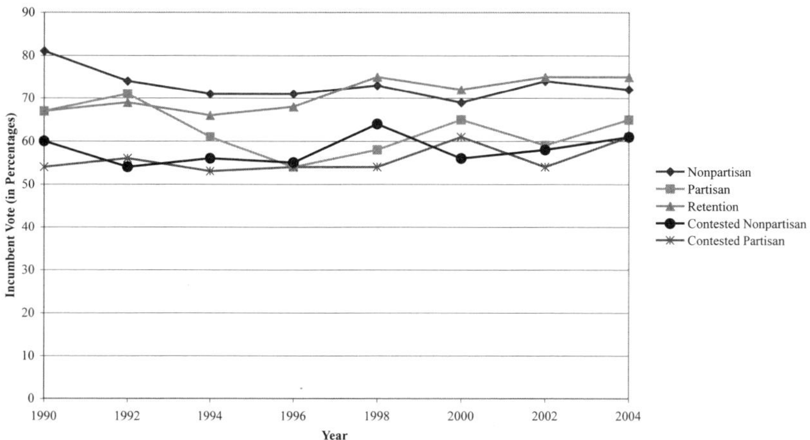

Figure 4.2 Average Vote for Incumbents in State Supreme Court Elections.

differences between 1996 when performance was at the lowest point and 1992 when incumbency was at its peak, at least from the perspective of average votes garnered by incumbents.

In Table 4.4, we consider the third indicator of competition, electoral defeats, which certainly is the most extreme sanction the electorate performs. Immediately apparent are the dramatic differences in defeat rates among the three election systems. Retention elections are, in practice, appointive systems. Only 1.3 percent, or three of 231 incumbents seeking reelection, were defeated in retention elections over a fourteen-year period. Nonpartisan elections were more competitive by this standard, with an overall defeat rate of 5.2 percent. Finally, partisan elections are highly competitive, with a defeat rate of 31 percent. Remarkably, one of every three justices seeking reelection in partisan elections was removed from office during this fourteen-year period. We will have much more to say about this below, but generally whether this is good news or bad news depends on the basis for the electorate's choices. If defeats are random events or decisions driven by the best-financed campaigns, then the concerns of judicial reform advocates are merited. Alternatively, if the electoral performance of incumbents is determined by substantive considerations and a host of other contingencies in the electoral environment, the criticisms are overdrawn or misplaced.

Trends in defeat rates among the various selection systems are depicted graphically in Figure 4.3. Generally, we see defeat rates rising in partisan elections to a fairly dramatic peak in 2000, followed by significant declines in 2002 and 2004. In fact, partisan defeat rates were lower in 2002 than in any of the six preceding electoral cycles. Otherwise, nonpartisan and

Table 4.4 State Supreme Court Incumbents Defeated, 1990–2004, by Type of Election System

Year	*Retention Elections*		*Nonpartisan Elections*		*Partisan Elections*		*All Elections*	
	Incumbents running n	*Incumbents defeated % (n)*	*Incumbents running n*	*Incumbents defeated % (n)*	*Incumbents running n*	*Incumbents defeated % (n)*	*Incumbents running n*	*Incumbents defeated % (n)*
1990	34	0.0 (0)	24	4.2 (1)	17	29.4 (5)	76	8.0 (6)
1992	23	4.3 (1)	22	9.1 (2)	20	25.0 (5)	65	12.3 (8)
1994	27	0.0 (0)	17	5.9 (1)	11	36.4 (4)	55	9.1 (5)
1996	23	8.7 (2)	23	4.3 (1)	11	36.4 (4)	57	12.3 (7)
1998	41	0.0 (0)	17	0.0 (0)	12	33.3 (4)	70	5.7 (4)
2000	30	0.0 (0)	25	8.0 (2)	11	45.5 (5)	67	10.4 (7)
2002	29	0.0 (0)	18	5.6 (1)	10	20.0 (2)	57	5.3 (3)
2004	24	0.0 (0)	25	4.0 (1)	10	30.0 (3)	59	6.8 (4)
Total	231	1.3 (3)	172	5.2 (9)	102	31.4 (32)	505	8.7 (44)

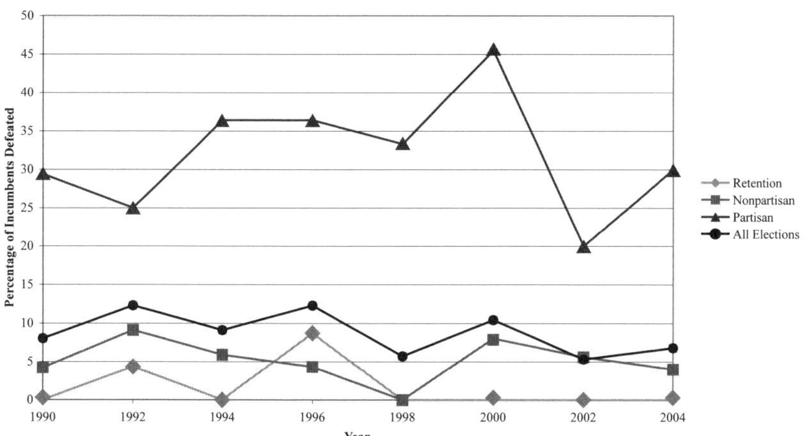

Figure 4.3 Defeat Rates in State Supreme Court Elections.

retention elections perform much more consistently over time. Defeats were nonexistent in retention elections from 1998 through 2004 and have never exceeded 9 percent, while nonpartisan elections show greater variability but the same overall parameters (0–9 percent).

Competition in state supreme court elections is placed into comparative perspective by the data reported in Table 4.5, which shows reelection rates from 1990 through 2004 for incumbents seeking reelection to the United States House of Representatives, United States Senate, statehouses, and state supreme courts. As Table 4.5 indicates, partisan state supreme court elections are less secure electorally than any of these other offices except statehouses. In three election cycles (1990, 2002, 2004) partisan state supreme court seats were safer than gubernatorial offices, were identical in one election cycle (1992), and were less safe in four election cycles (1994, 1996, 1998, 2000). Interestingly, the electoral security of governors has decreased since 2002 as the electoral safety of partisan supreme court seats has increased.

Overall, it makes a great deal of sense that partisan supreme court elections would look more like gubernatorial elections than elections to the national legislature. Relatively speaking, only a select handful of people ever hold these important offices, and opportunities to accede to office are rare. Because of the extraordinary importance of both institutions and the limited chances to capture these seats, we would expect competition to be intense, particularly in states characterized by healthy two-party competition. The fact that nonpartisan elections do not rise to this standard should be considered surprising and reflects in large measure the unwillingness of challengers to enter these races for years and the difficulty of overcoming the incumbency advantage when partisan labels are not on the ballot.

Table 4.5 Reelection Rates for Incumbents, 1990–2004

Election Cycle	*U.S. House*	*U.S. Senate*[a]	*Governor*[b]	*State Supreme Court (All Races)*	*State Supreme Court (Partisan Races Only)*	*State Supreme Court (Nonpartisan Races Only)*
1990	391 96.1%	29 96.7%	16 69.6%	70 92.0%	17 70.6%	24 95.8%
1992	325 88.3%	23 85.2%	3 75.0%	57 87.7%	20 75.0%	22 90.9%
1994	349 90.2%	24 92.3%	19 86.4%	50 90.9%	11 63.6%	17 94.1%
1996	361 94.0%	19 95.0%	8 100.0%	50 87.7%	11 63.6%	23 95.7%
1998	394 98.3%	26 89.7%	23 95.8%	66 94.3%	12 66.7%	17 100.0%
2000	394 97.8%	21 77.8%	5 83.3%	60 89.6%	11 54.5%	25 92.0%
2002	383 96.2%	23 88.5%	12 75%	54 94.7%	10 80.0%	18 94.4%
2004	395 97.8%	24 96.0%	4 50%	55 93.2%	10 70.0%	25 96.0%
Total	2992 94.9%	189 90.0%	90 81.1%	461 91.3%	102 68.8%	172 94.8%

a The House and Senate data are taken from Paul R Abramson, John H. Aldrich, and David W. Rohde, 2007. *Change and Continuity in the 2004 and 2006 Elections.* Washington, DC: CQ Press.

b These data are taken from Richard M. Scammon, Alice McGillivray, and Rhodes Cook, 2001. *America Votes 24: A Handbook of Contemporary American Election Statistics.* Washington, DC: CQ Press, Beyle, Thad. 2003. "2002 Gubernatorial Elections." *Spectrum: The Journal of State Government* 76 (Winter): 12–14 and Thad Beyle, 2005. "2004 Gubernatorial Elections." *Spectrum: The Journal of State Government* 78 (Winter): 12–14, 30,

Instead, nonpartisan elections look a lot more like those to the United States House of Representatives, although nonpartisan supreme court races were more competitive than House races in the last three election cycles to 2004. However, as voters increasingly are aware of the political importance of these seats, and as challengers increasingly seek to win them, we should see nonpartisan elections looking more like partisan elections. Of course, this is the nightmare of judicial reform advocates, but we suggest that when elections actually work like elections instead of pseudo-appointment systems, the public good is enhanced. After all, if elections are not really efficacious mechanisms for citizen control, why have them at all? On this point, we agree with judicial reform advocates. However, our solutions are opposite to the conventional wisdom. Instead of moving to formal appointment systems, we recommend eliminating retention elections and putting partisan labels back onto ballots. Indeed, it is these "reforms" of removing partisan labels and precluding challengers that caused elections to be less than optimal democratically in the first place.

Finally with regard to electoral competition, consider Table 4.6, which provides a snapshot of the states. As Table 4.6 indicates, the states differ considerably on all three dimensions. First, consider the extent to which challengers enter these races. In some states, supreme court elections almost always are contested (Alabama, Illinois, Michigan, Ohio, Texas), whereas in other states challengers are rare (Idaho, North Dakota, Oregon). The states also are quite dissimilar in the ways in which they vote for, or against, incumbents. On average, incumbents perform significantly less well in Alabama, Michigan, Mississippi, North Carolina, and Texas, where incumbents tend to receive 60 percent of the vote or less. In contrast, states such as Georgia, Idaho, Maryland, and Oregon tend to produce landslides for incumbents. In the same manner as contestation and electoral margins, defeat rates are markedly different across the states. Supreme court seats in Alabama, Illinois, North Carolina, and West Virginia are the least secure electorally, whereas twenty-two of thirty-eight states failed to oust any incumbents from 1990 through 2004 and another eight states saw only one electoral defeat in all of their races during the fourteen-year cycle. Clearly, electoral defeats are rare events in most states but only when partisan ballots are not used. Indeed, the incumbency advantage is remarkable in retention and nonpartisan election states when considered on a state-by-state basis.

Generally speaking, the extraordinary variations in electoral competition across election systems, election cycles, and states merit scientific explanation. What would cause elections to be highly competitive in some states but not others, or in particular election cycles but not others? Also, in multivariate models where the wide variety of factors influencing judicial elections are controlled, what do we learn about the effects of partisan elections, quality challengers, and campaign expenditures? We seek these answers in the analysis below.

Table 4.6 Competition in State Supreme Court Elections, 1990–2004, by State (Incumbent–Challenger Races Only)

State	*Election Type*	*Challenge Rate*	*Average Vote*	*Number of Defeats*	*Defeat Rate*	*N*
Alabama	Partisan	92.9	59.2	5	35.7	14
Alaska	Retention	n/a	62.9	0	0.0	7
Arizona	Retention	n/a	74.7	0	0.0	15
Arkansas[a]	Partisan to nonpartisan	50.0	82.6	0	0.0	6
California	Retention	n/a	67.5	0	0.0	15
Colorado	Retention	n/a	71.3	0	0.0	10
Florida	Retention	n/a	67.7	0	0.0	17
Georgia[b]	Partisan to nonpartisan	36.8	85.1	0	0.0	19
Idaho	Nonpartisan	25.0	88.4	1	8.3	12
Illinois[c]	Partisan or retention	100.0	68.0	1	25.0	4
Indiana	Retention	n/a	70.9	0	0.0	6
Iowa	Retention	n/a	75.4	0	0.0	12
Kansas	Retention	n/a	73.1	0	0.0	19
Kentucky	Nonpartisan	54.5	72.8	2	18.2	11
Louisiana	Partisan	44.4	78.0	1	22.2	9
Maryland	Retention	n/a	84.5	0	0.0	12
Michigan	Nonpartisan	100.0	57.9	0	0.0	15
Minnesota	Nonpartisan	68.8	76.0	0	0.0	16
Mississippi[d]	Partisan to nonpartisan	76.5	59.1	3	17.6	17
Missouri	Retention	n/a	62.2	0	0.0	11
Montana[e]	Nonpartisan or retention	100.0	70.3	1	8.3	12
Nebraska	Retention	n/a	71.0	1	6.3	16
Nevada	Nonpartisan	45.5	64.5	0	0.0	11

New Mexico	Partisan	80.0	69.5	1	11.1	9
North Carolina[f]	Partisan to nonpartisan	87.5	56.8	7	43.8	16
North Dakota	Nonpartisan	33.3	83.2	1	11.1	9
Ohio	Nonpartisan	93.3	62.2	0	0.0	15
Oklahoma[g]	Retention	n/a	63.6	0	0.0	40
Oregon	Nonpartisan	22.2	91.2	0	0.0	18
Pennsylvania[h]	Partisan or retention	n/a	74.7	0	0.0	3
South Dakota	Retention	n/a	79.6	0	0.0	8
Tennessee[i]	Partisan to retention	50.0	66.7	3	27.3	11
Texas[j]	Partisan	97.6	59.9	11	26.9	41
Utah[k]	Nonpartisan to retention	n/a	82.3	0	0.0	8
Washington	Nonpartisan	68.4	68.2	2	10.5	19
West Virginia	Partisan	75.0	61.8	2	50.0	4
Wisconsin	Nonpartisan	57.1	79.2	0	0.0	7
Wyoming	Retention	n/a	73.9	1	9.1	11
All states		68.2	70.2	44	8.7	505

Notes

a Arkansas changed from partisan elections to nonpartisan elections in 2002.
b Georgia changed from partisan elections to nonpartisan elections in 1984.
c Illinois uses partisan elections for initial terms and retention elections otherwise.
d Mississippi changed from partisan elections to nonpartisan elections in 1994.
e Montana uses nonpartisan elections in contested races, and retention elections otherwise.
f North Carolina changed from partisan elections to nonpartisan elections in 2004.
g The elections reported for Oklahoma are for the Supreme Court and Court of Criminal Appeals, both courts of the last resort.
h Pennsylvania uses partisan elections for initial terms and retention elections otherwise.
i Tennessee changed from partisan elections to retention elections in 1994.
j The elections reported for Texas are for the Supreme Court and Court of Criminal Appeals, both courts of last resort. Five of the eleven defeats were in the Supreme Court and six were from the Court of Appeals.
k Utah changed from nonpartisan elections to retention elections in 1982.

Modeling Competition in State Supreme Court Elections

To contribute to an understanding of electoral competition in state supreme court elections and to address squarely some of the most critical concerns of judicial reform advocates about the alleged inefficacy of judicial elections, we conduct a more rigorous examination of all 208 elections to the states' highest courts from 1990 through 2000 in the twenty-one states using partisan or nonpartisan elections to staff their benches.[42] Please note that in this chapter the data examined in the multivariate models do not extend to 2004. Similarly, we exclude retention elections in the models because challengers are never permitted, money rarely is spent, and there is little variation in the electoral performance of incumbents. As stated and shown earlier, retention elections are not really elections in any practical sense.

In this inquiry, our focus will be on the vote shares of state supreme court justices seeking reelection, and particularly whether challenger quality and campaign spending influence the electoral success of incumbents. In this analysis, we continue the practice conceptualizing supreme court elections as a two-stage process, in which (1) candidates first make decisions about whether to run, and (2) the electorate chooses between candidates when challengers become involved. Indeed, this is precisely the formula followed in chapters 2 and 3, where we evaluate ballot roll-off and the costs of campaigns. Theoretically, we expect challengers to be strategic when deciding whether to enter the electoral arena, basing their choices largely on the perceived vulnerability of incumbents. Moreover, we expect voters in the aggregate to be relatively rational when casting ballots, including differentiating between quality and non-quality challengers. Overall, we expect both challengers and the electorate to be responsive to the political and institutional context surrounding the election, court, and state.

Stage One: Challengers in State Supreme Court Elections

Specifically concerning stage one of the electoral process, or the factors that encourage challengers to enter the electoral arena, our dependent variable is whether a challenger is present in each race (Contested). As for independent variables, Bonneau and Hall[43] specified a model describing the conditions under which challengers to incumbents in state supreme court elections decide to run, and we replicate that model, as we did in chapters 2 and 3. The only departures from chapters 2 and 3 in this analysis are these: (1) the absence of a variable that measures the post-*White* period (because these data end in 2000), and (2) the absence of a variable for open-seat elections (because we are interested only in the performance of incumbents).

Generally, we expect challengers to run when incumbents are electorally vulnerable, supreme court seats are particularly attractive, the political and institutional context promotes competition, and a sizable candidate pool exists. Recall from chapters 2 and 3 the specific independent variables in this model: electoral vulnerability (measured as competitive seats and whether incumbents are newly appointed), attractiveness of the seat (salaries and term length), the political and institutional context (unified partisan control of state government, partisan elections, district-based constituencies), and candidate pool (lawyers). These variables predicting challengers, along with their measurement, are described in Table 4.7.

Table 4.7 Variable Descriptions for a Model of Challengers in State Supreme Court Elections

Variable	*Variable Description*
Dependent Variable	
Contested	1 if a challenger entered the supreme court race 0 otherwise
Electoral Vulnerability of the Incumbent	
Competitive Seat	1 if the incumbent supreme court justice won previously by a margin less than 60% 0 otherwise
New Appointee	1 if the election involves an incumbent initially appointed and facing his/her first election 0 otherwise
Attractiveness of Supreme Court Seats	
Salary	Supreme court base salary/state per capita disposable income, in dollars
Term	Length of the term of office for state supreme court, in years
Political and Institutional Context	
Unified Government	1 if the legislative and executive branches of state government are controlled by the same political party 0 otherwise
Partisan	1 if the election is a partisan election 0 otherwise
District	1 if the seat represents a district rather than the state 0 otherwise
Candidate Pool	
Lawyers	Number of lawyers in each state at the time of each election

Stage Two: The Vote Shares of Incumbents in State Supreme Court Elections

In the second stage of our model of state supreme court elections, we seek to assess the factors that encourage the electorate to cast ballots supporting or opposing the incumbent. Thus, our dependent variable is the percentage of the vote for the incumbent (Incumbent Vote). As such, higher values indicate lower levels of competition.

Consistent with Hall,[44] we posit a model of electoral choice that takes into account candidate- and issue-specific factors, along with institutional context. In this regard, we utilize some of the same variables from the first stage of our model but now have the goal of evaluating how these variables affect the decision calculus of the electorate rather than opponents. Generally, we expect voters in the aggregate to be able to distinguish between challengers with varying qualifications and also to be affected by context. We also expect money to matter but not in the defining way posited by judicial reform advocates. Table 4.8 provides a complete list of the variables used in stage two of our model and their exact measurement.

Candidate-Specific Characteristics

One of the primary findings in the literature on legislative elections is that quality challengers significantly reduce incumbents' electoral fortunes.[45] We expect this same effect in supreme court elections.

In the elections analyzed in this study, quality challengers were somewhat less common than non-quality challengers. From 1990 through 2000, only 47.1 percent of the elections drew challengers who were serving, or had served, on the bench. However, quality challengers were somewhat more successful than their novice counterparts. On average, incumbents facing non-quality challengers won with 59.7 percent of the vote whereas incumbents facing quality challengers did significantly less well with 52.2 percent. Thus, there is at least some reason to think that quality might matter.

To estimate systematically whether the electorate seemingly distinguishes qualified from nonqualified challengers, we follow the well-beaten path[46] of constructing a dichotomy (Quality Challenger) to distinguish experienced from inexperienced challengers. In the context of supreme courts, challengers who either have served, or are serving, on the bench can claim to possess the substantive expertise necessary for effective service while at the same time benefiting from the experience and name recognition garnered from previous election campaigns. Therefore, these quality challengers should negatively affect incumbents' vote shares relative to their neophyte counterparts. Recall, however, that the judicial reform literature predicts the absence of a relationship between challenger quality and election returns.

Table 4.8 Variable Descriptions for a Model of Incumbent Vote Shares in State Supreme Court Elections

Variable	*Variable Description*
Dependent Variable	
Incumbent Vote	Percentage of the vote received by the incumbent
Candidate Characteristics	
Quality Challenger	1 if the challenger currently holds, or has ever held, a judgeship 0 otherwise
Trial Court Challenger	1 if the challenger is a current or former trial court judge 0 otherwise
Appellate Court Challenger	1 if the challenger is a current or former appellate court judge 0 otherwise
Former Supreme Court Challenger	1 if the challenger is a defeated supreme court justice 0 otherwise
New Appointee	1 if the election involves an incumbent initially appointed and facing his/her first election 0 otherwise
Spending Difference	Difference between the log of the incumbent's spending and the log of the challenger's spending
Issues	
Murder Rate	State murders and non-negligent manslaughter per 100,000 population, lagged one year
Institutional Context	
No IAC	1 if the state has no intermediate appellate court 0 otherwise
Partisan	1 if the election is a partisan election 0 otherwise
Temporal Effects	
1990–91, 1992–93, 1994–95, 1996–97, 1998–99	1 if election occurred in the designated year 0 otherwise

Because of the critical importance of the challenger quality variable, however, we do not rely solely on a simple dichotomy to distinguish between experienced and inexperienced challengers. Instead, we estimate a second set of models using more detailed measures to capture the type of service each challenger has, or does not have, on the bench. Generally, by using the two types of measures of candidate quality found in the legislative literature, we can draw conclusions more confidently about the similarity or dissimilarity of judicial races to legislative elections. Further, the detailed measures will allow us to reach more refined conclusions about the ability of the electorate to distinguish among types of challengers in supreme court elections.

Specifically, thinking of courts as a hierarchy in which appellate court service is more valuable than trial court service, with the possible exception of defeated supreme court justices who may be at a disadvantage for having been thrown off the high court, we can generate a series of dichotomies that take into account these various types of experiences (Trial Court Challenger, Appellate Court Challenger, Former Supreme Court Challenger). Of course, we also must recognize that a small handful of states have no intermediate appellate courts (No IAC). Thus, in these states, trial court service becomes particularly important (Trial Court Challenger x No IAC).

Regarding other candidate-related factors, we include in stage two of our judicial elections model a measure of the incumbency advantage: whether the justice seeking reelection initially was appointed to the supreme court and is facing the electorate for the first time (New Appointee). We expect these justices not only to be more susceptible to challenge, as in stage one of our model, but also to be less successful at the polls. Voters should know less about these justices, not be able to recognize their names as easily, and thus be less inclined to support them. Also, voters may prefer candidates that they themselves select over candidates chosen by governors.

Finally concerning candidate-related variables, we include in stage two of our model a measure of the relative ability of incumbents and challengers to spend money. Studies of legislative elections, both congressional and state, indicate that spending affects electoral competition. Generally, spending by the incumbent is unrelated to vote margins whereas spending by the challenger has adverse effects on the incumbent.[47] Further, some studies consider spending an alternative measure of candidate quality.

Given our concerns with the potentially deleterious effects of money on election outcomes, we expect that the principal effect of spending will be found in *differences* between incumbents and challengers (Spending Difference) and not simply in the amount spent by either.[48] Overall we expect greater positive disparities to generate higher margins for incumbents. Conversely, as challengers narrow the gap, and in some cases outspend incumbents, we expect the electoral performance of incumbents to worsen. Consistent with standard practice in studies of legislative elections,[49] we log the spending variables to control for any nonlinearity and to make interpretation more intuitive by focusing on percentage increases rather than dollar increases. We also convert spending to 1990 dollars.

From 1990 through 2000, we see extraordinary variations across the states in dollars spent and in differences between incumbents and challengers. On average, incumbents outspent opponents, but in a few states challengers narrowed the gap or outspent incumbents. The largest differences are in Texas, for the civil court of last resort, and West Virginia, where disparities approach $700,000. The smallest differences are in Mississippi and Oregon, with the gap falling short of $4,000. In per capita terms, the biggest gaps are in Louisiana ($511) and Kentucky ($438), and the smallest are in Oregon ($1) and Texas for the criminal court of last resort ($5). We expect these variations in spending to provide considerable insight into the politics of supreme court elections.

Issue-Specific Characteristics

Whereas studies of gubernatorial and state legislative races have demonstrated that competition increases when the state of the economy is poor,[50] Hall has documented a similar form of retrospective voting in judicial elections based on the public safety; murder rate is significantly related to electoral support for supreme court justices seeking reelection.[51] Therefore, we include in our model a measure of each state's murder rate, lagged one year (Murder Rate), and predict that higher murder rates will decrease support for incumbents, other things being equal.

Institutional Context

Concerning institutional arrangements, we expect incumbents in partisan elections to fare less well with voters than their colleagues in nonpartisan elections. Historically, partisan elections have been more competitive, with regard to both attracting challengers[52] and lowering vote margins.[53] Thus, we include a variable (Partisan) to identify elections held on partisan rather than nonpartisan ballots. However, recall from Table 4.2 that incumbents in contested nonpartisan elections do not fare any better than their partisan colleagues. In contested nonpartisan elections, the average vote share for incumbents from 1990 through 2004 was 58 percent, whereas in partisan elections it was 56 percent.

Temporal Effects

Finally, we include dummy variables for each election cycle minus one (2000–01) to control for the effects of each specific election and other temporal effects in the models (1990–91, 1992–93, 1994–95, 1996–97, 1998–99).

Estimation Technique

Because we conceptualize elections to state supreme courts as a two-stage process, we utilize the Heckman procedure[54] first to estimate a model predicting the presence of challengers, as we did in chapter 2 and chapter 3.

We then correct for this selection bias in our model evaluating the vote shares of incumbents. Because supreme court elections are not uniformly contested and are not random events,[55] estimating vote shares without taking into account the likelihood of being challenged in the first place could lead to biased estimates and potentially erroneous inferences. Thus, in the first stage of our model, we analyze all elections, both contested and uncontested, and then correct for this nonrandom event in the second stage of our model examining contested elections only (or situations in which Incumbent Vote cannot be 100 percent).[56] Additionally, we use robust variance estimators, which are robust to assumptions about within-group (i.e., state) correlation.

Results

Which factors explain why challengers decide to take on state supreme court justices seeking reelection, and how well these incumbents fare with voters? We address these important questions in Tables 4.9 and 4.10. Table 4.9 includes our general dichotomous measure of candidate quality whereas Table 4.10 presents the detailed measures.

As Table 4.9 illustrates, the likelihood of challengers entering state supreme court elections is predictable and reflects, at least to some extent, strategic thinking about the probability of winning. Challengers go after incumbents who are the most electorally vulnerable, either because they hold marginal seats or because they suffer an attenuated incumbency advantage by virtue of never having been elected. Thus, many of the incumbents most susceptible to challenge are those who never were chosen by voters in the first place.

Similarly, political and institutional context matters. Challengers are less likely to enter the electoral arena in states characterized by unified government, or lower levels of partisan competition. Also, challengers are more likely to appear in statewide partisan elections (Partisan) and in district-based nonpartisan elections (District), but are less likely to run in district-based partisan elections (District x Partisan). As predicted, the effects of partisan electoral systems on the likelihood of contested state supreme court races are dependent on whether the election is held statewide or in a district.

Further, Table 4.9 documents that the size of the candidate pool is important for challengers to decide to run. The higher the number of lawyers, the more likely there is to be an opponent. This pattern is not surprising, given the requirement in every state that candidates for the high court bench be licensed attorneys.

At first glance, two of the results in stage one of our model are perplexing. Contrary to Bonneau and Hall, we find that the attractiveness of state supreme court seats, measured by Salary and Term, does not play a role in

Table 4.9 Competition, Challengers, and Spending in State Supreme Court Elections

Stage 1: Challengers in State Supreme Court Elections, 1990–2000

	Coefficient	*Robust SE*	*z*	*P > |z|*	*Expected β*
Competitive Seat	1.297	0.182	7.133	0.000	β > 0
New Appointee	1.314	0.196	6.707	0.000	β > 0
Salary	0.053	0.090	0.585	0.558	β > 0
Term	0.078	0.116	0.667	0.505	β > 0
Unified Government	−0.804	0.179	−4.499	0.000	β < 0
Partisan	1.398	0.434	3.223	0.001	β > 0
District	1.301	0.547	2.380	0.017	β > 0
District x Partisan	−2.618	0.447	−5.862	0.000	β < 0
Lawyers	0.000	0.000	3.936	0.000	β > 0
Constant	−2.385	1.044	−2.285	0.022	

Dependent variable: Contested.

Stage 2: Incumbent Vote Shares in State Supreme Court Elections, 1990–2000

	Coefficient	*Robust SE*	*z*	*P > |z|*	*Expected β*
Quality Challenger	−4.668	1.988	−2.348	0.019	β < 0
New Appointee	−3.332	1.244	−2.678	0.007	β < 0
Spending Difference	1.576	0.472	3.338	0.001	β > 0
Murder Rate	−0.011	0.216	−0.052	0.958	β < 0
Partisan	−2.781	1.557	−1.786	0.074	β < 0
1990–91	−0.923	1.899	−0.486	0.627	
1992–93	−1.425	2.497	−0.571	0.568	
1994–95	−1.171	2.531	−0.463	0.644	
1996–97	−2.653	2.967	−0.894	0.371	
1998–99	4.091	2.445	1.674	0.094	
Constant	59.569	2.488	23.938	0.000	

Dependent variable: Incumbent Vote
Mean of dependent variable = 56.85
Number of observations = 198
Censored observations = 69
Uncensored observations = 129
Log likelihood = −522.462.
χ^2 (5) = 11.36
Prob > χ^2 = 0.045
Test of independent equations: χ^2 (1) = 4.79
Prob > χ^2 = 0.029

determining whether supreme court elections are contested. However, we think the divergence is explained by differences in the time periods covered by our respective studies. Bonneau and Hall examined elections only up through 1995, whereas we include elections through 2000.[57] During the decade of the 1990s, challengers increasingly became interested in state supreme court elections, at a time when salaries and terms remained relatively constant. In 1990–91, half (50.0 percent) of all supreme court elections were uncontested, whereas only 25.0 percent were uncontested in 2000. In fact, in 1998–99, uncontested races hit a decade low of 17.9 percent. Thus, supreme court seats have become much more attractive overall, quite apart from such features as salary and term. Indeed, the results in this chapter are similar to those in chapters 2 and 3 with later data.

In sum, challengers' decisions to run are not random but instead are quite rational, politically speaking. As in congressional or state legislative elections, certain factors either increase or decrease the likelihood of contested supreme court elections. In this regard, an important fact to notice about Table 4.9 is the chi-square test of independent equations. The significant result provides empirical support for our theoretical argument: not taking into account the process by which state supreme court races are contested can lead to biased coefficients and potentially incorrect substantive inferences. Having controlled for this bias, we now turn to the second stage of our model, which examines the factors explaining the electoral fortunes of incumbents.

Looking at the results in Table 4.9, we see that the electorate does respond to candidate-specific forces in state supreme court elections. The significance of Quality Challenger suggests that voters are able to distinguish the candidates by their qualifications, a finding consistent with studies of legislative elections at both state and national levels. Challengers in supreme court elections with experience on the bench perform almost 5 percent better than their inexperienced counterparts. Although this may not immediately seem important, given that the average incumbent's vote is only 56.8 percent during the time frame of our study, the challenger's relative experience or inexperience could well mean the difference between an incumbent's reelection and defeat in many of these contests. Further, in a somewhat less dramatic manner, even if the incumbent were to survive the bid for reelection, the closeness of the race could alert the incumbent to the potential perils of ignoring constituency preferences on controversial matters of public policy while setting in motion a likely pattern of contested races in the future. In short, quality challengers enhance the democratic pressures on state supreme courts, and contrary to conventional wisdom voters appear to be quite capable of making smart political choices.

Other candidate characteristics also are significant influences on incumbents' vote shares in state supreme court elections. As with challengers' decisions to run, the incumbency advantage is important. Those justices who have not yet faced the electorate perform just over 3 percent worse, other things being equal, than their colleagues who have previously won elections to the high court bench. Again, this makes a great deal of sense when we consider that voters did not choose these candidates in the first place.

Similarly, differences in campaign spending between incumbents and challengers are important in determining incumbents' electoral performance in state supreme court elections. As Table 4.9 documents, money does matter, as in the case of legislative elections as well. A 1 percent increase in spending by the incumbent over the challenger can add about 1.6 percent to the incumbent's vote share, a substantively significant impact considering the average competitiveness of these elections. Given the powerful force of incumbency, it would take incredibly well-financed challengers and unpopular incumbents who could not raise money to tip the balance away from the status quo, *ceteris paribus.* And as clearly indicated in Table 4.1, incumbent spending on average significantly has outpaced challenger spending from 1990 through 2004. In every election cycle during that period, incumbents on average outspent challengers by sizable sums. Of course, there are individual races that deviate from these general tendencies.

Surprisingly, the coefficients for murder rate and partisan elections are not significant. Thus, our findings diverge from previous findings.[58] Again, we think time may explain these differences. Hall[59] examined elections from 1980 through 1995, and we know that supreme court elections (especially nonpartisan elections) increasingly began to attract challengers by the early 1990s. Whereas voters in the past may have voted retrospectively in the absence of challengers, they now have the ability to respond more directly to incumbents by favoring, or not favoring, alternative candidates. Regarding partisan elections, the differences between partisan elections and nonpartisan elections disappear once the seats are contested, and increasingly challengers are entering nonpartisan races. This finding is consistent with the descriptive data reported earlier.

Measuring candidate quality as a dichotomy is consistent with much of the work on legislative elections. However, given the crucial nature of this variable to our theoretical argument and our strong desire to make direct comparisons between judicial and legislative elections, we present a more refined set of indicators in Table 4.10, thus rendering this study even more comparable to the wide range of legislative studies on this subject and strengthening the robustness of any substantive conclusions. Please note that the specifications of both stage one and stage two in Table 4.10 are

Table 4.10 Competition, Type of Challenger, and Spending in State Supreme Court Elections

Stage 1: Challengers in State Supreme Court Elections, 1990–2000

	Coefficient	*Robust SE*	*z*	*P > |z|*	*Expected* β
Competitive Seat	1.260	0.190	6.630	0.000	$\beta > 0$
New Appointee	1.308	0.194	6.740	0.000	$\beta > 0$
Salary	0.059	0.107	0.560	0.578	$\beta > 0$
Term	0.077	0.119	0.650	0.517	$\beta > 0$
Unified Government	–0.814	0.182	–4.470	0.000	$\beta < 0$
Partisan	1.427	0.412	3.470	0.001	$\beta > 0$
District	1.333	0.542	2.460	0.014	$\beta > 0$
District x Partisan	–2.688	0.445	–6.040	0.000	$\beta < 0$
Lawyers	0.000	0.000	4.060	0.000	$\beta > 0$
Constant	–2.436	1.156	–2.110	0.035	

Dependent variable: Contested.

Stage 2: Incumbent Vote Shares in State Supreme Court Elections, 1990–2000

	Coefficient	*Robust SE*	*z*	*P > |z|*	*Expected* β
Trial Court Challenger	–4.379	1.832	–2.390	0.017	$\beta < 0$
Trial Court Challenger x No IAC	–8.705	3.004	–2.900	0.004	$\beta < 0$
Appellate Court Challenger	–5.022	2.867	–1.750	0.080	$\beta < 0$
Former Supreme Court Challenger	–3.197	6.538	–0.490	0.625	$\beta < 0$
No IAC	6.514	3.473	1.880	0.061	$\beta = 0$
New Appointee	–3.370	1.239	–2.720	0.007	$\beta < 0$
Spending Difference	1.615	0.467	3.460	0.001	$\beta > 0$
Murder Rate	0.104	0.194	0.540	0.592	$\beta < 0$
Partisan	–3.287	1.366	–2.410	0.016	$\beta < 0$
1990–91	–0.552	1.877	–0.290	0.769	
1992–93	–1.622	2.363	–0.690	0.492	
1994–95	–0.716	2.445	–0.290	0.770	
1996–97	–2.449	3.000	–0.820	0.414	
1998–99	4.681	2.305	2.030	0.042	
Constant	58.540	2.341	25.000	0.000	

Dependent variable: Incumbent Vote
Mean of dependent variable = 56.85
Number of observations = 198; Censored = 69, Uncensored = 129
Log likelihood = –522.425
χ^2 (5) = 18.93
Test of independent equations: χ^2 (1) = 4.15; Prob > χ^2 = 0.042.

identical to those in Table 4.9 with the exception of the candidate quality measures.

As Table 4.10 clearly indicates, the electorate not only responds to basic differences between challengers but also appears to differentiate between types of judicial experience. Generally, in states without intermediate appellate courts, the effects of trial court experience are about twice that of states providing more frequent opportunities to serve on the bench. Similarly, in states with intermediate appellate courts, trial court experience is important, but appellate service is even more so, albeit by a somewhat smaller increment. Interestingly, former justices seeking to reclaim their seats do not have a significant effect on incumbents' vote margins. However, this result should be viewed cautiously, since there are only two such cases in these data, and it is not at all certain whether this type of experience should be viewed theoretically as positive or negative.

The effects of trial court experience in states without intermediate appellate courts seem particularly significant. These challengers reduce the vote shares of incumbents by almost 9 percent, an effect that is quite dramatic given the competitiveness of state supreme court elections. Beyond this result, trial court and appellate court experience serves to reduce incumbent's margins from 4.4 percent to 5.0 percent, depending on the service involved. When incumbents win on average with only 56.8 percent of the vote, a 4 to 5 percent reduction can mean the difference between winning and losing many of these elections. In sum, the bottom line is that candidate quality in judicial elections matters.

Conclusion

In the preceding pages, we have argued that in order to understand the dynamics of state supreme court elections, scholars must consider carefully both the strategies of challengers and the choices of voters. Potential challengers must decide whether to enter the electoral arena, and the electorate must then decide whether to support the incumbent given available alternatives. Failure to consider both of these processes could lead to erroneous inferences about the politics of supreme court elections.

More specifically, our results indicate that the decisions of challengers and voters, at least in the aggregate, make a great deal of sense. Challengers take into account the electoral vulnerability of the incumbent as a primary factor in choosing whether to run. Similarly, the electorate takes into account judicial experience when selecting among candidates. Stated differently, challengers appear to enter state supreme court races when they might have a reasonable chance of winning, and voters in the aggregate cast ballots for incumbents after considering whether opponents may or may not be qualified for office. These important findings strike a considerable blow to the negative characterizations dominating the judicial reform literature. Indeed, it appears that both challengers and voters make rational political judgments in state supreme court elections. These elections simply are not games of chance.

Regarding campaign spending and the impact of big money in state supreme court elections, money does matter, as we would expect. However, it seems that the most serious problems with money are not in spending per se but rather are found in inequities between candidates. Campaign fundraising certainly favors incumbents, who already have an incredible advantage electorally simply by virtue of holding the office (except for those incumbents initially appointed and seeking their first victories). Moreover, as long as incumbents spend about as much as their challengers, incumbents should do quite well, other things considered. However, well-financed challengers running against unpopular incumbents could tip the balance in their favor by considerably outspending the incumbent. Thus, it seems that the focus of judicial reform should be on ways to make the spending game fair for incumbents and challengers rather than tossing out judicial elections altogether. Public financing with spending limits, for example, might be an effective solution, as long as the spending limits are set high enough so that incumbents would be likely to run up against them whereas challengers would not. Otherwise, spending limits simply would reinforce the incumbency advantage by not permitting challengers to spend enough money to gain voter familiarity. Of course, such plans would decrease the incumbency advantage, which contradicts the seeming goals of the judicial reform movement.

At the same time, we should recognize that not all incumbents deserve to be reelected and it is precisely these candidates who might have the most difficulty raising money. In essence, we cannot use the presence of challengers, narrow electoral margins for incumbents, and outright defeats as evidence of the failure of judicial elections. These are precisely the results we would expect when the democratic process is working well.

Further, our analysis reveals that judicial elections are governed by many of the same factors influencing legislative elections. Among other things, challengers are more likely to run in states characterized by competitive party politics, and the quality of challengers makes a great deal of difference to the electoral success of incumbents.

From a broader perspective, judicial politics scholars should think more systematically about the manner in which institutional arrangements, including selection and retention mechanisms, structure the politics of courts. This chapter, along with chapter 2 and chapter 3, joins a growing body of literature documenting these effects. In particular, partisan and nonpartisan elections are starting to look a great deal alike because challengers increasingly are taking on incumbents in nonpartisan races. Of course, this is precisely the problem that judicial reform advocates perceive. As elections (including partisan elections in some states) begin to operate like elections instead of *de facto* appointment systems, a very loud cry has been entered from judicial reform advocates to eliminate them. We disagree. Elections should be actual contests with competing candidates and alternative viewpoints, and these types of competitive races should only improve voter knowledge and participation while enhancing perceptions of democratic control and institutional legitimacy. In fact, removing partisan labels from ballots and precluding the possibility of challengers only served to impede the democratic process and institutionalize the incumbency advantage.

Most importantly, this work suggests that state supreme court elections may be more democratic, and their results more substantively meaningful, than opponents of these elections generally contend. Judicial reform advocates need to rethink traditional notions that the electorate is incapable of responding to candidate stimuli and that judicial elections inherently are an ineffective means for securing popular control over the bench. Our analysis reveals much to the contrary. Indeed, it would appear that two of the reform movement's primary arguments to discredit democratic politics—that voters cannot evaluate candidates at the same time that interest groups and other parties simply buy elections—are not accurate.

Chapter 5

Evaluating Recent Reforms and Proposals

In response to serious indictments against partisan elections by many of the nation's leading court reform advocacy groups in the United States, eighteen states have altered the means by which state supreme court justices are selected and retained, usually by replacing partisan elections with nonpartisan elections or the Missouri Plan. The most recent states to accede to the pressures of the critics are North Carolina and Arkansas, which replaced partisan elections with nonpartisan elections. In the process, Arkansas changed the timing of judicial elections to be out of sync with the regular November general election cycle. In the same manner, Minnesota currently is considering replacing nonpartisan elections with the Missouri Plan.

As less extreme measures, and more consistently with campaign finance reforms for nonjudicial elections, three states also are experimenting with public financing of supreme court elections. As mentioned, North Carolina jettisoned partisan elections for nonpartisan elections but at the same time created a system of public financing for judicial campaigns. New Mexico followed suit, and Wisconsin is in the process of making significant revisions to its existing system of public financing.

In this chapter, we discuss these recent alterations in the means by which state supreme courts are staffed and assess, to the extent that we can do so in the short time span since these changes, their consequences or likely consequences on the democratic process using descriptive data. In doing so, we draw on the systematic evidence presented in the previous chapters about the consequences of various institutional arrangements, including selection procedures, on the accountability function. Generally, we expect that removing partisan labels from ballots will inhibit the entry of challengers into races in which incumbents are seeking reelection and will reduce citizen participation in state supreme court elections. We also speculate that public financing will increase the incumbency advantage.

Public Financing of Judicial Election Campaigns

As we know, the electorate repeatedly has refused to relinquish the right to elect judges,[1] rejecting judicial reform advocates' most recent claims that appointment systems are necessary to correct for inherent deficiencies in elections to the American bench, including the seeming improprieties that flow from incumbent justices accepting campaign contributions and the purported negative impact of such actions on the legitimacy of courts. Whereas some influential scholars such as Geyh[2] and Averill[3] argue that nothing short of eliminating judicial elections will preserve independence and end the appearance of impropriety, others have become proponents of a more moderate reform: public funding of judicial elections.[4] By enacting public financing schemes, states can minimize the private contributions from businesses and attorneys that give rise to the perception that these contributors are favored when these parties appear in court.[5]

Indeed, a recent national Zogby survey indicates that 79 percent of businesses polled believe that campaign contributions made to judges influence their decisions. Additionally, 73 percent support the public funding of campaigns. As we discuss below, the public feels much the same way as businesses. Of course, these perceptions of impropriety may be false or have no impact at all on the legitimacy of courts. Moreover, even if the perceptions are inaccurate, public financing would not have the same dramatic consequences as eliminating electoral processes altogether.

Practically speaking, public financing of campaigns is far easier to achieve and less controversial than eliminating elections or altering their format. Public financing schemes do not require constitutional amendments approved by voters but simply can be enacted by the legislature through the regular legislative process.

That being said, there are serious issues and drawbacks to such arrangements, which lead some reformers to argue that public financing does not go far enough to correct for the negative consequences of elections. At the same time, advocates on the opposite side of the fence question whether public financing systems serve the democratic process. Consider the most obvious of these drawbacks.

First, public financing may reduce private contributions to candidates but does not eliminate any of the money raised and spent by independent groups. Indeed, "restricting fundraising activities makes these other forms of campaign support more important and increases the influence of the groups that provide them."[6] This should be a critical concern to judicial reform advocates, since the heavy hand of interest groups, particularly single-interest actors, are precisely the focus of their fears. Overall, public financing may not reduce the total sums of money spent in campaigns (even with spending limits on candidates) but may simply shift spending from one set of political actors to another.

Along these same lines, spending limits might heighten the incumbency advantage, because challengers typically need to spend more than incumbents to do well (recall our discussion in chapter 4). Of course, this would be fine for judicial reform advocates who tend to view the incumbency advantage as sacred, but for those concerned with the accountability function this would be a highly negative result. Moreover, public financing and the spending limits that go with the program are voluntary. Thus, candidates who know that they will be well financed can choose to opt out and circumvent spending regulations. The recent controversy in the American presidential election between Barack Obama (who refused public financing) and John McCain (who accepted it) is an excellent example of what might happen spending-wise, even with "rescue" provisions in place to counteract some of these inequities.

From a different perspective, proponents of public financing generally argue that these schemes will increase the range of candidates who are willing to enter the electoral arena, particularly challengers who want to take on established incumbents.[7] Thus, by reducing financial barriers to challengers, public financing should promote electoral competition and heighten the accountability function. However, as mentioned, electoral competition in judicial elections is not a desirable trait for all, particularly groups such as the American Bar Association.[8] That is, "increased competition may undermine ongoing efforts to cool judicial campaign rhetoric . . . by turning elections into referenda on the popularity of incumbent judges' isolated decisions."[9] By making it easier for candidates to run for office, public financing of judicial elections may actually make these elections *more* contentious and thus further contribute to the purported erosion of judicial independence. At this point, however, there is little empirical evidence that allows us to make any predictions about whether this goal of increasing the field of candidates is realized in practice.

Finally, and perhaps most important from a practical perspective, there is the critical issue of exactly how to fund such a system. When we discuss state-specific reforms below, we will talk more about the various funding options being tried in the states. For now, it is sufficient to note that there are significant challenges to funding judicial elections, particularly in the current economic crisis plaguing the United States. Overall, large proportions of taxpayers opt out, leaving these programs seriously under-funded. In sum, public financing of judicial elections may not be the panacea its proponents claim.

Changing Judicial Selection Systems in the American States

In this chapter, we examine five states that have either recently enacted significant structural changes to the judicial selection process or are seriously contemplating specific proposals to do so. As mentioned, North Carolina and Arkansas have enacted the most radical reforms, moving from partisan elections to nonpartisan elections. At the same time, North Carolina created a system for public financing of judicial elections whereas Arkansas chose not to enact the public financing option but instead changed the timing of judicial elections. Finally, New Mexico retained their current system of judicial selection but added public financing of judicial elections.

In addition to these three states that actually have enacted significant revisions to their systems of judicial selection in the past few years, Minnesota and Wisconsin are well along the road toward making major alterations. In Minnesota, the Quie Commission has recommended that nonpartisan elections be replaced with the Missouri Plan, of which retention elections are a part. This proposal has yet to be acted upon by the legislature but appears to have significant support in the state. Also, Wisconsin is considering a variety of plans to improve the system of public financing for judicial elections that has been "on the books" for several years but has been woefully under-funded. Indeed, very few judicial candidates have availed themselves of public funding in Wisconsin, despite the availability of some funds for this purpose. In response, the governor recently called a special session of the legislature to discuss providing meaningful changes to the system, and the ball seems to be well in motion on this issue.

In the following paragraphs, we examine each of these states and ask important questions about the likely consequences of recently enacted reforms. In particular, we consider each state separately to describe the rationale for each change while also assessing their successes or failures. Of course, because only a few elections have occurred since many of these transformations, our analysis necessarily will be suggestive and not definitive. More importantly, in three of these states (Arkansas, Minnesota, Wisconsin) we are not entirely clear why structural changes were/are needed in the first place, because supreme court elections in these states are far from competitive or expensive. However, available data suggests precisely what we would predict from the previous chapters: changing from partisan to nonpartisan elections disrupts the democratic process by inhibiting challengers and voting, whereas public financing either appears to be unimportant or increases the electoral security of incumbents, at least to the extent that we can tell with readily observable indicators.

North Carolina

The Reforms

North Carolina has been electing judges since 1868 and in the last couple of decades has produced some of the most contentious elections in the nation. In fact, a larger proportion of incumbents were defeated in North

Carolina than in any other state besides West Virginia during the period of 1990 through 2004 (see Table 4.6). Overall, seven of sixteen incumbents seeking reelection during this period were defeated. Interestingly, four of the seven were gubernatorial appointees seeking their first electoral victories to the state's highest court. Similarly, the challenge rate was 87.5 percent (compared with the national average of 68.2 percent), average vote for incumbents was 56.8 percent (compared with the national average of 70.2 percent), and the ballot roll-off rate was 14.1 percent (compared with the national average of 22.9 percent). By objective indicators, these elections were working precisely the way we would expect elections to operate in the United States: incumbents were being challenged, elections were competitive, and voters were participating (though at less than optimal levels). Of course, these patterns of effective elections in action are sources of alarm to judicial reform advocates.

After a series of failed efforts to replace partisan elections with the Missouri Plan (in 1974, 1977, 1989, 1991, 1995, and 1999), North Carolina finally succeeded in tossing out partisan elections for nonpartisan elections in 2002, beginning with the 2004 elections.[10] The North Carolina restructuring package has three components: replacing partisan elections with nonpartisan elections, providing full public financing for all appellate court elections, and providing voter guides to all registered voters.

Like public financing systems generally, the program in North Carolina is voluntary: candidates can choose to participate or not to participate. In order to qualify for the program, candidates must raise a minimum of 30 times the filing fee and spend no more than $10,000 in the year before the election.[11] Candidates are allowed to contribute up to $1,000 of their own money, and can receive the same amount from their immediate family (spouse, children, and siblings). Moreover, candidates must raise the qualifying amount from at least 350 contributors, and each contribution must be between $10 and $500.[12] This is to ensure that candidates have a broad base of support and thus are legitimate candidates.

In terms of disbursements, candidates receive 125 times the filing fee for the North Carolina Courts of Appeals and 175 times the filing fee for the Supreme Court.[13] There also are "rescue funds" for candidates who accept public funding but who face opponents who do not. If more money is spent by a candidate who opted out of public financing (or by an independent interest group), the candidate who does participate can receive matching funds up to twice the original spending limit.[14] This is an important provision to offset major financial disadvantages when opponents refuse public funding. Without this provision, candidates would be more reluctant to accept public funds. At the same time, there are caps on the additional funds for candidates in the system.

Money for the system is raised in three ways. First, there is a $3 "check-off" on state income tax returns, similar to the $3 check-off on federal income tax returns for federal elections. Second, each attorney licensed in North Carolina can make a $50 contribution to the fund when paying the professional license tax. Finally, any corporation, business, union, or professional association can make voluntary contributions.[15] It is important to note that the public financing program is funded *entirely* by voluntary contributions.

These major structural revisions in the ways judges are chosen in North Carolina were made, at least in part, because of seeming public concerns over the effects of money on judicial impartiality, as well as general voter ignorance about judicial elections. These concerns were identified in a poll conducted in the spring of 2002 by the North Carolina Center for Voter Education, which surveyed 600 North Carolina voters.[16] Some of these results are illuminating:

- 57 percent of the respondents claimed that they had little or no information about judicial candidates in the last election.[17]
- 77 percent of the respondents claimed to have been interested in the last election.
- 78 percent of the respondents felt that campaign contributions had some or a great deal of influence over judicial decisions.
- 85 percent of the respondents were concerned about the costs of running for judge and thought that good candidates were being deterred because of high campaign costs.
- 84 percent of the voters expressed concern that lawyers are the biggest campaign contributors to judicial elections.
- 81 percent of the voters felt that judges should be elected.

We should hasten to add that taking polls is quite common for advocacy groups and state governments, but that does not mean that these polls are accurate in the scientific sense. In order to constitute valid representations of citizen opinions, polls must be conducted with rigorous well-established standards for sample selection and neutral question wording. With this important disclaimer, not only for this poll but others mentioned in this book, we highlight the following findings.

First, voters strongly support the election of judges over appointment schemes. In fact, 75 percent of the respondents "strongly" felt that judges should be elected. This finding is consistent with public opinion poll results in other states. Second, voters want to elect judges but often do not feel that they have enough information to participate. This strikes us as an odd finding, considering the significantly below-average rates of roll-off in North Carolina Supreme Court elections. Third, voters feel that money is corrupting in judicial elections and the judicial system. This also is consistent with nonacademic polls about money and citizen perceptions of courts, such as those reported by the Justice at Stake Campaign.[18] It is in this context that North Carolina substantially altered the process for recruiting and retaining judges.

Assessing the Reforms

The structural revisions in North Carolina, though quite extreme, have had mixed results for the conduct of judicial elections. Of course, before assessing these consequences it is important to note that there have been only two election cycles since the reforms were enacted, rendering our conclusions highly tentative. Moreover, at this point we are not able to assess whether public perceptions of the judiciary have improved since public financing because there have been no subsequent public opinion surveys. However, there is limited empirical evidence on some aspects of the reforms that allow us to make some preliminary assessments of their successes and failures.

Let us begin with public financing. One way to think about the success of this program is to examine how many candidates have qualified (or attempted to qualify) for public funding. According to Democracy North Carolina, 71 percent (twenty of twenty-eight) candidates for the North Carolina Supreme Court and Court of Appeals qualified for public funding in the 2004 and 2006 elections.[19] Additionally, another three candidates attempted to qualify but failed, bringing the percentage of candidates who sought public funding to 82 percent. Clearly, candidates are participating in the program in sizable proportions. However, it remains to be seen which kinds of candidates opt out, and whether the candidates associated with single-interest politics and other high-roller campaigns simply side-step the public program and its corresponding limits. Such detailed data are not yet available.

Another way in which the reforms have been successful is in reducing the proportions of campaign funds provided by attorneys. According to the North Carolina Center for Voter Education,[20] 40 percent of the contributions to candidates in 2002 were made by attorneys. In 2004, the first election cycle after public financing, the percentage dropped to 11 percent. Interestingly, candidate contributions to their own campaigns also declined, from 9 percent in 2002 to 4 percent in 2004. Overall, 64 percent of the contributions in 2004 came from the public campaign fund. Thus, it would appear that the public financing of campaigns served to reduce campaign contributions from lawyers and other individuals who actually might appear in North Carolina courts.

In absolute numbers, more money was spent in 2004 than in 2002 in North Carolina appellate court elections. In 2004, over $1.2 million was spent,[21] compared with $807,320 in 2002. However, there were only six candidates running in 2002 whereas there were ten in 2004. Once we adjust spending by the number of candidates, we see that more money per candidate was spent in 2002 than in 2004. Based on these data, the reforms appear to have been successful, at least on this dimension.

Recall from the survey just mentioned that 85 percent of the public felt that excellent candidates were being discouraged from seeking judicial office because of the high costs of campaigns. If true, we should see more candidates running after the reforms than before the reforms, since public financing should remove financial deterrents to seeking office. Table 5.1 addresses this issue by listing each seat available on the Supreme Court by election cycle and the number of candidates seeking each seat, both in primaries and the general election. To consider the effects of public financing and the change to nonpartisan elections, we look at two election cycles before nonpartisan elections and public financing (2000 and 2002) and two after these changes (2004 and 2006).

The data indicate that nonpartisan elections and public financing seem to have had the effect of increasing competition for open seats but reducing competition for incumbents. In 2000 and 2002, the two election cycles before system changes, all four incumbents were challenged, and there was competition in the opposite political party during the primaries for two of these elections. In other words, in the two elections just before North Carolina made fundamental changes in the selection of judges, half of the incumbents were involved in elections that drew three candidates. However, after 2002, all four elections involving incumbents drew two candidates only. Thus, these changes appear to have strengthened the incumbency advantage rather than promote healthy electoral competition

Table 5.1 Candidates for the North Carolina Supreme Court, 2000–2006

Year	*Type of Election*	*Primary Candidates*	*General Election Candidates*	*Total Candidates*
2000	Inc: Frye (D)	0	2	2
2000	Inc: Freeman (D)	0	2	2
2002	Inc: Orr (R)	2 (D)	2	3
2002	Inc: Butterfield (D)	2 (R)	2	3
2004	Inc: Parker	0	2	2
2004	Open Seat	0	8	8
2006	Inc: Parker	0	2	2
2006	Inc: Martin	0	2	2
2006	Inc: Timmons-Goodson	0	2	2
2006	Open Seat	5	2*	5

* The two candidates in the general election were the top two vote winners in the primary election.

where incumbents are concerned. These findings are consistent with the data reported earlier on the increased incumbency advantage of nonpartisan elections generally.

Alternatively, open-seat elections now look like political free-for-alls. In the two open-seat elections in North Carolina since 2002, one race drew eight candidates and another drew five. Although this might be good news to those who were concerned about the sheer number of candidates entering supreme court elections, there really was no problem to fix. Historically open-seat elections in partisan and nonpartisan elections have been highly competitive. In fact, from 1990 though 2004, rates of contestation in open-seat partisan and nonpartisan supreme court elections nationally were, respectively, 90 percent and 92 percent.

What about the issue of voter participation? The survey results indicated that over three-fourths of the respondents in the poll conducted by the North Carolina Center for Voter Education were interested in judicial elections, but over half (57 percent) felt that they did not have enough information about the candidates or the issues. As part of the reform package, voter guides were provided that contained information on all candidates for the North Carolina courts.[22] If these voter guides were effective, then we should see higher proportions of voters participating after the reform than before.

In chapter 2, we argued that one way to measure voter participation is to examine the amount of ballot roll-off in a race. That is, given that some voters will have already turned out to vote for candidates in the most politically visible offices such as President and Governor, what percentage will vote in a state supreme court election? By comparing average rates of ballot roll-off before and after the reforms, we can ascertain whether voter participation was improved by the voter education initiative, which also should have counteracted the change from partisan to nonpartisan elections. Indeed, we would expect considerable improvement in voter participation in state supreme court elections, given the high percentage of respondents who claimed to have interest but little information upon which to base their votes. Table 5.2 shows votes cast in North Carolina Supreme Court elections and corresponding ballot roll-off rates from 2000 through 2006.

As Table 5.2 clearly indicates, voter participation has sharply *decreased* after the reform package in North Carolina in 2002. In fact, far *fewer* voters are now participating in state supreme court elections after the purported improvements in judicial selection relative to the period immediately before the changes. Comparing 2004 with 2000 (since both were presidential election years), we see that ballot roll-off was 23.3 percent in 2004 compared with 4.9 percent in 2000, an increase of over 18 percentage points. Looking at nonpresidential years, over 500,000 fewer votes were cast in supreme court elections in 2006 compared to 2002. Unfortunately,

Table 5.2 Average Votes Cast and Ballot Roll-Off in North Carolina State Supreme Court Races, General Elections 2000–2006

Year	*Average Votes Cast*	*Average Ballot Roll-Off (%)*
2000	2,797,000	4.9
2002	2,165,000	7.2
2004	2,645,000	23.3
2006	1,635,000	

we cannot compare ballot roll-off in these years because there were no presidential, gubernatorial, or senate races in North Carolina in 2006. Presumably, this is part of the reason why so few people participated in 2006. However, the decline in participation from 2000 (or even 2002) to 2004 indicates that more is going on than simply the absence of a top-of-the-ballot office. The early evidence suggests quite clearly that voters are participating less after the significant alterations in judicial selection than before these changes.

This is not surprising, considering the evidence we presented earlier, particularly in chapter 2. As we demonstrated empirically, ballot roll-off is significantly higher in nonpartisan elections than in partisan elections, even when a number of confounding factors such as contestation and candidate spending are controlled. The explanation is simple: the partisan affiliations of the candidates on the ballot serve as a meaningful cue and source of information to voters, thereby allowing them to participate in the election effectively with very little effort or other information costs. Removing this critical information serves to decrease voter participation. Perhaps more to the point, and as a voluminous literature in political science indicates, partisanship is a relatively rational way to vote, even in state supreme court elections.[23] It would appear that information guides simply cannot compensate for the absence of partisan labels on the ballot.

In sum, the evidence about the North Carolina reforms is mixed. On the positive side, at least from the perspective of the judicial reform movement, the amounts of money being raised and spent in state supreme court elections have decreased, along with the proportion of funds obtained from attorneys. Additionally, the large majority of candidates are opting for public campaign financing, which indicates that most candidates are in some measure supportive of the system. However, there are several observable consequences that do not support a positive evaluation of the 2002 reforms. Most seriously, voter participation has decreased dramatically since the shift from partisan to nonpartisan elections, public financing, and the production of voter guides. Furthermore, the incumbency advantage has been strengthened; in incumbent–challenger races for state supreme court, there now are fewer candidates on average for each seat. Indeed, in these races it would seem that the costs of running for office were not an important barrier to candidate entry. That being said, there has been a substantial increase in the number of candidates for open seats. Indeed, the changes in North Carolina appear to have generated lively competition for these seats, although highly surprising is the fact that fewer citizens are bothering to vote in them.

Of course, we must emphasize that these conclusions are tentative, because the reforms themselves still are fairly new. However, the picture is not that positive if the goal is to reduce the incumbency advantage and maintain any reasonable level of citizen participation in these elections. In short, the reforms appear to have been bad for democracy.

The Future

There are challenges that the North Carolina system of public financing is likely to face in the future, and how the state addresses these potential problems could affect the continued viability of the system. The most pressing problem is this: participation by the candidates has been high in seeking public funding but participation by voters in funding the system has been low. Only 7 percent of taxpayers contributed to the program when they filed their 2003 tax returns and only 12 percent of lawyers voluntarily contributed the $50 when paying the licensing tax.[24] These surprisingly low levels of support for the system by citizens and attorneys threaten the long-term sustainability of the program.

This problem is not unique to North Carolina. Other public financing schemes, such as the federal program for presidential candidates and the programs in Wisconsin and Minnesota for state office, are experiencing the same deficits.[25] According to select public opinion polls, the public seemingly wants to reduce the impact of private dollars on election outcomes but at the same time is not willing to fund systems that address their concerns, even when contributing involves no additional financial liability to them. This bizarre juxtaposition causes us to question the accuracy of the polls that report citizen concerns in the first place. But at a minimum, the poor participation rates in funding such systems remain a problem.

Thus, North Carolina will have to come up with a way to increase participation by those who fund the public financing system or devise alternative ways to support it financially. Bend offers several simple suggestions for doing this.[26] One proposal is to change the mechanism on personal income tax forms from an "opt-in" to an "opt-out" provision. Under this proposal, $3 would automatically be donated to the public financing system unless a voter specifically requested that this not occur. Doing this would probably increase the number of voters who participate. A second proposal is to make the $50 contribution from attorneys mandatory instead of voluntary. Of course, this also would raise the profile of attorneys in the funding scheme, a goal that was not desirable with reform advocates in the first place. A third option is to increase case filing fees, with the additional money going to supplement the public financing fund.

To date, none of these proposed modifications has received enough support to be enacted into law. However, in order to keep the public funding scheme financially viable, North Carolina will have to confront the issue of how to generate more money or make the hard choice of ending the program altogether.

Arkansas

The Reform

In November of 2000, the voters of Arkansas ratified Amendment 80 to the state constitution, which, among other things, provided for the nonpartisan election of all judges in the state.[27] Arkansas had elected judges in partisan elections since 1864 (when they changed from legislative appointment to partisan elections), and previous proposals to move away from partisan elections had failed on four other occasions (in 1980, 1991, 1995, and 1997). The closest this change came to being enacted prior to 2000 was in 1980, when the voters rejected a new state constitution. Otherwise, the various proposals died in the legislature (either in committee or on the floor). Although some political leaders in Arkansas favored the Missouri Plan over nonpartisan elections in 2000, this position garnered significant opposition from judges, legislators, and the media.[28] Thus, the change from partisan to nonpartisan elections was thought to be a compromise and a purported improvement over the status quo.

Of course, not everyone thought the change from partisan to nonpartisan elections was a good one. In writing about the Wyoming experience, Averill claimed that for a variety of reasons "a nonpartisan election system may be the worst of all selection methods."[29] One reason for this is that nonpartisan elections alone do not reduce the need for candidates to raise money from lawyers and groups likely to appear before them, and thus do nothing to reduce the appearance of impropriety. Second, in some states, political parties are highly active in nonpartisan elections, even going so far as to endorse candidates. (We discuss this in greater detail below.) Finally, as we have stated repeatedly, removing partisan labels from candidates takes away a valuable cue from voters, thereby decreasing participation while rendering election results more idiosyncratic.

Interestingly, it is not clear that the status quo in Arkansas suggested any need for constitutional revision, something we will also see when we discuss the cases of Minnesota and Wisconsin. In stark contrast to North Carolina, supreme court elections in Arkansas were not affected by many of the issues that capture the attention of judicial reform advocates. In

Arkansas, rates of contestation were low from 1990 through 2004. Only 50 percent of all incumbents seeking reelection were challenged, and incumbents averaged about an 82.6 percent vote share. In fact, no incumbents were defeated during that fourteen-year period. Even so, ballot roll-off was not that bad. Roll-off averaged about 16 percent, compared with the national average of 23 percent. In total campaign spending in elections between 1990 and 2004, Arkansas ranked seventeenth of twenty-two states electing judges.[30] Moreover, only the Texas Court of Criminal Appeals was lower in campaign spending among the states using partisan elections to choose judges. If we look only at the period from 1990 through 2000 (right before Arkansas changed from partisan to nonpartisan elections) we see a similar pattern.[31] Generally, Arkansas certainly has not had the kind of exorbitant spending in state supreme court elections prevalent in states such as Mississippi, Alabama, and Ohio.

Despite these trends, Arkansas abandoned partisan elections for nonpartisan elections yet maintained a rather interesting characteristic: no explicit prohibitions on endorsements from political parties, although there are restrictions on judicial candidates seeking such endorsements. Specifically, Canon 5A of the Arkansas Code of Judicial Conduct states that although a judge (or judicial candidate) is free to have his or her personal views on political issues, "as a member of Arkansas' non-partisan judiciary, a judge and judicial candidate must avoid any conduct which associates him or her with a political party." Similarly, Section 5C(1) states that a candidate for the bench cannot "directly or indirectly solicit or promote the candidate's name to appear in promotions on a political party's ticket or materials paid for by a political party." However, Section 5C(3) allows judicial candidates to "privately identify himself or herself as affiliated with a political party." What constitutes a "private" revelation seems wide open to interpretation.

In the transition from partisan to nonpartisan elections, Arkansas did not ban political parties from endorsing judicial candidates but did change the timing of judicial elections. Before the transition, political parties nominated candidates for judgeships at the same time they nominated candidates for other offices—in their partisan primary. After partisan nominations, judges then were elected in general elections held during the regular November election cycle, just as in the case for other elected offices. Now, judicial elections are held in conjunction with partisan primaries in May, although the judicial races are listed in a separate, nonpartisan portion of the ballot. All voters who vote in the primary—regardless of whether they participate in the Democratic primary or the Republican primary—vote for judges. If no candidate receives a majority of the vote, the top two vote-getters face each other in a run-off election at the same time as the general election in November. Interestingly, there are no rules prohibiting both candidates in the general election from being from the same political party. Given the potential for higher turnout in one party's primary versus the other, depending on the competitiveness of the other races, it is conceivable that two candidates from a single political party could face each other in the general election.

Assessing the Reforms

Unfortunately, we do not have public opinion data for Arkansas as we did for North Carolina, so we cannot examine the general concerns and expectations of Arkansas citizens. However, we can evaluate the changes in Arkansas based on the same objective criteria we used to evaluate North Carolina: candidate entry and voter participation. Has moving to nonpartisan elections opened the electoral process to challengers or increased voter participation?

In Table 5.3, we consider challenger entry in Arkansas Supreme Court elections before and after the change from partisan to nonpartisan elections in 2002, as well as the changes in timing that accompanied the switch. The table lists the number of candidates running for state supreme court both before (in 1996, 1998, 2000) and after (in 2002, 2004, 2006) the switch to nonpartisan elections.

Looking at the data, there is limited evidence that elections are less likely to be contested post-reform than pre-reform. Generally speaking, races in Arkansas do not draw challengers at the same rates as many other states. For all six election cycles, almost half (42 percent, or five of twelve races) did not attract challengers, even in two open-seat elections. Prior to the switch from partisan to nonpartisan elections, 60 percent (three of

Table 5.3 Candidates for the Arkansas Supreme Court, 1996–2006

Year	*Type of Election*	*Primary Candidates*	*General Election Candidates*	*Total Candidates*
1996	Open Seat	2	1	2
1996	Open Seat	0	1	1
1996	Open Seat	0	1	1
1998	Inc: Corbin	2	2	2
2000	Open Seat	2	2	2
2002	Inc: Glaze	1	0	1
2004	Open Seat	2	2	2
2004	Open Seat	3	0	3
2006	Inc: Corbin	2	0	2
2006	Inc: Imber	1	0	1
2006	Inc: Brown	1	0	1
2006	Open Seat	2	0	2

five) were contested; after the change, 57 percent (four of seven) were contested. Obviously, we are working with a small number of cases here. However, if anything, it appears as if *fewer* candidates are running for the Arkansas Supreme Court since the elections became nonpartisan. This is especially true with incumbents. The only incumbent–challenger race was contested in the earlier period, but after the change to nonpartisan elections only two of four incumbents have drawn challengers. This suggests, in a highly tentative and small way, that nonpartisan elections may have enhanced the incumbency advantage for the Arkansas Supreme Court.

Evaluating changes in voter participation in supreme court elections in Arkansas is complicated by the changes in timing that took place with the 2000 reform package. Recall that supreme court candidates appear on the general election ballot only if no candidate receives a majority of the vote in the primaries.

In Table 5.4, we calculate the average number of votes cast for all contested state supreme court general elections (in order to ensure that we are examining comparable units) as well as the percentage of ballot roll-off in these races. We examine only contested races because when a candidate is not opposed in Arkansas, the total number of votes is not reported. Instead, official statistics simply show that the candidate received 100 percent of the vote.

First, immediately observable in Table 5.4 are the stark contrasts between the 1998 election and the other two (2000 and 2004). Obviously the race involving incumbent Justice Corbin captured the attention of voters, resulting in the very low ballot roll-off rate of 6.4 percent. This is considered outstanding by any standard of evaluation. Of course, we also would expect lower ballot roll-off in the midterm election years than presidential election years, which draw more casual voters into the process who may not pay attention to down-ballot elections such as state supreme

Table 5.4 Average Votes Cast and Ballot Roll-Off in Arkansas State Supreme Court Races, General Elections 1996–2006

Year	*Average Votes Cast*	*Average Ballot Roll-Off (%)*
1996		
1998	661,000	6.4
2000	690,000	25.2
2002		
2004	843,000	19.2
2006		

Note: In 1996, the only contestation occurred in the Democratic primary for one of the three seats. In 2002, there was only one seat up for election and it was uncontested. In 2006, two of the four seats up for election were contested, but both were decided in the primary.

court. In fact, we documented in chapter 2 that roll-off tends to be much higher in presidential years than in non-presidential years.[32] Even so, a ballot roll-off rate of only 6.4 percent is excellent.

Otherwise, ballot roll-off rates in the presidential election years of 2000 and 2004 looks fairly similar, with lower roll-off in 2004 than in 2000. Again, we are only comparing two elections, but there is a decrease of six percentage points in ballot roll-off after the change to nonpartisan elections. Overall, however, the roll-off rates in 2000 and 2004 are terrible from the perspective of an active and interested electorate. In 2000, ballot roll-off was 25 percent and in 2004 it was 19 percent.

Moreover, in American elections generally, participation in primaries commonly is eclipsed by participation in general elections. Thus, we would strongly expect fewer voters overall to participate in judicial elections in Arkansas now, given the rather odd timing of these races.

Unfortunately, we cannot really compare campaign spending pre- and post-reforms in Arkansas because of the timing issue. If a candidate only has to get through the primaries in May to win, for instance, that candidate will raise and spend less money than if having to run all the way through November. Thus, we cannot draw any meaningful conclusions about campaign spending before and after the switch to nonpartisan elections in Arkansas. But as mentioned at the beginning of this discussion, there was no reason to think that Arkansas had any problems with "new style" campaigns in the first place. Thus, we are not sure what should have changed.

The Future

We do not expect state supreme court elections in Arkansas to change demonstrably as a result of the transition to nonpartisan elections, except in the case of citizen participation in these races. Given low levels of turnout in primaries versus general elections, we expect far fewer voters to participate in high court races in the future. We also predict some increase in the incumbency advantage because of the nature of nonpartisan elections, but given the incredible incumbency advantage already in place before the transition any changes are likely to be minimal.

It will be interesting to see whether political leaders in Arkansas will continue to push for the Missouri Plan now that nonpartisan elections have been entrenched. In the past, the Arkansas House was the death of such bills (either in committee or on the floor), but taking that huge step from partisan to nonpartisan elections may have opened the door to other revisions in the future and provided encouragement to election critics to continue their push toward ending democratic processes altogether. Even so, any further revisions must be ratified by the public, which at this point would still seem to be an uphill battle. Thus, we expect that nonpartisan elections will be the method of selection for the foreseeable future.

Minnesota

The Proposed Reform

Although Minnesotans have elected judges since 1857 and have done so using nonpartisan ballots since 1912,[33] Minnesota has long been categorized as the least contentious of all the states that elect judges. In fact, supreme court elections in Minnesota are even more low-key than in Arkansas. Although supreme court elections in Minnesota tend to be contested (69 percent of incumbents seeking reelection are challenged), these contests produce landslides for incumbents (averaging 76 percent of the vote). In fact, like Arkansas and in striking contrast to North Carolina, no state supreme court incumbents in Minnesota have ever been defeated.[34] Similarly, spending in these contests is incredibly low. For instance, Minnesota had the lowest levels of supreme court campaign spending for any state from 1990 through 2004, with just over $108,000 being spent per race on average.[35] When one looks at per capita spending instead of overall spending, only Texas Court of Criminal Appeals elections are cheaper. In short, supreme court elections in Minnesota are a far cry from highly politicized, big-money affairs.[36]

Nevertheless, after the United States Supreme Court decided *Republican Party of Minnesota* v. *White*, which struck down prohibitions on judicial candidates announcing their views on legal and political issues, there was a concern that highly contentious and expensive elections were on their way to Minnesota. To take up this issue, the Citizens Commission for the Preservation of an Impartial Judiciary was formed in 2006, and former Governor Al Quie was appointed to chair it. The Quie Commission, as the commission is called, subsequently made three recommendations for changing the judicial selection process in Minnesota.

First, the Quie Commission recommended that nonpartisan elections be replaced with the Missouri Plan, in which all judges initially would be appointed by the governor from a list assembled by a selection commission.[37] The initial term would be approximately four years (depending on when the judge was appointed). Second, the Quie Commission recommended that the state establish a performance evaluation commission consisting of appointees from all three branches of state government that would evaluate judges both in the middle and at the end of their terms. Moreover, the results of these evaluations would be publicized and listed on the ballot. Third, after serving an initial term each newly appointed judge would run in a retention election for an eight-year term. A judge who received more than 50 percent of "yes" votes would remain on the bench. If a judge were not retained, the process would begin anew in the manner described above. As noted, voters would be told on the ballot whether the judge was deemed "qualified" or "not qualified" by the performance evaluation commission.

This proposed selection system is a straightforward example of "merit selection," or the Missouri Plan, with one notable twist: the performance evaluation commission. Although some states have such commissions and publicize the results (such as Arizona and Colorado), Minnesota would be the only state to list the results of such an evaluation on the ballot for voters to consider at election time. This would provide voters with easy access to some information about the judge's performance but it is unclear exactly how the evaluations would be conducted or if critical information about the judge's decisions or other important proclivities on the bench would be disclosed.[38]

The Commission's recommendations seem to have the support of the public. According to a 2008 survey commissioned by the Justice at Stake Campaign, 74 percent of Minnesotans said they would vote "yes" on a constitutional amendment that would change the method of selection from nonpartisan elections to the retention election system proposed by the Quie Commission.[39] Moreover, 73 percent of the respondents reported that they "sometimes" or "almost always" vote in judicial elections. Of those who do not vote, 35 percent said that they "almost never" or "never" do so because of the lack of information. Thus, the performance evaluation commission recommendations might increase the percentage of voters who participate in these elections, although it is not clear what these reports would contain or whether they would serve the same function as a spirited challenger or partisan ballot. Finally, voters seem concerned with the amount of campaign spending and the appearance of impropriety in the courts, even though spending levels are extremely low in Minnesota. Only 22 percent agreed that Minnesota courts are free from the influence of special interest groups and 78 percent were at least somewhat concerned about judges needing to raise money for their campaigns (while 47 percent claimed that judges favor their campaign contributors).

Interestingly, these same strange tensions between wanting to elect judges and yet being critical of campaign activities appear to be present in other states as well, at least according to polls taken by advocacy groups such as the Justice at Stake Campaign. So, whereas the voters in Minnesota are concerned about judges raising money to campaign for office and the appearance of impropriety, a whopping 92 percent agree (or strongly agree) that it is important for judges to be elected. Moreover, 74 percent of respondents have at least "some" confidence in the Minnesota courts (and 76 percent in judges), compared with 56 percent for the governor and 58 percent for the state legislature. Finally, 82 percent believe that "fair" is an accurate description of the courts, and 78 percent think "impartial" is accurate.

These survey results show that voters are of two minds: voters are concerned about the process of electing judges but strongly believe that judges should be elected; voters are worried about the influence of special interest groups but think that courts are fair and impartial; voters are concerned with the corrupting influence of campaign spending but have more confidence in the courts than in any other institutions of government. These strange juxtapositions cause us to question the validity of these polls. Even so, these results hardly support the case to end the election of judges. Indeed, these results actually suggest that claims about the deleterious effects of campaigning on citizen perceptions of courts are overstated.

The Status of the Reform

Despite the seeming momentum for the recommendations of the Quie Commission, the legislature adjourned in 2008 without passing legislation to implement them. Part of the explanation is the conflict that unexpectedly emerged between the Quie Commission and the State Bar Association, which proposed ending elections entirely and replacing them with an appointment system.[40] Thus, although there seems to be considerable support for revising judicial selection procedures in Minnesota, the major players in the controversy are split on which reform is more desirable. Even with this split, however, a version of the Quie Commission platform passed one of the two committees in the House and Senate and we suspect that momentum will continue to build on these proposals, particularly since the Bar has agreed to support the Quie Commission report when it comes before the state legislature again in early 2009. An added incentive is the heightened competition in two supreme court seats in the 2008 election cycle. It appears that both seats were more competitive and contentious than traditionally has been the norm in Minnesota. Thus, Minnesota is the state to watch as a judicial reform experiment in action, although we are at a loss to understand exactly what purported problems are being fixed by the proposed switch to the Missouri Plan other than perhaps forestalling competitive elections in the future, which the reformers initially feared in the context of the *White* decision.

New Mexico

The Reform

New Mexico has an interesting history of judicial reform. Although judges have been chosen in partisan elections since 1912, New Mexico has modified several aspects of the judicial election process multiple times in recent years. In 1988, voters approved a constitutional amendment to replace a traditional partisan election system with an interesting hybrid system. Specifically, when a vacancy occurs in a New Mexico court, the state judicial nominating commission recommends a list of candidates to the governor, who then appoints one candidate from the list to assume office immediately. Then, during the next election cycle, this newly appointed judge runs in a partisan election for the remainder of the term. In subsequent elections, the judge runs in retention elections.[41]

In 1994, New Mexico altered the system again by raising the percentage of the vote to retain office to 57 percent instead of a bare majority. At present, the only other state to require a larger-than-simple-majority coalition to win is Illinois (which requires 60 percent).

Finally, in 1997 New Mexico created a judicial performance and evaluation commission, which evaluates judges at both the midpoint and end of their terms. These evaluations are based on the self-assessments of judges and on surveys of attorneys, law professors, and clerks. Although the midterm assessments are not released, evaluations of judges as they approach retention are published in newspapers and are available on the internet.[42]

In this context of reform over the past several decades, the extension of publicly financed campaigns to judicial elections in New Mexico was not much of a surprise.[43] In April 2007, after a special legislative session, Governor Bill Richardson signed legislation giving candidates for judicial office the option of seeking public funds for their campaigns in the first round of partisan elections only. Candidates are eligible for public funds if they raise $5 from each of a specified number of people (one-tenth of 1 percent of the number of voters in the state). Additionally, candidates may raise and spend "seed money" during the qualifying period as long as contributors do not give more than $100 per donor or committee (up to a maximum of $5,000). Thus, like North Carolina, New Mexico is trying to keep private money to a minimum in the selection and retention of judges.

Regarding the public financing system itself, the New Mexico program will be funded somewhat differently than the North Carolina and Wisconsin systems (to be discussed below). In New Mexico, the public financing system will be funded from qualified contributions to candidates, unspent funds from previous candidates and elections, unspent seed money, money received from the Uniform Unclaimed Property Act, and money appropriated by the legislature. There is nothing in the law that allows for an income tax check-off or direct contributions from attorneys or others.

In terms of how much money will be distributed, candidates in contested primary elections will receive $0.15 for each voter of the candidate's party in the state. If primaries are uncontested, candidates will receive 50 percent of that amount. For contested general elections, candidates will receive $0.15 for each voter in the state. If the general election is uncontested, then no money will be distributed. Importantly, if a general election appears to be uncontested but an opposition candidate later enters the race, money equal to the amount that the candidate should have received for contested races will be distributed to the candidate who opted for public financing. Like North Carolina, New Mexico has a "rescue funds" provision (called "matching funds") that allow a candidate who is participating in the system to respond to well-funded candidates who are not participating in public financing. This amount is limited to twice the original allocation of funds.

As mentioned, the public financing option is not available to candidates in New Mexico retention elections, and at present this simply is not an issue because retention elections rarely involve spending or campaigning.[44] Were this to change, the legislature could amend existing legislation quite readily to extend the public financing program to all elections in the state.

The Future

There have not been any elections in New Mexico since the enactment of public financing, so we cannot assess these reforms empirically. In terms of campaign spending before the reforms, New Mexico's partisan elections looked a lot like Arkansas: toward the bottom of states in average spending, though the rank increases somewhat with per capita spending.[45] Thus, judicial races in New Mexico were not the high-cost affairs that they were in other states. However, New Mexico is not as sleepy as Arkansas or Minnesota, electorally speaking. In the partisan elections, the challenge rate is 80 percent, which is considerably higher than the national average of 68 percent. The defeat rate also is higher, at 11.1 percent compared with the national average of only 8.7 percent. However, the average vote won by incumbents is 70 percent, which is right at the national average.

Thus, we might expect the new public financing system to have some impact but the exact nature of that impact remains to be seen. Partisan elections in New Mexico realistically are the only avenue of accession for many candidates seeking judgeships on the high court bench, particularly for candidates who may not share the governor's partisan affiliation or run in the same circles as the candidates typically identified by the judicial nominating commission. Under these conditions, we might expect competition to remain the norm, and for candidates with lavish resources to opt out of the public financing system.

Unfortunately, it is too soon to tell whether supreme court candidates will participate in the public financing system or if public financing will decrease the number of challengers in these races (as might be the case in North Carolina). At the same time, we will have to see how well the system garners financial support without the income tax check-off or direct contributions from attorneys and others. If the system is financially viable and successful, then New Mexico will serve as an important model for North Carolina, which is struggling.

Wisconsin

The Proposed Reform

Like the other states described in this chapter, Wisconsin has a long history of electing judges. Judges of the Wisconsin Supreme Court have been elected since the Court's creation in 1853. Traditionally, judges in Wisconsin are chosen on nonpartisan ballots, and judicial elections are held in times that do not correspond with the regular election cycle for other important political offices. Unlike the other states discussed here, however, Wisconsin started revising the election system as early as 1976 by offering partial public financing to candidates for major state offices, including the Supreme Court.[46] Like the campaign financing systems of the federal government and North Carolina, the Wisconsin system is funded by a state tax return check-off. However, in Wisconsin the amount per person from the check-off is only $1.

The Wisconsin public campaign financing system works like this: in years with supreme court elections, 8 percent of the money in the overall system is earmarked for those races, which are held in spring. Specifically, the primary for judicial elections is in February and the general election follows in April. Recall that Arkansas now holds its nonpartisan judicial elections at times other than the regular cycle as well.

Overall, Wisconsin is much more similar to Arkansas and Minnesota than to North Carolina and New Mexico, electorally speaking. Only just over half of all supreme court incumbents were challenged from 1990 through 2004, and they won by large margins (about 79 percent of the vote). Also, there have been no electoral defeats in decades (from 1967 to 2007).[47] In the one special election that was held during the regular election cycle in recent memory, ballot roll-off was a whopping 59 percent. Even so, in terms of campaign spending Wisconsin oddly ranks about in the middle of all states that elect judges (both in average amounts and average amounts per capita).[48]

In part because of campaign spending in Wisconsin, the state legislature is attempting to provide full public financing for judicial elections. Although there is a system already in place, taxpayer participation has declined over the years and recently there have been insufficient funds for candidates. Thus, many candidates have turned down public funding because of the inadequate amounts they would have received.[49] The new proposal to revive the public campaign financing system would provide complete financing to state supreme court candidates if they agree to limit their spending to no more than $400,000. Moreover, like the North Carolina system, candidates would be eligible for matching funds if targeted by special interest groups.[50] The proposal would be funded by raising the income tax check-off from $1 to $5 and by creating a Public Integrity

Endowment to which corporations, individuals, unions, foundations, or anyone else could contribute on a tax-deductible basis.

This reform appears to have the support of the justices and public alike. In fact, The Wisconsin Supreme Court sent a letter to the legislature urging them to enact meaningful campaign finance reform.[51] In early 2008, the Justice at Stake Campaign conducted a poll of the Wisconsin public (as they did in Minnesota), and according to the survey 75 percent support public funding for supreme court candidates.[52] Further, 52 percent of the public approved of the job the Wisconsin Supreme Court was doing, but 76 percent thought that campaign contributions had at least some influence on judicial decisions. Needless to say, there is a serious inconsistency between the strong support for public funding reported by Justice at Stake and the actual behavior of taxpayers in not funding the system.

The Status of the Reform

Despite a special legislative session called by the governor, no action has been taken on the proposed revisions to the campaign finance system in Wisconsin. The bill to increase public financing made it through legislative committee but did not receive a floor vote before the legislature adjourned. Just as in Minnesota, the pressure to enact this reform is not likely to end any time soon, with groups such as Common Cause and the Justice at Stake Campaign making this matter a priority.

Conclusion

As these five case studies illustrate, the movement to change the way judges are selected in the American states is alive and well. Although most states previously were opting for the Missouri Plan over partisan elections, this movement has stalled because of widespread public opposition (except in Minnesota). Now, reformers are focused on "cleansing" elections from partisanship and aggressive campaigning while working to end elections altogether. Indeed, removing partisan labels from ballots and restricting campaign activities have become paramount goals.

Although it is too early to assess with any confidence the effects of recent structural reforms on the conduct of elections to state supreme courts, early results are mixed. Regarding public financing, it appears that the amount of private contributions to supreme court election campaigns has been reduced, even if total spending has not changed much for the candidates who choose public financing. However, public financing schemes appear to have strengthened the incumbency advantage. At the same time, these systems are threatened by the lack of contributions, which can have serious consequences. As the case of Wisconsin illustrates, candidates will opt out of public financing if adequate sums of money are not available.

This is probably the most significant challenge facing North Carolina and New Mexico.

The switch from partisan elections to nonpartisan elections has had more readily observable consequences, which are highly consistent with empirical evidence generally about the effectiveness of partisan elections versus nonpartisan or retention elections for facilitating citizen participation in the selection process. In short, taking the candidates' partisan affiliations off the ballot significantly decreases voter participation. This is true even when states provide voter guides, as in the case of North Carolina. As Averill noted,[53] in many ways nonpartisan elections are the worst form of selecting judges, and the more systematic results reported by Hall[54] strongly support that contention. Thus, moving from partisan to nonpartisan elections, albeit not as extreme as eliminating judicial elections altogether, has much the same practical effect: larger proportions of citizens are removed from the process and the accountability function of elections is significantly impaired. At the same time, states with highly competitive nonpartisan elections continue to face issues with campaign activities and negative advertising even without partisan labels on the ballot. We cannot imagine how nonpartisan elections are a wise choice, and retention elections are only worse.

Chapter 6

Debunking Popular Myths of Judicial Reform

We started the discussion in this book by describing the intense controversy currently raging in the American states over the propriety of electing judges. With a full-scale war being waged against judicial elections, especially partisan elections, we asked whether many of the most fundamental criticisms being leveled against the democratic process have any merit, empirically speaking. Consistently throughout the preceding chapters, and as we would have predicted based on the voluminous empirical literature on a wide variety of elections to nonjudicial offices in the United States, we must conclude that judicial reform advocates are wrong about many of the most important assumptions underlying their case against judicial elections. In fact, elections to state supreme courts—especially when partisan in format or highly competitive and expensive otherwise—serve as powerful legitimacy-conferring institutions that enhance democracy and create an inextricable link between citizens and the judiciary.

Part of the problem with the court reform movement's position is its stubborn insistence in relying on outmoded theories of jurisprudence that portray judges as intrinsically different than other political actors. Based primarily on normative assertions that judges *should* base their decisions entirely in law, judicial election critics insist that any form of political behavior—including campaigning—harms the integrity of courts. However, legal realists and political scientists have long since discredited such naïve accounts of judicial decision making, and there is no empirical evidence supporting the contention that state court judges must be seen to be above the political fray to maintain public trust, or that campaigning or other office-seeking activities will have negative consequences for judges or the judiciary. In fact, given the notable absence of any identifiable crises of legitimacy in the states that have hosted competitive judicial elections for decades, we wonder if the real crisis is not the unrelenting assaults on the democratic process by judicial reform advocates and their never-ending cries that elections are poisoning the well of judicial independence and legitimacy. If hard-fought and expensive campaigns are so destructive, why do there not seem to be any observable negative consequences for citizens, judges, or courts?

Of course, the assault on judicial elections is a two-pronged attack. The first is to insist that competitive elections for judgeships are destroying citizen perceptions of impartiality upon which institutional legitimacy is founded. The other tactic is to insist that even if electing judges were not *de facto* inappropriate, modern judicial elections are ineffective. Specifically,

> [r]eformers argue that partisan elections, characterized by lackluster campaigns devoid of issue content, are disconnected from substantive evaluations of candidates or other meaningful considerations relevant to the judiciary, which renders them ineffective as a means of accountability.[1]

In other words, the debate over whether judges should or should not engage in electoral politics is irrelevant if elections fail to provide an efficacious means by which voters can participate in the judicial selection and retention process, including the critical function of effecting meaningful evaluations of candidates. The increasingly competitive and expensive nature of judicial elections only exacerbates these concerns because both judges seeking reelection and voters trying to make informed choices are being portrayed as entirely at the mercy of special interests that hijack the democratic process for their own political gain.

Because of the serious nature of the charges against judicial elections and the high political stakes for democratic processes in the United States, we decided to put the primary claims of judicial reform advocates through objective scientific tests to gauge their accuracy. Essentially, we identified many of the major criticisms of judicial elections, translated them into testable hypotheses, and evaluated these hypotheses using econometric techniques applied to actual evidence, specifically all state supreme court elections from 1990 through 2004.

Remarkably, our results lead to one striking conclusion: that the principal charges against judicial elections are factually inaccurate. In the paragraphs below, we review the allegations used to condemn judicial elections and the evidence we have produced to nullify them. In this way, our goal is to debunk popular myths of judicial reform and replace the serious inaccuracies in the conventional wisdom with scientifically verified facts.

Myth # 1: Citizens are not interested, or willing to participate, in state supreme court elections

In his classic study of state supreme court elections, Dubois cited the lack of citizen participation in judicial elections as "the leading indicator" that voters are "unwilling and incapable of holding its judiciary accountable through elections."[2] In the words of the National Center for State Courts, voters attach "limited importance to the work of the judicial branch of government and thus decline to vote."[3] Thus, high levels of ballot roll-off, a leading measure of citizen participation in down-ballot races, are seen by many as a simple reflection of the lack of interest in courts or the judicial selection process by state electorates. More importantly, consistent voter indifference to the judicial recruitment process would severely undermine the very premise upon which elections are held, thus rendering them irrelevant, ineffective, and obsolete.

However, as we have shown in chapter 2, public disengagement is not an inevitable characteristic of state supreme court elections. From 1990 through 2004, ballot roll-off ranged from the incredibly low rate of 1.6 percent to a whopping 65.1 percent in particular elections, and averaged from 12.5 percent (which is fairly low) to 59.2 percent (which is terrible) across the states. Obviously these extraordinary variations in citizen participation both across and within states do not speak to a consistently apathetic electorate.

Instead, we have demonstrated that voters in state supreme court elections are drawn into the electoral arena by the same factors that stimulate voting for elections to non-judicial offices. Stated succinctly by Hall, "voters vote when they have interest, readily available information, and choice."[4] Specifically, citizens participate in state supreme court elections in high proportions when the races are interesting because of aggressive challengers and well-financed campaigns. Also important as mobilizing agents are partisan ballots and, at least for nonpartisan elections, district-based constituencies.

Partisan ballots reduce information costs to voters and provide a relatively rational basis upon which to select among candidates. Nonpartisan elections remove this important resource and as a consequence dramatically decrease citizen participation in state supreme court elections. However, the effects of nonpartisan ballots can be counteracted somewhat by district-based constituencies. In district-based nonpartisan elections, the state minority party has an incentive to field candidates because of the increased odds of winning relative to statewide races, and smaller constituencies make it much easier to campaign. Voters are more likely to be contacted by a candidate or a candidate's campaign and thus are more likely to vote. In short, statewide partisan races and district-based nonpartisan elections are excellent agents of democracy. Both significantly reduce voter defection in state supreme court elections in a particularly strong way.

From a different perspective, removing partisan labels on ballots in statewide constituencies, the most common form of nonpartisan constituencies, significantly impairs citizen participation in supreme court elections, *ceteris paribus*. Thus, lack of interest and nonparticipation in some judicial elections is, to a large extent, a "self-fulfilling prophecy" of the judicial reform movement,[5] which insisted that such reforms were essential for improving the selection process. In practice, nonpartisan elections are an attack on the democratic process and meaningful citizen participation in the selection and retention of judges.

Myth # 2: Expensive, aggressive campaigns alienate voters and decrease citizen participation in judicial elections

The purported deleterious effects of money are at the center of the current controversy over electing judges. In chapter 2, we evaluated the conditions under which citizens are drawn into the electoral arena, and particularly whether rough-and-tumble campaigns and big-money politics alienate voters to the point that they refuse to participate in state supreme court elections. After considering the theoretically important variables that should affect the propensity to vote, we documented that campaign spending exerts a statistically significant impact on the willingness of voters to participate in state supreme court elections once these voters are at the polls, but that this influence is in the *opposite* direction of what judicial reform advocates predict.

In fact, campaign spending is one of the best mobilization agents in state supreme court elections. Rather than being alienated by costly campaigns, citizens embrace highly spirited expensive races by voting in much greater proportions than in more mundane contests. Why would well-financed campaigns improve voter participation? The answer is simple, and quite consistent with studies of elections to nonjudicial office: because successful campaigns stimulate interest in the races and provide information for making informed choices. Indeed, by promoting mass participation and giving voters ownership in the outcomes of these races, expensive campaigns strengthen the critical linkage between citizens and courts and enhance the quality of democracy.

Myth # 3: Nonpartisan elections "depoliticize" campaigns and reduce the costs to candidates of seeking these seats

In chapter 3, we examined the controversial issue of campaign spending, in an effort to ascertain why some candidates spend much more than others. Overall, we established that campaign costs are not rising uniformly for all candidates or all states. Instead, campaign spending in state supreme court elections reflects the types of considerations present in elections to other offices in the United States: the closeness of the race, the value of the seat, the institutional arrangements that define the election, and the overall political context.

Critical among these concerns is whether partisan labels are on the ballot. Contrary to conventional wisdom, nonpartisan elections increase the costs of campaigns, whereas partisan elections significantly decrease these costs, other things being equal. Rather than reducing demands on judges to solicit campaign contributions and generate large campaign war chests, nonpartisan elections do the opposite. And recall that nonpartisan elections are the creatures of the judicial reform movement. This increased spending that characterizes nonpartisan elections serves to intensify the efforts that candidates must make to elicit funds and exacerbates the problems of the seeming impropriety of doing so. Through the lens of campaign spending, nonpartisan elections are not the best choice among elections for minimizing the politics of big money in state supreme court contests. In fact, the very reform to improve electoral politics has had the opposite effect for those who consider the high costs of campaigns to be a serious problem.

That nonpartisan elections raise the costs of seeking office makes a great deal of sense. Candidates in nonpartisan elections must work harder to educate and mobilize voters to their particular candidacies. Although political parties are highly involved in these elections as would be the case in partisan elections, overcoming the information deficit of the lack of partisan labels on the ballot is formidable.

Competitive, well-financed campaigns substantially improve the willingness of citizens to participate in elections. In a healthy democracy, where citizens garner knowledge about candidates and are mobilized to vote through election campaigns, we should be open to the fact that lively well-financed campaigns actually might be preferable to lackluster and poorly financed campaigns that fail to serve voters. In this sense, the costs of campaigns should not be a cause for concern unless there is convincing evidence of adverse effects on candidate entry, quality recruitment, or other important aspects of the political process. Furthermore, mere conjecture and unsubstantiated claims from critics of judicial elections do not constitute convincing evidence.

Myth # 4: Money buys elections

Rising campaign costs in state supreme court elections are widely regarded by judicial reform advocates as one of the most serious and pressing threats to the integrity and legitimacy of American state judiciaries. Among other concerns are the necessity of judges soliciting campaign contributions from parties likely to appear before their courts and the high political stakes when financially flush interest groups and other political organizations seek to oust qualified incumbents over one or two hot-button political issues.

Are state supreme court justices simply at the mercy of special interests and other high rollers when their electoral fates are being determined, as many in the judicial reform literature suggest? In chapter 4, we answered this vitally important question about the impact of money on election outcomes in state supreme court races. Overall, we find exactly what studies of elections to nonjudicial offices have determined: that big spending is important in reelection campaigns but is only one of the many important factors that affect how well incumbents who are seeking reelection do with voters on election day. Also, the real concern should not be total spending per se in any election but rather the differentials in spending between the candidates. On average, campaign spending in incumbent–challenger races strongly favors incumbents. Also, given the powerful force of incumbency, it would take incredibly well-financed challengers and unpopular incumbents who could not raise money to tip the balance away from the status quo.

From a different perspective, money is a necessary condition for educating and mobilizing voters and for publicizing the candidacies of challengers. Without advertising and other forms of political information dissemination, challengers are incapable of discussing their credentials with voters and because of the incumbency advantage are highly likely to lose, regardless of their merits. In this way, the mere presence of money in an election is not reasonably a cause for concern.

Myth # 5: Citizens are incapable of assessing judicial qualifications when casting ballots in elections to the state high court bench

For decades, election critics have charged that the electorate is incapable of distinguishing between qualified and unqualified candidates for office. Stated succinctly by the American Bar Association, "voters often are unable to cast an informed ballot."[6] The initial fix for this problem was to replace partisan elections with nonpartisan elections and the Missouri Plan, which supposedly removes partisanship from the vote calculus and instead focuses campaigns on the professional merits of the candidates. The current solution to this purported problem is replacing elections of all sorts with appointment schemes.

In chapter 4 we addressed the question of whether state supreme court elections appeared to be devoid of meaningful choice. Specifically, we asked whether voters are capable of making candidate-based evaluations unrelated to incumbency. Our findings strongly contradict the negative stereotype that voters are ignorant and ineffective. Instead, we found that voters in state supreme court elections make fairly sophisticated candidate-based evaluations. When casting votes among supreme court candidates, voters distinguish challengers who have experience on the bench from challengers who lack it and thus are less suitable alternatives to incumbents. Moreover, voters differentiate among types of experience (trial court or appellate court service). Contrary to conventional wisdom, voters appear to be quite capable of making smart political choices. At the same time, quality challengers enhance the democratic pressures on state supreme courts by reducing the incumbency advantage.

Myth # 6: The United States Supreme Court's decision in *Republican Party of Minnesota* v. *White* transformed judicial elections into bitter, increasingly contentious races

One consistent theme in the nation's most prestigious law reviews, as well as publications by court reform advocacy groups, is an expected sea change in judicial elections because of the United States Supreme Court's decision in *Republican Party of Minnesota* v. *White*. By eliminating state restrictions in the form of "announce clauses" for candidates running for judgeships, the Supreme Court was feared to have ushered in an era of unrestrained, no-holds-barred competition in judicial elections.

In chapter 2 and chapter 3, we examined a series of political consequences that should have materialized if predictions about the destructive consequences of *White* were accurate. Specifically, we asked whether challengers increasingly are more prevalent after *White*, whether citizen participation has declined (as a manifestation of being "turned off" by nastier campaigns), and whether campaign expenditures have increased (as a consequence of intense competition and special-interest politics). Contrary to the conventional wisdom of a dramatic shift in judicial elections starting with the 2002 election cycle, we found no statistically discernable influence in state supreme court elections of the *White* decision on the propensity for challengers to take on incumbents, the willingness of citizens to vote, or the actual costs of campaigns. It would appear that the many predictions about the dire consequences of *White* were exaggerated or incorrect.

Myth # 7: State supreme court justices universally are being targeted by challengers, who themselves are driven in part by single-interest groups and other financial high rollers

Throughout the preceding chapters, we have demonstrated conclusively that the decisions of challengers to enter state supreme court races against incumbents are highly predictable and strategic, reflecting the same rational calculations that challengers manifest in elections for executive and legislative offices. Specifically, challengers run when incumbents are electorally vulnerable, supreme court seats are attractive, a sizable candidate pool exists, and the political and institutional context promotes competition.

Incumbents most susceptible to challenge are those who are not particularly popular with voters in the first place, evidenced by narrow margins of victory in the previous election bid, or who were appointed by governors to fill unexpired terms and are facing voters for the first time. With these electorally vulnerable incumbents, challengers actually have a chance to win relative to incumbents who are popular with voters and have established stable electoral coalitions. In the same manner, challengers are much more likely in open-seat races than races involving incumbents, *ceteris paribus*.

Otherwise, challengers are more likely to enter supreme court races when there is a substantial pool of candidates from which to draw. But most importantly from the perspective of our argument about the efficacy of judicial elections, statewide partisan elections and district-based nonpartisan elections enhance the likelihood of challengers. As with citizen participation in the election process, statewide partisan elections and district-based nonpartisan elections promote the entry of challengers, which in turn generates interesting and hard-fought campaigns that stimulate citizen interest and mobilize them to vote.

Other Relevant Evidence on the Success of Judicial Reform

The seven myths pervading the judicial reform literature that we have just debunked are considerably at odds with the empirical analysis presented in the first five chapters of this work. However, there are two other important contentions that merit discussion. The first is that judges chosen in partisan elections are less qualified for office than judges chosen by other means, and the second is that appointment schemes remove the stains of partisan politics and promote decisions that better reflect the rule of law. To address these points, we draw on recent scholarship on judicial performance and on the sizeable literature on the federal courts.

Myth # 8: Nonpartisan elections and the Missouri Plan improve the quality of the state court bench

One of the promises of the judicial reform movement was that nonpartisan elections and the Missouri Plan would dramatically improve the quality of the American bench. As the story goes, highly qualified judges are deterred from seeking office in partisan elections, because skilled jurists are not politicians and thus are not likely to have the political talent to organize campaigns and mobilize the electorate. The argument essentially is that the skills needed for quality judging and for winning elections are separate and distinct and are unlikely to be found in single individuals. To remove these supposed barriers for highly skilled attorneys and judges, reform advocates proposed that partisan elections be replaced with nonpartisan elections and the Missouri Plan for those states that continue to insist on the democratic process in some form. Today the argument has been extended to eliminate elections altogether in favor of appointment schemes.

Some political scientists immediately were skeptical of these claims, and in one of the first empirical studies of this subject Glick and Emmert[7] refuted the existence of quality differentials between state supreme court justices chosen in partisan elections and those chosen by other methods. In fact, Glick and Emmert[8] failed to detect any statistically discernable differences in various measures of quality across selection systems in the states.

In this enterprise, Glick and Emmert[9] operationalized quality using objective professional qualifications such as prestige of law degree and experience on the bench, as well as indicators of diversity such as race and gender. Recently, Hurwitz and Lanier[10] reexamined these findings and reconfirmed that diversity on the bench is not affected by the particular methods for staffing the bench. In other words, state supreme court justices tend to have the same overall characteristics, regardless of the method by which they initially were recruited. Partisan elections do not produce less qualified judges or disfavor women or minorities relative to nonpartisan elections, the Missouri Plan, or appointment systems.

Of course, one of the most difficult challenges in this work is defining quality and establishing objective indicators to measure it. As mentioned, Glick and Emmert[11] utilized measures of quality such as prestige of legal education. As we all realize, however, simply looking at the institutions where judges were educated is too crude a measure of quality. Surely there are outstanding judges who did not attend elite law schools just as there are inept judges who did.

Recently, there has been a breakthrough in this research with the use of behavioral indicators of judicial quality. Specifically, Choi, Gulanti, and Posner[12] measure quality as productivity, opinion quality, and independence. First, productivity is the number of opinions per judge per year, including dissents and concurrences. Quality judges should work harder and produce more efficiently than less capable jurists. Second, opinion quality is defined as the number of out-of-state citations. Carefully argued and well-crafted opinions should be cited more often in other states than less impressive opinions. Third, independence is manifested when judges write opinions against their co-partisans on the court.[13] Independent judges should follow the law rather than the interests of political parties and thus will dissent more often from their partisan allies.

Choi, Gulati, and Posner[14] applied these measures to the decisions of state supreme courts, including the Oklahoma and Texas Court of Criminal Appeals, in 1998, 1999, and 2000. Their results are notable and represent a considerable departure from the conventional wisdom. In a nutshell, "[e]lected judges write more opinions, and while their average cite counts per opinion are lower than those for appointed judges, they garner more citations overall."[15] Even more to the point, judges selected in partisan elections are the most productive of all.[16] Similarly, elected judges are more independent than appointed judges, and those chosen in partisan elections are the most independent of all.[17] In other words, judges chosen in elections, particularly in partisan elections, are *better* than judges chosen by other methods.

Certainly, we can take issue with the various indicators of quality used to date in the empirical research on recruitment. Even so, these studies regardless of measures share a consistent theme: that schemes other than partisan elections fail to improve the quality of the bench. Likewise, the highly negative portrayal of judges chosen by popular election are unfair and inaccurate. Indeed, the available empirical evidence suggests precisely the opposite: the best judges may, in fact, be the product of democratic politics.

Myth # 9: Appointment schemes take politics out of judicial selection and promote the rule of law

Finally, we examine the notion that appointment schemes remove the stains of partisan politics and promote judicial independence. We need look no further than our own discussion in chapter 1 to review the major pitfalls of appointment systems, which contained the very defects that gave rise to judicial election schemes in the first place. In essence, appointment schemes are characterized by intense partisanship, cronyism, and elitism and, depending on the method of retention, can significantly impair the function of judicial review or promote the unfettered exercise of personal preferences that may conflict with the rule of law. Additionally, appointment systems lack effective removal power for errant or incompetent judges.

Consider the United States Supreme Court as the most visible judicial appointment scheme operating in the nation. As everyone recognizes, Republican Presidents appoint Republicans and Democratic Presidents appoint Democrats to the Supreme Court, regardless of the composition of the United States Senate. Moreover, all of these nominees are well known in White House circles before their nominations. Indeed, the failed nomination of Harriet Miers by President George W. Bush is an outstanding example of the extent to which personal ties can influence these choices.

Moreover, there is an intense battle between Democrats and Republicans over Supreme Court nominations during every presidential election and vacancy on the Court. Why? Because we know that Democratic judges interpret the law differently than Republican judges. If this were not true, then it would not matter who sits on the Court as long as these candidates have adequate legal training and experience. The fact that politicians, organized interests, the media, and the public all are concerned about seats on the United States Supreme Court is *prima facie* evidence that judging is not the neutral, impartial enterprise some would have us believe. However, if that is not enough, an empirical literature spanning several decades supports this contention.

In short, judges are political beings who make political decisions. The notion that judges decide cases solely on the law as applied to facts of the cases has been widely discredited by scholars,[18] and no amount of "independence" can change this. United States Supreme Court Justices are appointed for life. They are as structurally independent as judges can be. Yet these are the very features that give rise to their ability to decide cases without sanction based on their personal philosophies of law and public policy, which may or may not correspond with the rule of law or strictures of constitutional adjudication. In sum, appointment systems merely relocate politics from the electorate to political elites, allow judges to decide cases based on personal preferences (whether consistent with the rule of law or not, whether unbiased or not), and create serious issues of legitimacy at the state level when sitting justices engage in improper conduct or consistently make decisions not supported in law.[19] Appointment schemes are not a miracle cure for the ills of judicial elections. In many ways, the pathologies of appointment systems are worse. Stated differently, electoral independence does not guarantee impartiality or prudence in the exercise of judicial power.

Final Thoughts on Electing Judges in the American States

The judicial reform movement has come full circle. Beginning with the attempts to eliminate appointment schemes for selecting judges by introducing judicial elections, to the attempts to end judicial elections by reintroducing appointment schemes, judicial reform advocates have run the range of possibilities for staffing state court systems. The lesson from this is clear: there is no perfect system for selecting judges in the American states. Each system represents a series of tradeoffs about who is best suited to make political judgments, exactly where partisanship will be most manifest, and the basis upon which judges will cast votes once seated.

In sharp contradistinction to the claims of election critics, we have demonstrated conclusively that partisan elections to the American bench are a far cry from the institutional failures that they are purported to be among court reform advocates, legal scholars, and the media. Instead of lacking the capacity to fulfill their very basic function of accountability, judicial elections are highly efficacious institutions of democracy that in many ways serve as the prototype for what state elections should be in the United States. On every major point of contention that could be addressed by empirical analysis, the evidence strongly suggests that critics of judicial elections are incorrect. At a minimum, this evidence should help to alleviate the concerns of those who fear competitive judicial elections. We also hope that our work will promote a more informed discussion of how best to select and retain judges in the American states.

As an important corollary of this work, we suggest that instead of continuing to coddle judicial reform advocates as though they have some special wisdom to which we all should defer, we should examine the barrage of attacks on judicial elections and the unsubstantiated claims that underlie them, and demand that evidence be produced to support their attacks. Indeed, we consider skepticism a highly prudent course, considering the range of inaccuracies that have plagued the judicial reform movement historically. In this controversy, the stakes are high. Judicial reform advocates are not just assaulting a method for choosing judges but also are waging war on democratic processes and the rights of citizens to maintain control over government.

Of course, elections are not perfect either. Citizens rightly are concerned about problems plaguing elections right now—not only judicial elections but also those for other political offices in the United States. Perhaps most significant are negative tone and the politics of single-interest actors in election campaigns. However, these issues are better handled by thinking about ways of reforming campaign finance schemes and truth-in-advertising standards rather than the extreme reaction of ending elections altogether. In fact, demands for better information and transparency should be the order of the day with all American elections.

From our vantage point, democratic politics is alive and well in the American states. Given a choice between citizen control of the American state court bench and elite control that serves to constrain the exercise of judicial review and impairs the capacity of courts to act as a co-equal branch of government while protecting arrogant and incompetent judges, we think the better choice is obvious. Similarly, we think the nation would be better served by ending nonpartisan elections and the Missouri Plan, both of which impede the democratic process and exacerbate some of the most potentially negative consequences of judicial elections. In sum, partisan elections are a highly effective mechanism for selecting state court judges and should be reconsidered.

Notes

1 The Controversy over Electing Judges

1 Sandra Day O'Connor, 2007. "Justice for Sale: How Special-Interest Money Threatens the Integrity of our Courts." *Wall Street Journal*, November 15.

2 American Bar Association Commission on the 21st Century Judiciary. 2003. *Justice in Jeopardy*. Chicago: American Bar Association, p. 96.

3 Roy A. Schotland, 2001. "Financing Judicial Elections, 2000: Change and Challenge." *Law Review of Michigan State University–Detroit College of Law* 2001 (Fall): 849–899; and Anthony Champagne, 2003. "The Politics of Judicial Selection." *Policy Studies Journal* 31 (August): 413–419.

4 For example, Thomas R. Phillips, 2002. "When Money Talks, the Judiciary Must Balk." *Washington Post*, April 14, p. B2; and O'Connor, "Justice for Sale."

5 For example, National Center for State Courts. 2002. *Call to Action: Statement of the National Summit on Improving Judicial Selection*. Williamsburg, VA: National Center for State Courts; and American Bar Association Commission on the 21st Century Judiciary, *Justice in Jeopardy*.

6 For example, Deborah Goldberg, Sarah Samis, Edwin Bender, and Rachel Weiss, 2005. *The New Politics of Judicial Elections, 2004*. Washington, DC: Justice at Stake Campaign.

7 For example, Roy A. Schotland, 1985. "Elective Judges' Campaign Financing: Are State Judges' Robes the Emperor's Clothes of American Democracy." *Journal of Law and Politics* 2 (Spring): 57–167; and Charles Gardner Geyh, 2003. "Why Judicial Elections Stink." *Ohio State Law Journal* 64 (1): 43–79.

8 See, for example, Matthew J. Streb, ed. 2007. *Running for Judge: The Rising Political, Financial, and Legal Stakes of Judicial Elections*. New York: New York University Press.

9 Philip L. Dubois, 1980. *From Ballot to Bench: Judicial Elections and the Quest for Accountability*. Austin, TX: University of Texas Press; and Melinda Gann Hall, 2001a. "State Supreme Courts in American Democracy: Probing the Myths of Judicial Reform." *American Political Science Review* 95 (June): 315–330..

10 Melinda Gann Hall, 2009a. "The Controversy over Electing Judges and Advocacy in Political Science." *Justice System Journal* 30 (3): Forthcoming; and Melinda Gann Hall, 2009b. "On the Cataclysm of Judicial Elections and Other Popular Anti-Democratic Myths." Paper presented at the What's Law

Got to Do With It? Conference at the Indiana University School of Law, March 26–27.

11 Some states have altered appointment plans also. Rhode Island abandoned legislative selection for gubernatorial appointment with lifetime terms. Also, Vermont changed from legislative to gubernatorial appointment for initial accession, with legislative renewal for six-year terms.

12 Schotland, "Elective Judges' Campaign Financing."

13 Of the twelve states that currently appoint justices to the high court bench, only one (Hawaii) is not one of the original states of the Union or a state that once was part of an original state; Maine initially was part of Massachusetts, and Vermont originally was part of New York. In Maine and Vermont, governors appoint supreme court justices. Further, only two of the original thirteen states (Georgia and North Carolina) have competitive elections for supreme court. Although Pennsylvania justices initially are elected in partisan elections, they are retained for subsequent terms in retention elections.

14 Charles H. Sheldon and Linda S. Maule, 1997. *Choosing Justice: The Recruitment of State and Federal Judges.* Pullman, WA: Washington State University Press.

15 Ibid.

16 Interestingly, most appointive schemes in the states do not provide life tenure for judges. Remarkably, only Rhode Island has such a system in the strictest sense, and two other states (Massachusetts and New Hampshire) have terms of office for their judges that expire when judges reach age 70 (the mandatory retirement age).

17 Sheldon and Maule, *Choosing Justice.*

18 Paul Brace, Melinda Gann Hall, and Laura Langer, 2001. "Placing State Supreme Courts in State Politics." *State Politics and Policy Quarterly* 1 (Spring): 81–108.

19 Langer confirms these results across other areas of law. See Laura Langer, 2002. *Judicial Review in State Supreme Courts: A Comparative Study.* Albany: SUNY Press.

20 Sheldon and Maule, *Choosing Justice*, p. 3.

21 It is interesting to note that even states that did not change the method by which they chose judges "added restraint by shortening the terms for judges" (see Sheldon and Maule, *Choosing Justice*, p. 4), which also serves to reduce judicial independence, albeit in a different way.

22 Sheldon and Maule, *Choosing Justice*, p. 4.

23 Lawrence M. Friedman, 1985. *History of American Law.* New York: Simon and Schuster., pp. 129–130.

24 Kermit L. Hall, 1984. "Progressive Reform and the Decline of Democratic Accountability: The Popular Election of State Supreme Court Judges, 1850–1920." *American Bar Foundation Research Journal* 9 (Spring): 345–369.

25 See Hall, "The Controversy over Electing Judges and Advocacy in Political Science" for a fuller discussion of this issue and the argument that elections might bring justices into line with the rule of law rather than negate it.

26 For example, O'Connor, "Justice for Sale"; and Geyh, "Why Judicial Elections Stink."

27 Hall, "State Supreme Courts in American Democracy," p. 316.

28 Sheldon and Maule, *Choosing Justice.*

29 Interestingly, the Progressives appear to be wrong on both counts. Glick and

Emmert, Bonneau, and Hurwitz and Lanier find no differences in the quality of judges between selection systems, and Hall finds that nonpartisan and retention elections are driven by political factors, just as in partisan elections. Moreover, Choi, Gulati, and Posner document that elected judges actually perform *better* than appointed judges. See Henry R. Glick and Craig F. Emmert, 1987. "Selection Systems and Judicial Characteristics: The Recruitment of State Supreme Court Judges." *Judicature* 70 (December–January): 228–235; Chris W. Bonneau, 2001. "The Composition of State Supreme Courts, 2000." *Judicature* 85 (July–August): 26–31; Mark S. Hurwitz and Drew Noble Lanier, 2003. "Explaining Judicial Diversity: The Differential Ability of Women and Minorities to Attain Seats on State Supreme and Appellate Courts." *State Politics and Policy Quarterly* 3 (Winter): 329–352; Hall, "State Supreme Courts in American Democracy"; and Stephen J. Choi, G. Mitu Gulati, and Eric A. Posner, 2007. "Professionals or Politicians: The Uncertain Case for an Elected Rather than Appointed Judiciary." Unpublished manuscript. August 2007.

30 Hall, "Progressive Reform and the Decline of Democratic Accountability."

31 Melinda Gann Hall, 2007a. "Competition as Accountability in State Supreme Court Elections." In *Running for Judge: The Rising Political, Financial, and Legal Stakes of Judicial Elections*, ed. by Matthew Streb. New York: New York University Press.

32 Ibid.

33 See Bonneau, "The Composition of State Supreme Courts, 2000"; Glick and Emmert, "Selection Systems and Judicial Characteristics"; and Hurwitz and Lanier, "Explaining Judicial Diversity." Similarly, these races are not immune from political considerations (see Hall, "State Supreme Courts in American Democracy").

34 Melinda Gann Hall, 1999. "State Judicial Politics: Rules, Structure, and the Political Game." In *American State and Local Politic: Directions for the Twenty-First Century*, ed. by Ronald E. Weber and Paul Brace. Chatham, NJ: Chatham House.

35 For example, Paul Brace and Melinda Gann Hall, 1997. "The Interplay of Preferences, Case Facts, Context, and Structure in the Politics of Judicial Choice." *Journal of Politics* 59 (November): 1206–1231; Brace, Hall, and Langer, "Placing State Supreme Courts in State Politics"; Melinda Gann Hall, 1987. "Constituent Influence in State Supreme Courts: Conceptual Notes and a Case Study." *Journal of Politics* 49 (November): 1117–1124; Melinda Gann Hall, 1992. "Electoral Politics and Strategic Voting in State Supreme Courts." *Journal of Politics* 54 (May): 427–446; and Melinda Gann Hall, 1995. "Justices as Representatives: Elections and Judicial Politics in the American States." *American Politics Quarterly* 23 (October): 485–503.

36 For example, Hall, "State Supreme Courts in American Democracy"; Hall, "Competition as Accountability in State Supreme Court Elections"; Hall, "Courts and Judicial Politics in the American States"; Chris W. Bonneau, 2005a. "What Price Justice(s)? Understanding Campaign Spending in State Supreme Court Elections." *State Politics and Policy Quarterly* 5 (Summer): 107–125; and Chris W. Bonneau, 2007c. "The Effects of Campaign Spending in State Supreme Court Elections." *Political Research Quarterly* 60 (September): 489–499.

37 Hall, "State Supreme Courts in American Democracy"; Melinda Gann Hall, 2001b. "Voluntary Retirements from State Supreme Courts: Assessing

Democratic Pressures to Relinquish the Bench." *Journal of Politics* 63 (November): 1112–1140; and Hall, "Competition as Accountability in State Supreme Court Elections."

38 For example, Philip L. Dubois, 1979. "The Significance of Voting Cues in State Supreme Court Elections." *Law and Society Review* 13 (Spring): 757–779; Donald W. Jackson and James W. Riddlesperger, Jr., 1991. "Money and Politics in Judicial Elections: The 1988 Election of the Chief Justice of the Texas Supreme Court." *Judicature* 74 (December–January): 184–189; and David Klein and Lawrence Baum, 2001. "Ballot Information and Voting Decisions in Judicial Elections." *Political Research Quarterly* 54 (December): 709–728.

39 Hall, "Courts and Judicial Politics in the American States."

40 Hall, "Competition as Accountability in State Supreme Court Elections."

41 Chris W. Bonneau, 2007a. "Campaign Fundraising in State Supreme Court Elections." *Social Science Quarterly* 88 (March): 68–85.

42 American Bar Association Commission on the 21st Century Judiciary, *Justice in Jeopardy*.

43 National Center for State Courts, *Call to Action*.

44 Democracy North Carolina, "A Profile on the Judicial Public Financing Program, 2004–06."

45 Citizens Commission for the Preservation of an Independent Judiciary, 2007. *Final Report and Recommendations*. http://www.keepmnjusticeimpartial.org/FinalReportAndRecommendation.pdf

46 Judith Davidoff, 2007. "Justices Endorse Public Funding for Supreme Court Races." *Capital Times*, December 10.

47 Jeffrey A. Segal and Harold J. Spaeth, 2002. *The Supreme Court and the Attitudinal Model Revisited*. New York: Cambridge University Press.

48 C. Herman Pritchett, 1941. "Divisions of Opinion among Justices on the U.S. Supreme Court, 1939–1941." *American Political Science Review* 35 (October), p. 890.

49 Rohde and Spaeth provide a detailed discussion of the importance of institutional arrangements in United States Supreme Court decision making. See Rohde and Spaeth, *Supreme Court Decision Making*.

50 See Paul Brace and Melinda Gann Hall, 1993. "Integrated Models of Judicial Dissent." *Journal of Politics* 55 (November): 914–935; Brace and Hall, "The Interplay of Preferences, Case Facts, Context, and Structure in the Politics of Judicial Choice"; Hall, "Constituent Influence in State Supreme Courts"; Hall, "Electoral Politics and Strategic Voting in State Supreme Courts"; Hall, "Justices as Representatives"; and Melinda Gann Hall and Paul Brace. 1992. "Toward an Integrated Model of Judicial Voting Behavior." *American Politics Quarterly* 20 (April): 147–168.

51 See Paul Brace, Melinda Gann Hall, and Laura Langer, 1999. "Judicial Choice and the Politics of Abortion: Institutions, Context, and the Autonomy of Courts." *Albany Law Review* 62 (April): 1265–1303; and Brace, Hall, and Langer, "Placing State Supreme Courts in State Politics."

52 See Paul Brace and Melinda Gann Hall, 2001. "'Haves' Versus 'Have Nots' in State Supreme Courts: Allocating Docket Space and Wins in Power Asymmetric Cases." *Law and Society Review* 35 (2): 393–417.

53 Hall, "The Controversy Over Electing Judges and Advocacy in Political Science."

54 Melinda Gann Hall, 2007c. "Voting in State Supreme Court Elections:

Competition and Context as Democratic Incentives." *Journal of Politics* 69 (November), p. 1147.

55 Hall, "The Controversy Over Electing Judges and Advocacy in Political Science"; and Hall, "The Cataclysm of Judicial Elections and Other Popular Anti-Democratic Myths."

2 Mobilizing Citizens to Vote

1 Council of State Governments, 2006. *The Book of the States.* Lexington, KY: Council of State Governments.

2 Dubois, *From Ballot to Bench.*

3 Ibid., p. 36.

4 Geyh, "Why Judicial Elections Stink."

5 David Adamany and Philip Dubois, 1976. "Electing State Judges." *Wisconsin Law Review* 1976 (3), p. 743.

6 National Center for State Courts, *Call to Action.*

7 Hall, "The Controversy over Electing Judges and Advocacy in Political Science"; and Hall, "The Cataclysm of Judicial Elections and Other Popular Anti-Democratic Myths."

8 Dubois, *From Ballot to Bench*, p. 36.

9 Hall, "Voting in State Supreme Court Elections," p. 1147.

10 Zoltan Hajnal and Jessica Trounstine, 2005. "Where Turnout Matters: The Consequences of Uneven Turnout in City Politics." *Journal of Politics* 67 (May): 515–535.

11 For example, Martin P. Wattenberg, Ian McAllister, and Anthony Salvanto, 2000. "How Voting is Like Taking an SAT Test: An Analysis of American Voter Rolloff." *American Politics Quarterly* 28 (April): 234–250.

12 For example, Brian F. Schaffner, Matthew Streb, and Gerald Wright, 2001. "Teams without Uniforms: The Nonpartisan Ballot in State and Local Elections." *Political Research Quarterly* 54 (March): 7–30.

13 For example, Charles S. Bullock, III, and Richard E. Dunn, 1996. "Election Roll-Off: A Test of Three Explanations." *Urban Affairs Review* 32 (September): 71–86; and Schaffner, Streb, and Wright, "Teams without Uniforms."

14 For example, Shaun Bowler, Todd Donovan, and Trudi Happ, 1992. "Ballot Propositions and Information Costs: Direct Democracy and the Fatigued Voter." *Western Political Quarterly* 45 (June): 559–568; and David B. Magleby, 1984. *Direct Legislation: Voting on Ballot Propositions in the United States.* Baltimore: Johns Hopkins University Press.

15 David B. Rottman and Roy A. Schotland. 2001. "What Makes Judicial Elections Unique?" *Loyola of Los Angeles Law Review* 34 (June), p. 1369.

16 Dubois, *From Ballot to Bench*, p. 33.

17 Hall, "State Supreme Courts in American Democracy"; Chris W. Bonneau, 2005b. "Electoral Verdicts: Incumbent Defeats in State Supreme Court Elections." *American Politics Research* 33 (November): 818–841; and Melinda Gann Hall and Chris W. Bonneau, 2006. "Does Quality Matter? Challengers in State Supreme Court Elections." *American Journal of Political Science* 50 (January): 20–33.

18 Twenty-three states use partisan or nonpartisan elections to select judges. However, Tennessee holds elections in August (and switched to retention elections after 1990), Idaho and Wisconsin in April, and Pennsylvania (with

a few exceptions) in odd-numbered years. Thus, because there are no presidential, senatorial, or gubernatorial elections from which to gauge supreme court participation, no cases are included from Idaho, Pennsylvania, Tennessee, or Wisconsin. Moreover, Michigan, Pennsylvania, and West Virginia hold multimember elections for some seats, depending on vacancies and term rotations. Any elections reported for these states are single-member only. Finally, North Dakota has no reporting requirements on campaign spending and thus is excluded.

19 For example, Hall, "Voting in State Supreme Court Elections"; and Wattenberg, McAllister, and Salvanto, "How Voting is Like Taking an SAT Test."

20 For example, Dubois, *From Ballot to Bench*, Hall, "Voting in State Supreme Court Elections"; and William K. Hall and Larry T. Aspin, 1987a. "The Roll-Off Effect in Judicial Retention Elections." *Social Science Journal* 24 (4): 415–427.

21 For example, Wattenberg, McAllister, and Salvanto, "How Voting is Like Taking an SAT Test."

22 For example, Bullock and Dunn, "Election Roll-Off"; Stephen M. Nichols and Gregory A. Strizek, 1995. "Electronic Voting Machines and Ballot Roll-Off." *American Politics Quarterly* 23 (July): 300–318; and James M. Vanderleeuw and Richard L. Engstrom, 1987. "Race, Referendums, and Roll-Off." *Journal of Politics* 49 (November): 1081–1092.

23 Dubois, *From Ballot to Bench*, p. 66

24 Consistent with common practice, two types of elections that preclude a calculation of roll-off are excluded: (1) elections held in November but without a presidential, senatorial, or gubernatorial race on the ballot; and (2) elections held at times other than the regular November cycle. For these situations, scholars have yet to calculate normal turnout and thus there is no baseline from which to gauge participation in judicial elections. More importantly, we have strong theoretical reasons to expect that the factors influencing citizen participation in that minority of supreme court elections not held contemporaneously with major elections will differ significantly from the regular elections. Thus, pooling these observations is problematic, and simply looking at turnout rather than roll-off does not address the problem. Similarly, multimember races are excluded because of the difficulty of coding critical variables such as competition and incumbency. In total, 132 of 786 elections, or 16.8 percent, are excluded by these criteria. In general, the conclusions in this chapter should not be generalized to these races.

25 In three states (Idaho, Louisiana, Wisconsin) only one case is included for each, because supreme court elections in these states usually are scheduled at times other than November or because the elections are usually decided in the primaries. These three races are exceptions to those rules.

26 Ballot roll-off in state supreme court elections is less on average than the four mayoral elections recently analyzed by Schaffner, Streb, and Wright, which ranged from between 33 and 35 percent in partisan elections to between 37 and 43 percent in nonpartisan contests. See Schaffner, Streb, and Wright, "Teams without Uniforms."

27 Hall, "Voting in State Supreme Court Elections."

28 Ibid.

29 For example, American Bar Association, *Justice in Jeopardy*; Damon M. Cann, 2007. "Justice for Sale? Campaign Contributions and Judicial

Decisionmaking." *State Politics and Policy Quarterly* 7 (Fall): 281–297; and Geyh, "Why Judicial Elections Stink."

30 National Center for State Courts, *Call to Action*, p. 7.

31 American Bar Association, *Justice in Jeopardy*, p. 89.

32 Ibid., p. 125.

33 National Center for State Courts, *Call to Action*, p. 14.

34 For example, Cann, "Justice for Sale?"; Geyh, "Why Judicial Elections Stink"; and Eric N. Waltenburg and Charles S. Lopeman, 2000. "Tort Decisions and Campaign Dollars." *Southeastern Political Review* 28 (2): 241–263.

35 Chris W. Bonneau and Melinda Gann Hall, 2003. "Predicting Challengers in State Supreme Court Elections: Context and the Politics of Institutional Design." *Political Research Quarterly* 56 (September): 337–349; Hall, "State Supreme Courts in American Democracy"; Hall, "Competition as Accountability in State Supreme Court Elections"; and Hall, "Voting in State Supreme Court Elections."

36 Hall, "State Supreme Courts in American Democracy"; Hall, "Competition as Accountability in State Supreme Court Elections"; and Hall, "Voting in State Supreme Court Elections."

37 Chris W. Bonneau, 2004. "Patterns of Campaign Spending and Electoral Competition in State Supreme Court Elections." *Justice System Journal* 25 (1): 21–38; Bonneau, "Electoral Verdicts"; and Bonneau, "Campaign Fundraising in State Supreme Court Elections."

38 American Bar Association, *Justice in Jeopardy*.

39 Bonneau, "Electoral Verdicts."

40 Ibid.

41 For example, John J. Coleman and Paul F. Manna, 2000. "Congressional Campaign Spending and the Quality of Democracy." *Journal of Politics* 62 (August): 757–789.

42 For example, American Bar Association, *Justice in Jeopardy*; Dubois, *From Ballot to Bench*; Marie Hojnacki and Lawrence Baum, 1992. "'New Style' Judicial Campaigns and Voters: Economic Issues and Union Members in Ohio." *Western Political Quarterly* 45 (December): 921–948 and Schotland, "Financing Judicial Elections, 2000."

43 James Sample, Lauren Jones, and Rachel Weiss, 2007. *The New Politics of Judicial Elections 2006*. Washington, DC: Justice at Stake.

44 Hall, "State Supreme Courts in American Democracy"; Hall, "Voluntary Retirements from State Supreme Courts"; Hall, "Competition as Accountability in State Supreme Court Elections"; and Hall "Voting in State Supreme Court Elections."

45 Bonneau, "Patterns of Campaign Spending and Electoral Competition in State Supreme Court Elections"; Bonneau, "Electoral Verdicts"; and Bonneau, "The Effects of Campaign Spending in State Supreme Court Elections."

46 Bonneau and Hall, "Predicting Challengers in State Supreme Court Elections"; and Hall and Bonneau, "Does Quality Matter?"

47 For example, Dubois, *From Ballot to Bench*; and Hall, "Voting in State Supreme Court Elections."

48 For example, Schaffner, Streb, and Wright, "Teams without Uniforms"; and Wattenberg, McAllister, and Salvanto, "How Voting is Like Taking an SAT Test."

49 Bonneau and Hall, "Predicting Challengers in State Supreme Court Elections"; and Hall and Bonneau, "Does Quality Matter?"

50 Ibid.
51 For example, James C. Garand, Kenneth Wink, and Bryan Vincent, 1993. "Changing Meanings of Election Marginality in U.S. House Elections, 1824–1978." *Political Research Quarterly* 46 (March): 27–48.
52 Malcolm E Jewell, 1982. *Representation in State Legislatures*. Lexington, KY: University Press of Kentucky.
53 Hall, "State Supreme Courts in American Democracy"; and Hall, "Voting in State Supreme Court Elections."
54 For example, Harold D. Clarke, Frank B. Feigert, Barry J. Seldon, and Marianne C. Stewart, 1999. "More Time with My Money: Leaving the House and Going Home in 1992 and 1994." *Political Research Quarterly* 52 (March): 67–85; Timothy Groseclose and Keith Krehbiel, 1994. "Golden Parachutes, Rubber Checks, and Strategic Retirements in the 102nd House." *American Journal of Political Science* 38 (February): 75–99; and Richard L. Hall and Robert van Houweling, 1995, "Avarice and Ambition in Congress: Representatives' Decisions to Run or Retire from the U.S. House." *American Political Science Review* 89 (March): 121–136.
55 James F. Spriggs, II, and Paul J. Wahlbeck, 1995. "Calling It Quits: Strategic Retirement on the Federal Courts of Appeals, 1893–1991." *Political Research Quarterly* 48 (September): 573–597; and Peverill Squire, 1988. "Politics and Personal Factors in the Retirement from the United States Supreme Court." *Political Behavior* 10 (June): 180–190.
56 Bonneau and Hall, "Predicting Challengers in State Supreme Court Elections"; and Hall and Bonneau, "Does Quality Matter?"
57 For example, Hall, "State Supreme Courts in American Democracy"; Hall, "Voluntary Retirements from State Supreme Courts"; Hall, "Voting in State Supreme Court Elections"; and Hall and Bonneau, "Does Quality Matter?"
58 For example, Dubois, *From Ballot to Bench*; Hall, "State Supreme Courts in American Democracy"; and Kevin M. Leyden and Stephen A. Borrelli, 1995. "The Effect of State Economic Conditions on Gubernatorial Elections: Does Unified Government Make a Difference?" *Political Research Quarterly* 48 (June): 275–290.
59 For example, Bonneau, "Patterns of Campaign Spending and Electoral Competition in State Supreme Court Elections"; Dubois, *From Ballot to Bench*; and Hall, "State Supreme Courts in American Democracy."
60 For example, John R. Hibbing and Sara L. Brandes, 1983. "State Population and Electoral Success of U.S. Senators." *American Journal of Political Science* 27 (November): 808–819.
61 Bonneau and Hall, "Predicting Challengers in State Supreme Court Elections"; and Hall and Bonneau, "Does Quality Matter?"
62 Bonneau and Hall, "Predicting Challengers in State Supreme Court Elections."
63 For example, Anthony Champagne and Greg Thielemann, 1991. "Awareness of Trial Court Judges." *Judicature* 74 (February–March): 271–276; and Schotland, "Elective Judges' Campaign Financing."
64 For example, Hall, "State Supreme Courts in American Democracy"; and Bonneau, "Patterns of Campaign Spending and Electoral Competition in State Supreme Court Elections."
65 For example, Geyh, "Why Judicial Elections Stink."
66 For example, Gary C. Jacobson, 1997. *The Politics of Congressional Elections*, 4th edn. New York: Longman; Scott J. Thomas, 1989. "Do Incumbent

Campaign Expenditures Matter?" *Journal of Politics* 51 (November): 965–976; and Chris W. Bonneau, 2007b. "The Dynamics of Campaign Spending in State Supreme Court Elections." In *Running for Judge: The Rising Political, Financial, and Legal Stakes of Judicial Elections*, ed. by Matthew Streb. New York: New York University Press.

67 For example, Bonneau, "The Dynamics of Campaign Spending in State Supreme Court Elections."

68 For example, Dubois, *From Ballot to Bench*; and Kim Quaile Hill and Jan E. Leighley, 1993. "Party Ideology, Organization, and Competitiveness as Mobilizing Forces in Gubernatorial Elections." *American Journal of Political Science* 37 (November): 1158–1178.

69 For example, Dubois, *From Ballot to Bench*; and Hall, "Voting in State Supreme Court Elections."

70 Robert A. Jackson, 1995. "Clarifying the Relationship between Education and Turnout." *American Politics Quarterly* 23 (July): 279–299; and Nicholas P. Lovrich, Jr. and Charles H. Sheldon, 1983. "Voters in Contested, Nonpartisan Judicial Elections: A Responsible Electorate or a Problematic Public?" *Western Political Quarterly* 36 (June): 241–256.

71 Sande Milton, 1983. "A Cross-Sectional Analysis of the Roll-Off Vote in New York State, 1948–1974." *Polity* 15 (Summer): 613–629.

72 Dubois, "The Significance of Voting Cues in State Supreme Court Elections"; and Hall, "Voting in State Supreme Court Elections."

73 Paul D. Beechen, 1974. "Can Judicial Elections Express the People's Choice?" *Judicature* 57 (January): 242–246; and Hall and Aspin, "The Roll-Off Effect in Judicial Retention Elections."

74 Hall, "State Supreme Courts in American Democracy"; and Hall "Voting in State Supreme Court Elections."

75 Alan S. Gerber and Donald P. Green, 2000. "The Effects of Canvassing, Telephone Calls, and Direct Mail on Voter Turnout: A Field Experiment." *American Political Science Review* 94 (September): 653–663.

76 For example, Bonneau and Hall, "Predicting Challengers in State Supreme Court Elections."

77 We do not use dummy variables for each year simply because the Presidential Elections variable is a linear combination of those variables and because of the large number of years in this dataset. Instead, we follow established practice (for example, Brace and Hall, "The Interplay of Preferences, Cases Facts, Context, and Structure in the Politics of Judicial Choice") and use summary variables that also have a meaningful substantive component. When we estimate with single years, two are dropped to avoid collinearity, and Presidential Election falls to the 0.10 level of statistical significance in each model. Otherwise, the substantive conclusions remain the same.

78 Hojnacki and Baum, "'New Style' Judicial Campaigns and Voters."

79 Hall and Bonneau, "Does Quality Matter?"

80 Ibid.

81 Bonneau, "Patterns of Campaign Spending and Electoral Competition in State Supreme Court Elections"; Bonneau and Hall, "Predicting Challengers in State Supreme Court Elections"; and Hall, "State Supreme Courts in American Democracy."

82 In this model, when all other variables are at their means, predicted ballot roll-off is 9.4 percent when per capita spending is set at two standard deviations above the mean. However, roll-off increases to 22.0 percent with

two-standard-deviation decrease in per capita spending. With over one-third (38 percent) of the incumbents in this study winning by 60 percent of the vote or less, the potential effect of spending on election outcomes is considerable.

83 Sara Benesh, 2006. "Understanding Public Confidence in American Courts." *Journal of Politics* 68 (August): 697–707.

84 Damon M. Cann and Jeff Yates, 2008. "Homegrown Institutional Legitimacy: Assessing Citizens' Diffuse Support for State Courts." *American Politics Research* 36 (March): 297–329.

85 Hall, "Voting in State Supreme Court Elections."

3 Explaining Campaign Spending

1 Goldberg, Samis, Bender, and Weiss, *The New Politics of Judicial Elections, 2004*, p. 1.

2 Schotland, "Elective Judges' Campaign Financing."

3 For example, National Center for State Courts, 1999. *How the Public Views the State Courts: A 1999 National Survey*. Williamsburg, VA: National Center for State Courts; Cann, "Justice for Sale?"; Damon M. Cann, 2002. "Campaign Contributions and Judicial Behavior." *American Review of Politics* 23 (Fall): 261–274; and Cann and Yates, "Homegrown Institutional Legitimacy."

4 Bonneau's various works on this subject are the most comprehensive studies to date. However, those studies consider total spending by candidates only.

5 Goldberg, Samis, Bender, and Weiss, *The New Politics of Judicial Elections, 2004*.

6 Ibid.

7 Using experimental vignettes embedded in a public opinion survey in Kentucky (a state that selects supreme court justices in nonpartisan elections), James L. Gibson ("Challenges to the Impartiality of State Supreme Courts: Legitimacy Theory and 'New-Style' Judicial Campaigns." *American Political Science Review* 102 (February 2008): 59–75) finds that attack ads reduce citizen perceptions of judicial impartiality. However, it is unclear what effects (if any) this has, what the duration of any effects might be, or whether these experimental results have "real world" applications (or sufficient external validity). We also do not know if the Kentucky case is generalizable, particularly to states using partisan elections or states with electoral histories more competitive than Kentucky.

8 Goldberg, Samis, Bender, and Weiss, *The New Politics of Judicial Elections, 2004*.

9 But see Gibson, "Challenges to the Impartiality of State Supreme Courts."

10 For example, Linda Campbell, 2002. "An Absurd System Gets Even Worse." *Fort Worth Star-Telegram*, November 21; David Hampton, 2002. "Political and Special-Interest Influence on Judges Worsens." *Jackson Clarion-Ledger*, October 27; Adam Liptak, 2004. "Judicial Races in Several States Become Partisan Battlegrounds." *New York Times*, October 24; and *Sheboygan Press Gazette*, 2007. "Heed High Court's Advice on Financing Judicial Elections." *Sheboygan Press Gazette*, December 23, p. 5A.

11 For example, William Glaberson, 2000b. "State Chief Justices Plan to Meet on Judicial Candidates' Abuses." *New York Times*, September 8, p. A14; Phillips, "When Money Talks, the Judiciary Must Balk"; Tony Mauro, 2006.

"Chief Justices Sound Alarm on Judicial Elections." *Legal Times*, August 23; and Davidoff, "Justices Endorse Public Funding for Supreme Court Races."

12 For example, Schotland, "Elective Judges' Campaign Financing"; and Bonneau, "The Dynamics of Campaign Spending in State Supreme Court Elections."

13 The averages in chapter 3 vary somewhat from those in chapter 2 because of a small variation in the numbers of cases being examined due to missing data in the multivariate models.

14 Bonneau, "Patterns of Campaign Spending and Electoral Competition in State Supreme Court Elections."

15 Robert E. Hogan and Keith E. Hamm, 1998. "Variations in District-Level Campaign Spending in State Legislatures." In *Campaign Finance in State Legislative Elections*, ed. by Joel A. Thompson and Gary F. Moncrief. Washington, DC: CQ Press; Robert E. Hogan, 2000. "The Costs of Representation in State Legislatures: Explaining Variations in Campaign Spending." *Social Science Quarterly* 81 (December): 941–956; and Randall W. Partin, 2002. "Assessing the Impact of Campaign Spending in Governors' Races." *Political Research Quarterly* 55 (March): 213–233.

16 See Bonneau, "Electoral Verdicts."

17 Bonneau and Hall, "Predicting Challengers in State Supreme Court Elections."

18 See chapter 4 of this book; Hall, "State Supreme Courts in American Democracy."

19 Hall's studies ("Constituent Influence in State Supreme Courts," "Electoral Politics and Strategic Voting in State Supreme Courts," "Justices as Representatives") of constituency influence indicate that supreme court justices in competitive districts and other strategic contingencies engage in strategies to retain their seats, including voting with court majorities instead of dissenting.

20 For example, Melinda Gann Hall, and Paul Brace, 1989. "Order in the Courts: A Neo-Institutional Approach to Judicial Consensus." *Western Political Quarterly* 42 (September): 391–407; Hall and Brace, "Toward an Integrated Model of Judicial Voting Behavior"; Paul Brace and Melinda Gann Hall, 1995. "Studying Courts Comparatively: The View from the American States." *Political Research Quarterly* 48 (March): 5–29; and Brace and Hall, "The Interplay of Preferences, Case Facts, Context, and Structure in the Politics of Judicial Choice."

21 Kenneth A. Shepsle and Barry R. Weingast, 1987. "The Institutional Foundations of Committee Power." *American Political Science Review* 81 (March): 85–104.

22 For example, Terry M. Moe, 1987. "An Assessment of the Positive Theory of 'Congressional Dominance.'" *Legislative Studies Quarterly* 12 (November): 475–520.

23 For example, Dubois, "The Significance of Voting Cues in State Supreme Court Elections"; Philip L. Dubois, 1984. "Voting Cues in Nonpartisan Trial Court Elections: A Multivariate Assessment." *Law and Society Review* 18 (3): 395–436; Larry T. Aspin and William K. Hall, 1987. "The Friends and Neighbors Effect in Judicial Retention Elections." *Western Political Quarterly* 40 (December): 703–715; Larry T. Aspin and William K. Hall, 1989. "Friends and Neighbors Voting in Judicial Retention Elections: A Research Note Comparing Trial and Appellate Court Elections." *Western Political Quarterly* 42

(December): 587–595; and Klein and Baum, "Ballot Information and Voting Decisions in Judicial Elections."

24 For example, Gary C. Jacobson, 1980. *Money in Congressional Elections*. New Haven, CT: Yale University Press, Gary C. Jacobson, 1997. *The Politics of Congressional Elections*, 4th edn. New York: Longman; Donald Philip Green and Jonathan S. Krasno, 1988. "Salvation for the Spendthrift Incumbent: Reestimating the Effects of Campaign Spending in House Elections." *American Journal of Political Science* 32 (November): 884–907; Peverill Squire and John R. Wright, 1990. "Fundraising by Nonincumbent Candidates for the U.S. House of Representatives." *Legislative Studies Quarterly* 15 (February): 89–98; Anthony Gierzynski and David A. Breaux, 1991. "Money and Votes in State Legislative Elections." *Legislative Studies Quarterly* 16 (May): 203–217; and Anthony Gierzynski and David A. Breaux, 1996. "Legislative Elections and the Importance of Money." *Legislative Studies Quarterly* 21 (August): 337–358.

25 For example, Dubois, "Voting Cues in Nonpartisan Trial Court Elections"; Philip L. Dubois, 1986. "Penny for Your Thoughts? Campaign Spending in California Trial Court Elections, 1976–1982." *Western Political Quarterly* 39 (June): 265–284; Gregory S. Thielemann, 1993. "Local Advantage in Campaign Financing: Friends, Neighborhoods, and Their Money in Texas Supreme Court Elections." *Journal of Politics* 55 (May): 472–478; but see Theodore S. Arrington, 1996. "When Money Doesn't Matter: Campaign Spending for Minor Statewide Judicial and Executive Offices in North Carolina." *Justice System Journal* 18 (3): 257–266.

26 For example, Jacobson, *Money in Congressional Elections*; Aspin and Hall, "The Friends and Neighbors Effect in Judicial Retention Elections"; Alvarez, *Information and Elections*.

27 Coleman and Manna, "Congressional Campaign Spending and the Quality of Democracy."

28 R. Michael Alvarez, 1997. *Information and Elections*. Ann Arbor: University of Michigan Press.

29 Melinda Gann Hall and Chris W. Bonneau, 2008. "Mobilizing Interest: The Effects of Money on Citizen Participation in State Supreme Court Elections." *American Journal of Political Science* 52 (July): 457–470.

30 Although North Dakota does require candidates to file reports detailing their list of contributors and the amount of each contribution, it does not require candidates to file expenditure reports. Thus, we omitted all contested races in North Dakota. In New Mexico, we were unable to locate campaign finance reports prior to 2000. At the time we began data collection, according to the Secretary of State's office, these records were destroyed five years after an election, which eliminated all elections prior to 1998. Moreover, New Mexico requires justices to stand for partisan elections only for open seats or when they are appointed to fill a vacancy (after winning an initial partisan election, justices are retained in retention elections). We include elections in New Mexico after 2000, but omit elections prior to that point.

31 Heckman, "Sample Selection Bias as a Specification Error."

32 See Bonneau and Hall, "Predicting Challengers in State Supreme Court Elections"; Hall and Bonneau, "Does Quality Matter?"; and Hall and Bonneau, "Mobilizing Interest."

33 Hall and Bonneau, "Mobilizing Interest."

34 We use the log of total spending to be consistent with standard practice and also to make interpretation more intuitive by focusing on percentage increases rather than dollar increases. The dependent variable is coded in constant (1990) dollars. See Partin, "Assessing the Impact of Campaign Spending in Governors' Races."
35 For example, Bonneau, "The Dynamics of Campaign Spending in State Supreme Court Elections"; Jacobson, *Money in Congressional Elections*; and Thomas, "Do Incumbent Campaign Expenditures Matter?"
36 Hogan and Hamm, "Variations in District-Level Campaign Spending in State Legislatures."
37 For example, Jacobson, *Money in Congressional Elections*; Jacobson, *The Politics of Congressional Elections*; and Green and Krasno, "Salvation for the Spendthrift Incumbent."
38 Frank J. Sorauf, 1988. *Money in American Elections.* Glenview, IL: Scott, Foresman.
39 Hogan, "The Costs of Representation in State Legislatures."
40 Bonneau, "Patterns of Campaign Spending and Electoral Competition in State Supreme Court Elections"; and Bonneau, "The Dynamics of Campaign Spending in State Supreme Court Elections."
41 Jacobson, *The Politics of Congressional Elections.*
42 Bonneau, "Electoral Verdicts."
43 Anthony Gierzynski, 1998. "A Framework for the Study of Campaign Finance." In *Campaign Finance in State Legislative Elections*, ed. by Joel A. Thompson and Gary F. Moncrief. Washington, DC: CQ Press.
44 Benjamin A. Webster, Clyde Wilcox, Paul S. Herrnson, Peter L. Francia, John C. Green, and Lynda Powell, 2001. "Competing for Cash: The Individual Financiers of Congressional Elections." In *Playing Hardball: Campaigning for the U.S. Congress*, ed. by Paul S. Herrnson. Upper Saddle River, NJ: Prentice Hall.
45 Indeed, this is the reason given for estimating these kinds of models using two stage least squares. See Jacobson, *Money in Congressional Elections*; and Green and Krasno, "Salvation for the Spendthrift Incumbent."
46 Jacobson, *Money in Congressional Elections*; and Gierzynski and Breaux, "Money and Votes in State Legislative Elections."
47 For example, William Glaberson, 2000a. "Fierce Campaigns Signal a New Era for State Courts." *New York Times*, June 5, p. A1; and Phillips, "When Money Talks, the Judiciary Must Balk."
48 Gierzynski, "A Framework for the Study of Campaign Finance."
49 For example, Hall and Brace, "Order in the Courts"; Hall and Brace, "Toward an Integrated Model of Judicial Voting Behavior"; Brace and Hall, "Studying Courts Comparatively"; and Brace and Hall, "The Interplay of Preferences, Case Facts, Context, and Structure in the Politics of Judicial Choice."
50 Gierzynski, "A Framework for the Study of Campaign Finance."
51 Bonneau and Hall, "Predicting Challengers in State Supreme Court Elections."
52 For example, Peverill Squire, 1989. "Challengers in U.S. Senate Elections." *Legislative Studies Quarterly* 14 (November): 531–547; Gierzynski, "A Framework for the Study of Campaign Finance"; and Partin, "Assessing the Impact of Campaign Spending in Governors' Races."
53 Hogan and Hamm, "Variations in District-Level Campaign Spending in State Legislatures."

54 Hogan, "The Costs of Representation in State Legislatures."
55 Hogan, "The Costs of Representation in State Legislatures"; Stephen B. Burbank and Barry Friedman, 2002. "Reconsidering Judicial Independence." In *Judicial Independence at the Crossroads: An Interdisciplinary Approach*, ed. by Stephen B. Burbank and Barry Friedman. Thousand Oaks, CA: Sage; and Partin, "Assessing the Impact of Campaign Spending in Governors' Races."
56 Hall, "Courts and Judicial Politics in the American States"; and Herbert M. Kritzer, Paul Brace and Melinda Gann Hall, and Brent T. Boyea. 2007. "The Business of State Supreme Courts, Revisited." *Journal of Empirical Legal Studies* 4 (July): 427–439.
57 Glaberson, "Fierce Campaigns Signal a New Era for State Courts"; and Phillips, "When Money Talks, the Judiciary Must Balk."
58 Note that the salary, term of office, staff, and other institutional features of these Texas courts are the same.
59 We do not use dummy variables for each year because of both the number of additional variables in the dataset and the number of dummy variables we would need to include if we did so for each year. Instead, we follow the established practice of using summary variables that also have a meaningful substantive component. See, for example, Brace and Hall, "Studying Courts Comparatively"; and Hall and Bonneau, "Mobilizing Interest."
60 Heckman, "Sample Selection Bias as a Specification Error."
61 Hall and Bonneau, "Mobilizing Interest."
62 Ibid.
63 Ibid.
64 It may be too soon to see such an effect. However, other studies report a rise in contestation well before the Court's decision in this case. See Bonneau, "Patterns of Campaign Spending and Electoral Competition in State Supreme Court Elections"; Bonneau and Hall, "Predicting Challengers in State Supreme Court Elections"; Hall, "State Supreme Courts in American Democracy"; and Hall, "Competition as Accountability in State Supreme Court Elections."
65 Matthew J. Streb and Brian Frederick, 2008. "Paying a Price for a Seat on the Bench: Campaign Spending in Contested Intermediate Appellate Court Elections." *State Politics and Policy Quarterly* 8 (Winter): 410-429.
66 Bonneau, "What Price Justice(s)?"
67 Streb and Frederick, "Paying a Price for a Seat on the Bench."
68 Hogan and Hamm, "Variations in District-Level Campaign Spending in State Legislatures."
69 See, for example, Sorauf, *Money in American Elections*; and Hogan, "The Costs of Representation in State Legislatures."

4 Quality Challengers, Money, and the Choices of Voters

1 For example, Bonneau and Hall, "Predicting Challengers in State Supreme Court Elections"; Stone, Maisel, and Maestas, "Quality Counts"; and Hall, "State Supreme Courts in American Democracy."
2 House and Senate rates were calculated from Abramson, Aldrich, and Rohde, *Change and Continuity in the 2004 and 2006 Elections*, and the gubernatorial data were obtained from Scammon, McGillivray, and Cook, *American Votes 24: A Handbook of Contemporary American Election Statistics* and Beyle "2002 Gubernatorial Elections" and "2004 Gubernatorial Elections."

3 American Bar Association Commission on the 21st Century Judiciary, *Justice in Jeopardy*, p. 19.
4 Dubois, *From Ballot to Bench*, p. 64.
5 Ibid., p. 5.
6 American Bar Association Commission on the 21st Century Judiciary, *Justice in Jeopardy*, p. 129.
7 Citizens for Independent Courts Task Force on Selecting State Court Judges, 2000. "Choosing Justice: Reforming the Selection of State Judges." In *Uncertain Justice: Politics in America's Courts.* New York: Century Foundation.
8 Rottman and Schotland, "What Makes Judicial Elections Unique?," pp. 1371–1372.
9 For example, Lawrence Baum, 1987. "Explaining the Vote in Judicial Elections: The 1984 Ohio Supreme Court Elections." *Western Political Quarterly* 40 (June): 361–371; Dubois, *From Ballot to Bench*; Hall, "State Supreme Courts in American Democracy"; Hall, "Voluntary Retirements from State Supreme Courts"; and Lovrich and Sheldon, "Voters in Contested, Nonpartisan Judicial Elections."
10 For example, Dubois, *From Ballot to Bench*; Hall, "State Supreme Courts in American Democracy"; Hall, "Voluntary Retirements from State Supreme Courts"; Hall, "Voting in State Supreme Court Elections"; and Klein and Baum, "Ballot Information and Voting Decisions in Judicial Elections."
11 Emily Van Dunk, 1997. "Challenger Quality in State Legislative Elections." *Political Research Quarterly* 50 (September): 793–807.
12 For example, Alan I. Abramowitz, 1991. "Incumbency, Campaign Spending, and the Decline of Competition in U. S. House Elections." *Journal of Politics* 53 (February): 34–56; Jacobson, *Money in Congressional Elections*, in Judicial Elections." *Political Research Quarterly* 54 (December): 709–728; Jonathan S Krasno, 1994. *Challengers, Competition, and Reelection: Comparing Senate and House Elections.* New Haven, CT: Yale University Press; and Lyn Ragsdale, 1981. "Incumbent Popularity, Challenger Invisibility, and Congressional Voters." *Legislative Studies Quarterly* 6 (May): 201–218.
13 For example, Michael Berkman and James Eisenstein, 1999. "State Legislators as Congressional Candidates: The Effects of Prior Experience on Legislative Recruitment and Fundraising." *Political Research Quarterly* 52 (September): 487–598; Jon R. Bond, Cary Covington, and Richard Fleisher. 1985. "Explaining Challenger Quality in Congressional Elections." *Journal of Politics* 47 (May): 510–529; Jacobson, *The Politics of Congressional Elections*; and Stone, Maisel, and Maestas, "Quality Counts."
14 Abramowitz, "Incumbency, Campaign Spending, and the Decline of Competition in U.S. House Elections"; Gary C. Jacobson, 1989. "Strategic Politicians and the Dynamics of U.S. House Elections, 1946–86." *American Political Science Review* 83 (September): 773–793; Lublin, "Quality not Quantity: Strategic Politicians in U.S. Senate Elections, 1952–1990"; Stephen P. Nicholson and Gary M. Segura, 1999. "Midterm Elections and Divided Government: An Information-Driven Theory of Electoral Volatility." *Political Research Quarterly* 52 (September): 609–629; and Squire, "Challengers in U.S. Senate Elections."
15 For example, Alan I. Abramowitz, 1988. "Explaining Senate Election Outcomes." *American Political Science Review* 82 (June): 385–403.
16 For example, Bond, Covington, and Fleisher, "Explaining Challenger Quality

in Congressional Elections"; Jonathan S. Krasno and Donald Philip Green. 1988. "Preempting Quality Challengers in House Elections." *Journal of Politics* 50 (November): 920–936; David I. Lublin, 1994. "Quality, Not Quantity: Strategic Politicians in U.S. Senate Elections, 1952–1990." *Journal of Politics* 56 (February): 228–241; and Squire, "Challengers in U.S. Senate Elections."

17 Bond, Covington, and Fleisher, "Explaining Challenger Quality in Congressional Elections."

18 For example, James Garand, 1991. "Electoral Marginality in State Legislative Elections, 1968–86." *Legislative Studies Quarterly* 16 (February): 7–28; Thomas M. Holbrook and Charles M. Tidmarch, 1991. "Sophomore Surge in State Legislative Elections, 1968–86." *Legislative Studies Quarterly* 16 (February): 49–63; and Malcolm E. Jewell and David A. Breaux, 1988. "The Effect of Incumbency on State Legislative Elections." *Legislative Studies Quarterly* 13 (November): 495–514.

19 Van Dunk, "Challenger Quality in State Legislative Elections."

20 For example, Lawrence Baum, 1983. "The Electoral Fates of Incumbent Judges in the Ohio Court of Common Pleas." *Judicature* 66 (April): 42–50; Baum, "Explaining the Vote in Judicial Elections"; Bonneau, "Patterns of Campaign Spending and Electoral Competition in State Supreme Court Elections"; Bonneau, "Electoral Verdicts"; Bonneau, "Campaign Fundraising in State Supreme Court Elections"; Bonneau, "The Effects of Campaign Sending in State Supreme Court Elections"; Bonneau and Hall, "Predicting Challengers in State Supreme Court Elections"; Dubois, *From Ballot to Bench*, Hall, "State Supreme Courts in American Democracy"; Hall, "Voluntary Retirements from State Supreme Courts"; Hall, "Voting in State Supreme Court Elections"; William K. Hall and Larry T. Aspin, 1987b. "What Twenty Years of Judicial Retention Elections Have Told Us." *Judicature* 70 (April–May): 340–347; and Lovrich and Sheldon, "Voters in Contested, Nonpartisan Judicial Elections."

21 Dubois, "Voting Cues in Nonpartisan Trial Court Elections."

22 Klein and Baum, "Ballot Information and Voting Decisions in Judicial Elections."

23 Currently, thirty states require appellate court judges to be members of the state bar for five to ten years, twelve states require bar membership without specifying a minimum time, four states require judges to be "learned in the law" without additional clarification, and four states have no qualifications related to any of the factors just listed. See Council of State Governments, 1999. *Book of the States.* Lexington, KY: Council of State Governments.

24 For example, Champagne, "The Politics of Judicial Selection"; Phillips, "When Money Talks, the Judiciary Must Balk"; and Geyh, "Why Judicial Elections Stink."

25 Dubois, *From Ballot to Bench*, p. 28.

26 Glaberson, "State Chief Justices Plan to Meet on Judicial Candidates' Abuses," p. 1.

27 American Bar Association, 1998. *Report and Recommendations of the Task Force on Lawyers' Political Contributions: Part II.* Chicago, IL: American Bar Association; Mark Hansen, 1998. "A Run for the Bench." *ABA Journal* 84 (October): 68–72; Glaberson, "Fierce Campaigns Signal a New Era for State Courts"; and Glaberson, "State Chief Justices Plan to Meet on Judicial Candidates' Abuses."

28 Dawson Bell, 2001. "Engler to Ask for Appointed High Court." *Detroit Free Press*, January 27; Brian Dickerson, 2001. "Belatedly, Engler Seeks Court Reform." *Detroit Free Press*, January 29; and *Pittsburgh Post-Gazette*, 2001. "Editorial: Ridge the Reformer." *Pittsburgh Post-Gazette*, February 14.

29 For example, Jeffrey S. Banks and D. Roderick Kiewiet, 1989. "Explaining Patterns of Candidate Competition in Congressional Elections." *American Journal of Political Science* 33 (November): 997–1015; Green and Krasno, "Salvation for the Spendthrift Incumbent"; Gary C. Jacobson, 1978. "The Effects of Campaign Spending in Congressional Elections." *American Political Science Review* 72 (June): 469–491; Jacobson, *Money in Congressional Elections*; Jacobson, "Strategic Politicians and the Dynamics of U.S. House Elections, 1946–86"; Gary C. Jacobson, 1990. "The Effects of Campaign Spending in House Elections: New Evidence for Old Arguments." *American Journal of Political Science* 34 (May): 334–362; and Peverill Squire, 1995. "Candidates, Money, and Voters—Assessing the State of Congressional Elections Research." *Political Research Quarterly* 48 (December): 891–917.

30 For example, William E. Cassie and David A. Breaux, 1998. "Expenditures and Election Results." In *Campaign Finance in State Legislative Elections*, ed. by Joel A. Thompson and Gary F. Moncrief. Washington, DC: CQ Press; Gierzynski and Breaux, "Money and Votes in State Legislative Elections"; and Micheal W. Giles and Anita Pritchard, 1985. "Campaign Expenditures and Legislative Elections in Florida." *Legislative Studies Quarterly* 10 (February): 71–88.

31 Lonna Rae Atkeson and Randall W. Partin, 1995. "Economic and Referendum Voting: A Comparison of Gubernatorial and Senate Elections." *American Political Science Review* 89 (March): 99–107; Kedron Bardwell, 2002, "Money and Challenger Emergence in Gubernatorial Primaries." *Political Research Quarterly* 55 (September): 653–667; Thomas M. Carsey and Gerald R. Wright, 1998. "State and National Forces in Gubernatorial and Senate Elections." *American Journal of Political Science* 42 (July): 994–1002; Partin, "Assessing the Impact of Campaign Spending in Governors' Races"; and Craig J. Svoboda, 1995. "Retrospective Voting in Gubernatorial Elections: 1982 and 1986." *Political Research Quarterly* 48 (March): 135–150.

32 For example, Bonneau, "The Effects of Campaign Spending in State Supreme Court Elections"; Hall, "State Supreme Courts in American Democracy"; Hall, "Voluntary Retirements from State Supreme Courts"; Hall, "Competition as Accountability in State Supreme Court Elections"; and Hall and Bonneau, "Does Quality Matter?"

33 For example, Schotland, "Elective Judges' Campaign Financing"; and Geyh, "Why Judicial Elections Stink."

34 For example Michael R. Dimino, 2004. "The Futile Quest for a System of Judicial 'Merit' Selection." *Albany Law Review* 67 (Spring): 803–819; Michael R. Dimino, Sr, 2005. "The Worst Way of Selecting Judges—Except All the Others that Have Been Tried." *Northern Kentucky Law Review* 32 (2): 267–304; and Hall, "The Controversy over Electing Judges and Advocacy in Political Science."

35 For example, Anthony Champagne and Judith Haydel, 1993. *Judicial Reform in the States*. Lanham, MD: University Press of America; Geyh, "Why Judicial Elections Stink"; Dimino, "The Worst Way of Selecting Judges"; and Matthew J. Streb and Brian Frederick, 2007. "Judicial Reform and the Future of Judicial Elections." In *Running for Judge: The Rising Political, Financial, and*

Legal Stakes of Judicial Elections, ed. by Matthew Streb. New York: New York University Press.

36 Jacobson, *Money in Congressional Elections*; Aspin and Hall, "The Friends and Neighbors Effect in Judicial Retention Elections"; and Alvarez, *Information and Elections*.

37 For example, Jacobson, *Money in Congressional Elections*; Thielemann, "Local Advantage in Campaign Financing"; and Arrington, "When Money Doesn't Matter."

38 Hall, "Competition as Accountability in State Supreme Court Elections," p. 166.

39 Hall, "State Supreme Courts in American Democracy"; Hall, "Voting in State Supreme Court Elections"; and Bonneau "Electoral Verdicts."

40 Hall, "Voting in State Supreme Court Elections"; and Hall and Bonneau, "Mobilizing Interest."

41 Hall, "State Supreme Courts in American Democracy;" and Hall, "Voluntary Retirements from State Supreme Courts."

42 The results of this portion of the chapter are taken from one of our earlier works on judicial elections. We did not extend the data to 2004 for the purposes of this book. However, time should not affect the robustness of the conclusions, which are quite consistent with the results in chapters 2 and 3.

43 Bonneau and Hall, "Predicting Challengers in State Supreme Court Elections."

44 Hall, "State Supreme Courts in American Democracy."

45 For example, Abramowitz, "Explaining Senate Election Outcomes"; Abramowitz, "Incumbency, Campaign Spending, and the Decline of Competition in U.S. House Elections"; Bond, Covington, and Fleisher, "Explaining Challenger Quality in Congressional Elections"; Jacobson, *Money in Congressional Elections*; Jacobson, "Strategic Politicians and the Dynamics of U.S. House Elections"; Jacobson, *The Politics of Congressional Elections*; Krasno, *Challengers, Competition and Reelection*; Krasno and Green, "Preempting Quality Challengers in House Elections"; Nicholson and Segura, "Midterm Elections and Divided Government"; Ragsdale, "Incumbent Popularity, Challenger, Invisibility, and Congressional Voters"; Squire, "Challengers in U.S. Senate Elections"; and Van Dunk, "Challenger Quality in State Legislative Elections."

46 For example, Jacobson, "Strategic Politicians and the Dynamics of U.S. House Elections"; and Van Dunk, "Challenger Quality in State Legislative Elections."

47 For example, Gierzynski and Breaux, "Money and Votes in State Legislative Elections"; Gierzynski and Breaux, "Legislative Elections and the Importance of Money"; Green and Krasno, "Salvation for the Spendthrift Incumbent"; Jacobson, *Money in Congressional Elections*; and Jacobson, "The Effects of Campaign Spending in House Elections."

48 As an alternative to spending differences, we estimated the models using separate measures of incumbent and challenger spending. In the model reported in Table 4.9, incumbent spending produces a coefficient of 1.477, significant at .046, and challenger spending has a coefficient of –1.577, significant at .001. Similarly, in the model in Table 4.10, incumbent spending produces a coefficient of 1.451, significant at .068, and challenger spending a coefficient of –1.616, significant at .001. Moreover, the substitution of individual spending for differences in spending does not alter any other substantive result.

Thus, the findings about the effects of spending appear to be robust with regard to measurement and are generally consistent with legislative research.

49 For example, Jacobson, *Money in Congressional Elections.*

50 Atkeson and Partin, "Economic and Referendum Voting"; Carsey and Wright, "State and National Forces in Gubernatorial and Senate Elections"; Leyden and Borrelli, "The Effect of State Economic Conditions on Gubernatorial Elections"; Richard G. Niemi, Harold W. Stanley, and Ronald J. Vogel, 1995. "State Economies and State Taxes: Do Voters Hold Governors Accountable?" *American Journal of Political Science* 39 (November): 936–957; and Svoboda, "Retrospective Voting in Gubernatorial Elections."

51 Hall, "State Supreme Courts in American Democracy."

52 Bonneau and Hall, "Predicting Challengers in State Supreme Court Elections."

53 Dubois, *From Ballot to Bench;* and Hall, "State Supreme Courts in American Democracy."

54 Heckman, "Sample Selection Bias as a Specification Error."

55 Bonneau and Hall, "Predicting Challengers in State Supreme Court Elections."

56 Since the second stage of our model examines the effects of different types of quality challengers, one might argue that we should use the factors predicting the likelihood of *quality* challengers, versus any type of challenger, in stage one. However, Bonneau and Hall found that the *same* factors predict both situations: whether an incumbent is likely to be challenged at all and whether quality challengers emerge. See Bonneau and Hall, "Predicting Challengers in State Supreme Court Elections."

57 Bonneau and Hall, "Predicting Challengers in State Supreme Court Elections."

58 Hall, "State Supreme Courts in American Democracy."

59 Ibid.

5 Evaluating Recent Reforms and Proposals

1 Deborah Goldberg, 2002. *Public Funding of Judicial Elections: Financing Campaigns for Fair and Independent Courts.* New York: Brennan Center for Justice.

2 Geyh, "Why Judicial Elections Stink."

3 Lawrence H. Averill, Jr., 1995. "Observations on the Wyoming Experience with Merit Selection of Judges: A Model for Arkansas." *University of Arkansas–Little Rock Law Journal* 17 (Winter): 281–342.

4 American Bar Association, *Justice in Jeopardy.*

5 Charles Gardner Geyh, 2001. "Publicly Funded Judicial Elections: An Overview." *Loyola of Los Angeles Law Review* 34 (June): 1467–1487; and Goldberg, *Public Funding of Judicial Elections.*

6 Owen G. Abbe and Paul S. Herrnson, 2003. "Public Financing of Judicial Elections? A Judicious Perspective on the ABA's Proposal for Campaign Finance Reform." *Polity* 35 (July), p. 547.

7 Ibid.

8 For example, see Goldberg, *Public Funding of Judicial Elections.*

9 Geyh, "Publicly Funded Judicial Elections," p. 1480.

10 For district court judges, this change took effect in the 2002 elections. See

American Judicature Society, 2008c. *Judicial Selection in the States, Minnesota.* http://www.ajs.org/js/MN.htm

11 Bend, "North Carolina's Public Financing of Judicial Campaigns."

12 Ibid.

13 Ibid.

14 Ibid.

15 Ibid.

16 The survey was conducted by American Viewpoint and has a margin of error of ± 4.0 percent.

17 Unfortunately, the survey does not appear to differentiate between different levels of courts. It would be interesting to know if there were any significant differences in this figure depending on the level of court.

18 For example, Goldberg, *Public Funding of Judicial Elections.*

19 Democracy North Carolina, 2006. "A Profile of the Judicial Public Financing Program, 2004–06." http://www.democracy-nc.org/nc/judicialcampaignreform/impact06–06.pdf

20 North Carolina Center for Voter Education, 2008. "How the Public Campaign Fund has Reduced the Role of Private Money in Elections for the N.C. Supreme Court." http://www.ncjudges.org/jcra/graphic_contributions.html

21 In constant (2002) dollars, this is just over $1.1 million.

22 Bend, "North Carolina's Public Financing of Judicial Campaigns."

23 Hall, "Voting in State Supreme Court Elections."

24 Bend, "North Carolina's Public Financing of Judicial Campaigns."

25 Ibid.

26 Ibid.

27 The amendment also reorganized and consolidated the jurisdiction of lower courts. More significantly, the Amendment permits the legislature to refer the issue of merit selection of appellate judges to the voters at any future general election, thereby making it easier for such a change to occur.

28 American Judicature Society, 2008b. *Judicial Selection in the States, Arkansas.* http://www.ajs.org/js/AR.htm

29 Averill, "Observations on the Wyoming Experience with Merit Selection of Judges," p. 322.

30 Bonneau, "The Dynamics of Campaign Spending in State Supreme Court Elections."

31 Bonneau, "Patterns of Campaign Spending and Electoral Competition in State Supreme Court Elections."

32 Hall and Bonneau, "Mobilizing Interest."

33 George W. Soule, 2008. "The Threats of Partisanship to Minnesota's Judicial Elections." *William Mitchell Law Review* 34 (2): 701–728.

34 This may be in part because Minnesota denotes on the ballot which candidate is the incumbent. Because many judges retire before the end of their terms (thereby allowing the governor to appoint their replacement), most races involve an incumbent—even if not an incumbent who has previously won an election.

35 Bonneau, "The Dynamics of Campaign Spending in State Supreme Court Elections."

36 Soule, "The Threats of Partisanship to Minnesota's Judicial Elections."

37 Currently, the governor makes *ad interim* appointments without formal

constraint. However, although there is no mandated consultative process, the governor in practice uses an informal merit process to select candidates. Making this a requirement is an important component of the Quie Commission's proposed reforms. See American Judicature Society, 2008c. *Judicial Selection in the States, Minnesota.*

38 This provision was deleted from the reform bill considered by the Minnesota Legislature. Thus, although the Quie Commission recommended this, it is very unlikely to be part of any enacted bill.

39 Justice at Stake, 2008. *Minnesota Public Opinion Poll on Judicial Selection.* http://www.gavelgrab.org/wpcontent/resources/polls/MinnesotaJusticeatStakeSurvey.pdf. Interestingly, 85 percent report that they would not support a system that removed the electoral component of the Missouri Plan. A key element to the public's support seems to be the inclusion of retention elections.

40 Although the Bar still prefers a lifetime appointment system, it currently supports the reform bill (a slightly modified version of the Quie Commission proposal) introduced in the legislature.

41 American Judicature Society, 2008d. *Judicial Selection in the States, New Mexico.* http://www.ajs.org/js/NM.htm

42 Ibid.

43 Previously, only candidates for the Public Regulation Commission were eligible for public financing.

44 For example, Bonneau, "Patterns of Campaign Spending and Electoral Competition in State Supreme Court Elections."

45 Bonneau, "The Dynamics of Campaign Spending in State Supreme Court Elections."

46 American Judicature Society, 2008e. *Judicial Selection in the States, Wisconsin.* http://www.ajs.org/js/WI.htm

47 Jason J. Czarnezki, 2005. "A Call for Change: Improving Judicial Selection Methods." *Marquette Law Review* 89 (Fall): 169–178.

48 Bonneau, "The Dynamics of Campaign Spending in State Supreme Court Elections."

49 American Judicature Society, *Judicial Selection in the States, Wisconsin.*

50 Common Cause of Wisconsin, 2008. "'Impartial Justice' Measure Passes Senate 23–10." http://www.commoncause.org/site/pp.asp?c=dkLNK1MQIwG&b=1776959

51 *Sheboygan Press Gazette*, "Heed High Court's Advice on Financing Judicial Elections."

52 Additionally, 77 percent agreed that the governor and legislature needed to address this issue before the next election, but 76 percent agreed that there were more important priorities for spending tax dollars (such as education and healthcare) and that the "legislature should not be spending this money to fund political campaigns for judges." Try as we might, we cannot reconcile this glaring inconsistency. Voters in Wisconsin, like in Minnesota, seem to be of two minds on this issue. Alternatively, the survey may be flawed.

53 Averill, "Observations on the Wyoming Experience with Merit Selection of Judges."

54 Hall, "State Supreme Courts in American Democracy"; and Hall, "Voting in State Supreme Court Elections."

6 Debunking Popular Myths of Judicial Reform

1 Hall, "State Supreme Courts in American Democracy," p. 316.
2 Dubois, *From Ballot to Bench*, p. 36.
3 National Center for State Courts, *Call to Action*, p. 38.
4 Hall, "Voting in State Supreme Court Elections," p. 1151.
5 Hall, "Voting in State Supreme Court Elections."
6 American Bar Association, *Justice in Jeopardy*, p. 87.
7 Glick and Emmert, "Selection Systems and Judicial Characteristics."
8 Ibid.
9 Ibid.
10 Mark S. Hurwitz and Drew Noble Lanier, 2003. "Explaining Judicial Diversity: The Differential Ability of Women and Minorities to Attain Seats on State Supreme and Appellate Courts." *State Politics and Policy Quarterly* 3 (Winter): 329–352.
11 Glick and Emmert, "Selection Systems and Judicial Characteristics."
12 Choi, Gulati, and Posner, "Professionals or Politicians."
13 Ibid, p. 17.
14 Choi, Gulati, and Posner, "Professionals or Politicians."
15 Ibid, p. 39.
16 Ibid, p. 27.
17 Ibid, p. 15.
18 For example, Segal and Spaeth, *The Supreme Court and the Attitudinal Model Revisited*.
19 See Hall, "The Controversy over Electing Judges and Advocacy in Political Science"; and Melinda Gann Hall, 2009b. "On the Cataclysm of Judicial Elections and Other Popular Anti-Democratic Myths." Paper presented at the What's Law Got to Do With It? Conference at the Indiana University School of Law, March 26–27, for a more detailed discussion of the lack of conceptual clarity in contemporary discussions of judicial independence and electoral accountability and their relationship to the rule of law and judicial impartiality.

References

Abbe, Owen G. and Paul S. Herrnson. 2003. "Public Financing of Judicial Elections? A Judicious Perspective on the ABA's Proposal for Campaign Finance Reform." *Polity* 35 (July): 535–554.

Abramowitz, Alan I. 1988. "Explaining Senate Election Outcomes." *American Political Science Review* 82 (June): 385–403.

Abramowitz, Alan I. 1991. "Incumbency, Campaign Spending, and the Decline of Competition in U. S. House Elections." *Journal of Politics* 53 (February): 34–56.

Abramson, Paul R., John H. Aldrich, and David W. Rohde. 2007. *Change and Continuity in the 2004 and 2006 Elections.* Washington, DC: CQ Press.

Adamany, David and Philip Dubois. 1976. "Electing State Judges." *Wisconsin Law Review* 1976 (3): 731–779.

Alvarez, R. Michael. 1997. *Information and Elections.* Ann Arbor: University of Michigan Press.

American Bar Association. 1998. *Report and Recommendations of the Task Force on Lawyers' Political Contributions: Part II.* Chicago, IL: American Bar Association.

American Bar Association Commission on the 21st Century Judiciary. 2003. *Justice in Jeopardy.* Chicago: American Bar Association.

American Judicature Society. 2008a. *Judicial Selection in the States, North Carolina.* http://www.ajs.org/js/NC.htm

American Judicature Society. 2008b. *Judicial Selection in the States, Arkansas.* http://www.ajs.org/js/AR.htm

American Judicature Society. 2008c. *Judicial Selection in the States, Minnesota.* http://www.ajs.org/js/MN.htm

American Judicature Society. 2008d. *Judicial Selection in the States, New Mexico.* http://www.ajs.org/js/NM.htm

American Judicature Society. 2008e. *Judicial Selection in the States, Wisconsin.* http://www.ajs.org/js/WI.htm

Arrington, Theodore S. 1996. "When Money Doesn't Matter: Campaign Spending for Minor Statewide Judicial and Executive Offices in North Carolina." *Justice System Journal* 18 (3): 257–266.

Aspin, Larry T. and William K. Hall. 1987. "The Friends and Neighbors Effect in Judicial Retention Elections." *Western Political Quarterly* 40 (December): 703–715.

Aspin, Larry T. and William K. Hall. 1989. "Friends and Neighbors Voting in Judicial Retention Elections: A Research Note Comparing Trial and Appellate Court Elections." *Western Political Quarterly* 42 (December): 587–595.

Atkeson, Lonna Rae and Randall W. Partin. 1995. "Economic and Referendum Voting: A Comparison of Gubernatorial and Senate Elections." *American Political Science Review* 89 (March): 99–107.

Averill, Lawrence H, Jr. 1995. "Observations on the Wyoming Experience with Merit Selection of Judges: A Model for Arkansas." *University of Arkansas–Little Rock Law Journal* 17 (Winter): 281–342.

Banks, Jeffrey S. and D. Roderick Kiewiet. 1989. "Explaining Patterns of Candidate Competition in Congressional Elections." *American Journal of Political Science* 33 (November): 997–1015.

Bardwell, Kedron. 2002. "Money and Challenger Emergence in Gubernatorial Primaries." *Political Research Quarterly* 55 (September): 653–667.

Baum, Lawrence. 1983. "The Electoral Fates of Incumbent Judges in the Ohio Court of Common Pleas." *Judicature* 66 (April): 42–50.

Baum, Lawrence. 1987. "Explaining the Vote in Judicial Elections: The 1984 Ohio Supreme Court Elections." *Western Political Quarterly* 40 (June): 361–371.

Beechen, Paul D. 1974. "Can Judicial Elections Express the People's Choice?" *Judicature* 57 (January): 242–246.

Bell, Dawson. 2001. "Engler to Ask for Appointed High Court." *Detroit Free Press*, January 27.

Bend, Doug. 2005. "North Carolina's Public Financing of Judicial Campaigns: A Preliminary Analysis." *Georgetown Journal of Legal Ethics* 18 (Summer): 597–609.

Benesh, Sara. 2006. "Understanding Public Confidence in American Courts." *Journal of Politics* 68 (August): 697–707.

Berkman, Michael and James Eisenstein. 1999. "State Legislators as Congressional Candidates: The Effects of Prior Experience on Legislative Recruitment and Fundraising." *Political Research Quarterly* 52 (September): 487–598.

Beyle, Thad. 2003. "2002 Gubernatorial Elections." *Spectrum: The Journal of State Government* 76 (Winter): 12–14.

Beyle, Thad. 2005. "2004 Gubernatorial Elections." *Spectrum: The Journal of State Government* 78 (Winter): 12–14, 30.

Bond, Jon R., Cary Covington, and Richard Fleisher. 1985. "Explaining Challenger Quality in Congressional Elections." *Journal of Politics* 47 (May): 510–529.

Bonneau, Chris W. 2001. "The Composition of State Supreme Courts, 2000." *Judicature* 85 (July–August): 26–31.

Bonneau, Chris W. 2004. "Patterns of Campaign Spending and Electoral Competition in State Supreme Court Elections." *Justice System Journal* 25 (1): 21–38.

Bonneau, Chris W. 2005a. "What Price Justice(s)? Understanding Campaign Spending in State Supreme Court Elections." *State Politics and Policy Quarterly* 5 (Summer): 107–125.

Bonneau, Chris W. 2005b. "Electoral Verdicts: Incumbent Defeats in State Supreme Court Elections." *American Politics Research* 33 (November): 818–841.

Bonneau, Chris W. 2007a. "Campaign Fundraising in State Supreme Court Elections." *Social Science Quarterly* 88 (March): 68–85.

Bonneau, Chris W. 2007b. "The Dynamics of Campaign Spending in State Supreme Court Elections." In *Running for Judge: The Rising Political, Financial, and Legal Stakes of Judicial Elections*, ed. by Matthew Streb. New York: New York University Press.

Bonneau, Chris W. 2007c. "The Effects of Campaign Spending in State Supreme Court Elections." *Political Research Quarterly* 60 (September): 489–499.

Bonneau, Chris W. and Melinda Gann Hall. 2003. "Predicting Challengers in State Supreme Court Elections: Context and the Politics of Institutional Design." *Political Research Quarterly* 56 (September): 337–349.

Bowler, Shaun, Todd Donovan, and Trudi Happ. 1992. "Ballot Propositions and Information Costs: Direct Democracy and the Fatigued Voter." *Western Political Quarterly* 45 (June): 559–568.

Brace, Paul and Melinda Gann Hall. 1993. "Integrated Models of Judicial Dissent." *Journal of Politics* 55 (November): 914–935.

Brace, Paul and Melinda Gann Hall. 1995. "Studying Courts Comparatively: The View from the American States." *Political Research Quarterly* 48 (March): 5–29.

Brace, Paul and Melinda Gann Hall. 1997. "The Interplay of Preferences, Case Facts, Context, and Structure in the Politics of Judicial Choice." *Journal of Politics* 59 (November): 1206–1231.

Brace, Paul and Melinda Gann Hall. 2001. " 'Haves' Versus 'Have Nots' in State Supreme Courts: Allocating Docket Space and Wins in Power Asymmetric Cases." *Law and Society Review* 35 (2): 393–417.

Brace, Paul, Melinda Gann Hall, and Laura Langer. 1999. "Judicial Choice and the Politics of Abortion: Institutions, Context, and the Autonomy of Courts." *Albany Law Review* 62 (April): 1265–1303.

Brace, Paul, Melinda Gann Hall, and Laura Langer. 2001. "Placing State Supreme Courts in State Politics." *State Politics and Policy Quarterly* 1 (Spring): 81–108.

Bullock, Charles S., III, and Richard E. Dunn. 1996. "Election Roll-Off: A Test of Three Explanations." *Urban Affairs Review* 32 (September): 71–86.

Burbank, Stephen B. and Barry Friedman. 2002. "Reconsidering Judicial Independence." In *Judicial Independence at the Crossroads: An Interdisciplinary Approach*, ed. by Stephen B. Burbank and Barry Friedman. Thousand Oaks, CA: Sage.

Campbell, Linda. 2002. "An Absurd System Gets Even Worse." *Fort Worth Star-Telegram*, November 21.

Cann, Damon M. 2002. "Campaign Contributions and Judicial Behavior." *American Review of Politics* 23 (Fall): 261–274.

Cann, Damon M. 2007. "Justice for Sale? Campaign Contributions and Judicial Decisionmaking." *State Politics and Policy Quarterly* 7 (Fall): 281–297.

Cann, Damon M. and Jeff Yates. 2008. "Homegrown Institutional Legitimacy: Assessing Citizens' Diffuse Support for State Courts." *American Politics Research* 36 (March): 297–329.

Carsey, Thomas M., and Gerald R. Wright. 1998. "State and National Forces in Gubernatorial and Senate Elections." *American Journal of Political Science* 42 (July): 994–1002.

Cassie, William E. and David A. Breaux. 1998. "Expenditures and Election Results." In *Campaign Finance in State Legislative Elections*, ed. by Joel A. Thompson and Gary F. Moncrief. Washington, DC: CQ Press.

Champagne, Anthony. 2003. "The Politics of Judicial Selection." *Policy Studies Journal* 31 (August): 413–419.

Champagne, Anthony and Judith Haydel. 1993. *Judicial Reform in the States.* Lanham, MD: University Press of America.

Champagne, Anthony and Greg Thielemann. 1991. "Awareness of Trial Court Judges." *Judicature* 74 (February–March): 271–276.

Choi, Stephen J., G. Mitu Gulati, and Eric A. Posner. 2007. "Professionals or Politicians: The Uncertain Case for an Elected Rather than Appointed Judiciary." Unpublished manuscript. August 2007.

Citizens Commission for the Preservation of an Independent Judiciary. 2007. *Final Report and Recommendations.* http://www.keepmnjusticeimpartial.org/FinalReportAndRecommendation.pdf

Citizens for Independent Courts Task Force on Selecting State Court Judges. 2000. "Choosing Justice: Reforming the Selection of State Judges." In *Uncertain Justice: Politics in America's Courts.* New York: Century Foundation.

Clarke, Harold D., Frank B. Feigert, Barry J. Seldon, and Marianne C. Stewart. 1999. "More Time with My Money: Leaving the House and Going Home in 1992 and 1994." *Political Research Quarterly* 52 (March): 67–85.

Coleman, John J. and Paul F. Manna. 2000. "Congressional Campaign Spending and the Quality of Democracy." *Journal of Politics* 62 (August): 757–789.

Common Cause of Wisconsin. 2008. "'Impartial Justice' Measure Passes Senate 23–10." http://www.commoncause.org/site/pp.asp?c=dkLNK1MQIwG&b=1776959

Council of State Governments. 1999. *Book of the States.* Lexington, KY: Council of State Governments.

Council of State Governments. 2006. *The Book of the States.* Lexington, KY: Council of State Governments.

Czarnezki, Jason J. 2005. "A Call for Change: Improving Judicial Selection Methods." *Marquette Law Review* 89 (Fall): 169–178.

Davidoff, Judith. 2007. "Justices Endorse Public Funding for Supreme Court Races." *Capital Times*, December 10.

Democracy North Carolina. 2006. "A Profile of the Judicial Public Financing Program, 2004–06." http://www.democracy-nc.org/nc/judicialcampaignreform/impact06–06.pdf

Dickerson, Brian. 2001. "Belatedly, Engler Seeks Court Reform." *Detroit Free Press*, January 29.

Dimino, Michael R. 2004. "The Futile Quest for a System of Judicial 'Merit' Selection." *Albany Law Review* 67 (Spring): 803–819.

Dimino, Michael R., Sr. 2005. "The Worst Way of Selecting Judges—Except All the Others that Have Been Tried." *Northern Kentucky Law Review* 32 (2): 267–304.

Dubois, Philip L. 1979. "The Significance of Voting Cues in State Supreme Court Elections." *Law and Society Review* 13 (Spring): 757–779.

Dubois, Philip L. 1980. *From Ballot to Bench: Judicial Elections and the Quest for Accountability.* Austin, TX: University of Texas Press.

Dubois, Philip L. 1984. "Voting Cues in Nonpartisan Trial Court Elections: A Multivariate Assessment." *Law and Society Review* 18 (3): 395–436.

Dubois, Philip L. 1986. "Penny for Your Thoughts? Campaign Spending in

California Trial Court Elections, 1976–1982." *Western Political Quarterly* 39 (June): 265–284.

Friedman, Lawrence M. 1985. *History of American Law.* New York: Simon and Schuster.

Garand, James. 1991. "Electoral Marginality in State Legislative Elections, 1968–86." *Legislative Studies Quarterly* 16 (February): 7–28.

Garand, James C., Kenneth Wink, and Bryan Vincent. 1993. "Changing Meanings of Election Marginality in U.S. House Elections, 1824–1978." *Political Research Quarterly* 46 (March): 27–48.

Gerber, Alan S. and Donald P. Green. 2000. "The Effects of Canvassing, Telephone Calls, and Direct Mail on Voter Turnout: A Field Experiment." *American Political Science Review* 94 (September): 653–663.

Geyh, Charles Gardner. 2001. "Publicly Funded Judicial Elections: An Overview." *Loyola of Los Angeles Law Review* 34 (June): 1467–1487.

Geyh, Charles Gardner. 2003. "Why Judicial Elections Stink." *Ohio State Law Journal* 64 (1): 43–79.

Gibson, James L. 2008. "Challenges to the Impartiality of State Supreme Courts: Legitimacy Theory and 'New-Style' Judicial Campaigns." *American Political Science Review* 102 (February): 59–75.

Gierzynski, Anthony. 1998. "A Framework for the Study of Campaign Finance." In *Campaign Finance in State Legislative Elections*, ed. by Joel A. Thompson and Gary F. Moncrief. Washington, DC: CQ Press.

Gierzynski, Anthony and David A. Breaux. 1991. "Money and Votes in State Legislative Elections." *Legislative Studies Quarterly* 16 (May): 203–217.

Gierzynski, Anthony and David A. Breaux. 1996. "Legislative Elections and the Importance of Money." *Legislative Studies Quarterly* 21 (August): 337–358.

Giles, Micheal W. and Anita Pritchard. 1985. "Campaign Expenditures and Legislative Elections in Florida." *Legislative Studies Quarterly* 10 (February): 71–88.

Glaberson, William. 2000a. "Fierce Campaigns Signal a New Era for State Courts." *New York Times*, June 5, p. A1.

Glaberson, William. 2000b. "State Chief Justices Plan to Meet on Judicial Candidates' Abuses." *New York Times*, September 8, p. A14.

Glick, Henry R. and Craig F. Emmert. 1987. "Selection Systems and Judicial Characteristics: The Recruitment of State Supreme Court Judges." *Judicature* 70 (December–January): 228–235.

Goldberg, Deborah. 2002. *Public Funding of Judicial Elections: Financing Campaigns for Fair and Independent Courts.* New York: Brennan Center for Justice.

Goldberg, Deborah, Sarah Samis, Edwin Bender, and Rachel Weiss. 2005. *The New Politics of Judicial Elections, 2004.* Washington, DC: Justice at Stake Campaign.

Green, Donald Philip and Jonathan S. Krasno. 1988. "Salvation for the Spendthrift Incumbent: Reestimating the Effects of Campaign Spending in House Elections." *American Journal of Political Science* 32 (November): 884–907.

Groseclose, Timothy and Keith Krehbiel. 1994. "Golden Parachutes, Rubber Checks, and Strategic Retirements in the 102nd House." *American Journal of Political Science* 38 (February): 75–99.

Hajnal, Zoltan and Jessica Trounstine. 2005. "Where Turnout Matters: The Consequences of Uneven Turnout in City Politics." *Journal of Politics* 67 (May): 515–535.

Hall, Kermit L. 1984. "Progressive Reform and the Decline of Democratic Accountability: The Popular Election of State Supreme Court Judges, 1850–1920." *American Bar Foundation Research Journal* 9 (Spring): 345–369.

Hall, Melinda Gann. 1987. "Constituent Influence in State Supreme Courts: Conceptual Notes and a Case Study." *Journal of Politics* 49 (November): 1117–1124.

Hall, Melinda Gann. 1992. "Electoral Politics and Strategic Voting in State Supreme Courts." *Journal of Politics* 54 (May): 427–446.

Hall, Melinda Gann. 1995. "Justices as Representatives: Elections and Judicial Politics in the American States." *American Politics Quarterly* 23 (October): 485–503.

Hall, Melinda Gann. 1999. "State Judicial Politics: Rules, Structure, and the Political Game." In *American State and Local Politic: Directions for the Twenty-First Century*, ed. by Ronald E. Weber and Paul Brace. Chatham, NJ: Chatham House.

Hall, Melinda Gann. 2001a. "State Supreme Courts in American Democracy: Probing the Myths of Judicial Reform." *American Political Science Review* 95 (June): 315–330.

Hall, Melinda Gann. 2001b. "Voluntary Retirements from State Supreme Courts: Assessing Democratic Pressures to Relinquish the Bench." *Journal of Politics* 63 (November): 1112–1140.

Hall, Melinda Gann. 2007a. "Competition as Accountability in State Supreme Court Elections." In *Running for Judge: The Rising Political, Financial, and Legal Stakes of Judicial Elections*, ed. by Matthew Streb. New York: New York University Press.

Hall, Melinda Gann. 2007b. "Courts and Judicial Politics in the American States." In *Politics in the American States: A Comparative Analysis*, ed. by Virginia Gray and Russell L. Hanson. Washington, DC: Congressional Quarterly Press.

Hall, Melinda Gann. 2007c. "Voting in State Supreme Court Elections: Competition and Context as Democratic Incentives." *Journal of Politics* 69 (November): 1147–1159.

Hall, Melinda Gann. 2009a. "The Controversy over Electing Judges and Advocacy in Political Science." *Justice System Journal* 30 (3): Forthcoming.

Hall, Melinda Gann. 2009b. "On the Cataclysm of Judicial Elections and Other Popular Anti-Democratic Myths." Paper presented at the What's Law Got to Do With It? Conference at the Indiana University School of Law, March 26-27.

Hall, Melinda Gann and Chris W. Bonneau. 2006. "Does Quality Matter? Challengers in State Supreme Court Elections." *American Journal of Political Science* 50 (January): 20–33.

Hall, Melinda Gann and Chris W. Bonneau. 2008. "Mobilizing Interest: The Effects of Money on Citizen Participation in State Supreme Court Elections." *American Journal of Political Science* 52 (July): 457–470.

Hall, Melinda Gann and Paul Brace. 1989. "Order in the Courts: A Neo-Institutional Approach to Judicial Consensus." *Western Political Quarterly* 42 (September): 391–407.

Hall, Melinda Gann and Paul Brace. 1992. "Toward an Integrated Model of Judicial Voting Behavior." *American Politics Quarterly* 20 (April): 147–168.

Hall, Richard L. and Robert van Houweling. 1995. "Avarice and Ambition in

Congress: Representatives' Decisions to Run or Retire from the U.S. House." *American Political Science Review* 89 (March): 121–136.

Hall, William K. and Larry T. Aspin. 1987a. "The Roll-Off Effect in Judicial Retention Elections." *Social Science Journal* 24 (4): 415–427.

Hall, William K. and Larry T. Aspin. 1987b. "What Twenty Years of Judicial Retention Elections Have Told Us." *Judicature* 70 (April–May): 340–347.

Hampton, David. 2002. "Political and Special-Interest Influence on Judges Worsens." *Jackson Clarion-Ledger*, October 27.

Hansen, Mark. 1998. "A Run for the Bench." *ABA Journal* 84 (October): 68–72.

Heckman, James J. 1979. "Sample Selection Bias as a Specification Error." *Econometrica* 47 (January): 153–162.

Hibbing, John R. and Sara L. Brandes. 1983. "State Population and Electoral Success of U.S. Senators." *American Journal of Political Science* 27 (November): 808–819.

Hill, Kim Quaile and Jan E. Leighley. 1993. "Party Ideology, Organization, and Competitiveness as Mobilizing Forces in Gubernatorial Elections." *American Journal of Political Science* 37 (November): 1158–1178.

Hogan, Robert E. 2000. "The Costs of Representation in State Legislatures: Explaining Variations in Campaign Spending." *Social Science Quarterly* 81 (December): 941–956.

Hogan, Robert E., and Keith E. Hamm. 1998. "Variations in District-Level Campaign Spending in State Legislatures." In *Campaign Finance in State Legislative Elections*, ed. by Joel A. Thompson and Gary F. Moncrief. Washington, DC: CQ Press.

Hojnacki, Marie and Lawrence Baum. 1992. "'New Style' Judicial Campaigns and Voters: Economic Issues and Union Members in Ohio." *Western Political Quarterly* 45 (December): 921–948.

Holbrook, Thomas M. and Charles M. Tidmarch. 1991. "Sophomore Surge in State Legislative Elections, 1968–86." *Legislative Studies Quarterly* 16 (February): 49–63.

Hurwitz, Mark S. and Drew Noble Lanier. 2003. "Explaining Judicial Diversity: The Differential Ability of Women and Minorities to Attain Seats on State Supreme and Appellate Courts." *State Politics and Policy Quarterly* 3 (Winter): 329–352.

Hurwitz, Mark S. and Drew Noble Lanier. 2008. "Diversity in State and Federal Appellate Courts: Change and Continuity Across 20 Years." *Justice System Journal* 29 (1): 47–70.

Jackson, Donald W. and James W. Riddlesperger, Jr. 1991. "Money and Politics in Judicial Elections: The 1988 Election of the Chief Justice of the Texas Supreme Court." *Judicature* 74 (December–January): 184–189.

Jackson, Robert A. 1995. "Clarifying the Relationship between Education and Turnout." *American Politics Quarterly* 23 (July): 279–299.

Jacobson, Gary C. 1978. "The Effects of Campaign Spending in Congressional Elections." *American Political Science Review* 72 (June): 469–491.

Jacobson, Gary C. 1980. *Money in Congressional Elections.* New Haven, CT: Yale University Press.

Jacobson, Gary C. 1989. "Strategic Politicians and the Dynamics of U.S. House

Elections, 1946–86." *American Political Science Review* 83 (September): 773–793.

Jacobson, Gary C. 1990. "The Effects of Campaign Spending in House Elections: New Evidence for Old Arguments." *American Journal of Political Science* 34 (May): 334–362.

Jacobson, Gary C. 1997. *The Politics of Congressional Elections*, 4th edn. New York: Longman.

Jewell, Malcolm E. 1982. *Representation in State Legislatures.* Lexington, KY: University Press of Kentucky.

Jewell, Malcolm E. and David A. Breaux. 1988. "The Effect of Incumbency on State Legislative Elections." *Legislative Studies Quarterly* 13 (November): 495–514.

Justice at Stake. 2008. *Minnesota Public Opinion Poll on Judicial Selection.* http://www.gavelgrab.org/wpcontent/resources/polls/MinnesotaJusticeatStakeSurvey.pdf.

Klein, David and Lawrence Baum. 2001. "Ballot Information and Voting Decisions in Judicial Elections." *Political Research Quarterly* 54 (December): 709–728.

Krasno, Jonathan S. 1994. *Challengers, Competition, and Reelection: Comparing Senate and House Elections.* New Haven, CT: Yale University Press.

Krasno, Jonathan S. and Donald Philip Green. 1988. "Preempting Quality Challengers in House Elections." *Journal of Politics* 50 (November): 920–936.

Kritzer, Herbert M., Paul Brace, and Melinda Gann Hall, and Brent T. Boyea. 2007. "The Business of State Supreme Courts, Revisited." *Journal of Empirical Legal Studies* 4 (July): 427–439.

Langer, Laura. 2002. *Judicial Review in State Supreme Courts: A Comparative Study.* Albany: SUNY Press.

Leyden, Kevin M. and Stephen A. Borrelli. 1995. "The Effect of State Economic Conditions on Gubernatorial Elections: Does Unified Government Make a Difference?" *Political Research Quarterly* 48 (June): 275–290.

Liptak, Adam. 2004. "Judicial Races in Several States Become Partisan Battlegrounds." *New York Times*, October 24.

Lovrich, Nicholas P., Jr. and Charles H. Sheldon. 1983. "Voters in Contested, Nonpartisan Judicial Elections: A Responsible Electorate or a Problematic Public?" *Western Political Quarterly* 36 (June): 241–256.

Lublin, David I. 1994. "Quality, Not Quantity: Strategic Politicians in U.S. Senate Elections, 1952–1990." *Journal of Politics* 56 (February): 228–241.

Magleby, David B. 1984. *Direct Legislation: Voting on Ballot Propositions in the United States.* Baltimore: Johns Hopkins University Press.

Mauro, Tony. 2006. "Chief Justices Sound Alarm on Judicial Elections." *Legal Times*, August 23.

Milton, Sande. 1983. "A Cross-Sectional Analysis of the Roll-Off Vote in New York State, 1948–1974." *Polity* 15 (Summer): 613–629.

Moe, Terry M. 1987. "An Assessment of the Positive Theory of 'Congressional Dominance.'" *Legislative Studies Quarterly* 12 (November): 475–520.

National Center for State Courts. 1999. *How the Public Views the State Courts: A 1999 National Survey.* Williamsburg, VA: National Center for State Courts.

National Center for State Courts. 2002. *Call to Action: Statement of the National Summit on Improving Judicial Selection.* Williamsburg, VA: National Center for State Courts.

Nichols, Stephen M. and Gregory A. Strizek. 1995. "Electronic Voting Machines and Ballot Roll-Off." *American Politics Quarterly* 23 (July): 300–318.

Nicholson, Stephen P. and Gary M. Segura. 1999. "Midterm Elections and Divided Government: An Information-Driven Theory of Electoral Volatility." *Political Research Quarterly* 52 (September): 609–629.

Niemi, Richard G., Harold W. Stanley, and Ronald J. Vogel. 1995. "State Economies and State Taxes: Do Voters Hold Governors Accountable?" *American Journal of Political Science* 39 (November): 936–957.

North Carolina Center for Voter Education. 2008. "How the Public Campaign Fund has Reduced the Role of Private Money in Elections for the N.C. Supreme Court." http://www.ncjudges.org/jcra/graphic_contributions.html

O'Connor, Sandra Day. 2007. "Justice for Sale: How Special-Interest Money Threatens the Integrity of our Courts." *Wall Street Journal*, November 15.

Partin, Randall W. 2002. "Assessing the Impact of Campaign Spending in Governors' Races." *Political Research Quarterly* 55 (March): 213–233.

Phillips, Thomas R. 2002. "When Money Talks, the Judiciary Must Balk." *Washington Post*, April 14, p. B2.

Pittsburgh Post-Gazette. 2001. "Editorial: Ridge the Reformer." *Pittsburgh Post-Gazette*, February 14.

Pritchett, C. Herman. 1941. "Divisions of Opinion among Justices on the U.S. Supreme Court, 1939–1941." *American Political Science Review* 35 (October): 890–898.

Ragsdale, Lyn. 1981. "Incumbent Popularity, Challenger Invisibility, and Congressional Voters." *Legislative Studies Quarterly* 6 (May): 201–218.

Republican Party of Minnesota v. *White*. 2002. 536 *U.S.* 765.

Rohde, David W. and Harold J. Spaeth. 1976. *Supreme Court Decision Making*. San Francisco: W. H. Freeman.

Rottman, David B. and Roy A. Schotland. 2001. "What Makes Judicial Elections Unique?" *Loyola of Los Angeles Law Review* 34 (June): 1369–1373.

Sample, James, Lauren Jones, and Rachel Weiss. 2007. *The New Politics of Judicial Elections 2006*. Washington, DC: Justice at Stake.

Scammon, Richard M., Alice McGillivray, and Rhodes Cook. 2001. *America Votes 24: A Handbook of Contemporary American Election Statistics*. Washington, DC: CQ Press.

Schaffner, Brian F., Matthew Streb, and Gerald Wright. 2001. "Teams without Uniforms: The Nonpartisan Ballot in State and Local Elections." *Political Research Quarterly* 54 (March): 7–30.

Schotland, Roy A. 1985. "Elective Judges' Campaign Financing: Are State Judges' Robes the Emperor's Clothes of American Democracy." *Journal of Law and Politics* 2 (Spring): 57–167.

Schotland, Roy A. 2001. "Financing Judicial Elections, 2000: Change and Challenge." *Law Review of Michigan State University–Detroit College of Law* 2001 (Fall): 849–899.

Segal, Jeffrey A. and Harold J. Spaeth. 2002. *The Supreme Court and the Attitudinal Model Revisited*. New York: Cambridge University Press.

Sheboygan Press Gazette. 2007. "Heed High Court's Advice on Financing Judicial Elections." *Sheboygan Press Gazette*, December 23, p. 5A.

Sheldon, Charles H. and Linda S. Maule. 1997. *Choosing Justice: The Recruitment of State and Federal Judges.* Pullman, WA: Washington State University Press.

Shepsle, Kenneth A. and Barry R. Weingast. 1987. "The Institutional Foundations of Committee Power." *American Political Science Review* 81 (March): 85–104.

Sorauf, Frank J. 1988. *Money in American Elections.* Glenview, IL: Scott, Foresman.

Soule, George W. 2008. "The Threats of Partisanship to Minnesota's Judicial Elections." *William Mitchell Law Review* 34 (2): 701–728.

Spriggs, James F., II, and Paul J. Wahlbeck. 1995. "Calling It Quits: Strategic Retirement on the Federal Courts of Appeals, 1893–1991." *Political Research Quarterly* 48 (September): 573–597.

Squire, Peverill. 1988. "Politics and Personal Factors in the Retirement from the United States Supreme Court." *Political Behavior* 10 (June): 180–190.

Squire, Peverill. 1989. "Challengers in U.S. Senate Elections." *Legislative Studies Quarterly* 14 (November): 531–547.

Squire, Peverill. 1995. "Candidates, Money, and Voters—Assessing the State of Congressional Elections Research." *Political Research Quarterly* 48 (December): 891–917.

Squire, Peverill and John R. Wright. 1990. "Fundraising by Nonincumbent Candidates for the U.S. House of Representatives." *Legislative Studies Quarterly* 15 (February): 89–98.

Stone, Walter J., Sandy Maisel, and Cherie D. Maestas. 2004. "Quality Counts: Extending the Strategic Politician Model of Incumbent Deterrence." *American Journal of Political Science* 48 (July): 479–495.

Streb, Matthew J., ed. 2007. *Running for Judge: The Rising Political, Financial, and Legal Stakes of Judicial Elections.* New York: New York University Press.

Streb, Matthew J. and Brian Frederick. 2007. "Judicial Reform and the Future of Judicial Elections." In *Running for Judge: The Rising Political, Financial, and Legal Stakes of Judicial Elections*, ed. by Matthew Streb. New York: New York University Press.

Streb, Matthew J. and Brian Frederick. 2008. "Paying a Price for a Seat on the Bench: Campaign Spending in Contested Intermediate Appellate Court Elections." *State Politics and Policy Quarterly* 8 (Winter): 410-429.

Svoboda, Craig J. 1995. "Retrospective Voting in Gubernatorial Elections: 1982 and 1986." *Political Research Quarterly* 48 (March): 135–150.

Thielemann, Gregory S. 1993. "Local Advantage in Campaign Financing: Friends, Neighborhoods, and Their Money in Texas Supreme Court Elections." *Journal of Politics* 55 (May): 472–478.

Thomas, Scott J. 1989. "Do Incumbent Campaign Expenditures Matter?" *Journal of Politics* 51 (November): 965–976.

Van Dunk, Emily. 1997. "Challenger Quality in State Legislative Elections." *Political Research Quarterly* 50 (September): 793–807.

Vanderleeuw, James M. and Richard L. Engstrom. 1987. "Race, Referendums, and Roll-Off." *Journal of Politics* 49 (November): 1081–1092.

Waltenburg, Eric N. and Charles S. Lopeman. 2000. "Tort Decisions and Campaign Dollars." *Southeastern Political Review* 28 (2): 241–263.

Wattenberg, Martin P., Ian McAllister, and Anthony Salvanto. 2000. "How Voting is Like Taking an SAT Test: An Analysis of American Voter Rolloff." *American Politics Quarterly* 28 (April): 234–250.

Webster, Benjamin A., Clyde Wilcox, Paul S. Herrnson, Peter L. Francia, John C. Green, and Lynda Powell. 2001. "Competing for Cash: The Individual Financiers of Congressional Elections." In *Playing Hardball: Campaigning for the U.S. Congress*, ed. by Paul S. Herrnson. Upper Saddle River, NJ: Prentice Hall.

Index

A library at your fingertips!

eBooks are electronic versions of printed books. You can store them on your PC/laptop or browse them online.

They have advantages for anyone needing rapid access to a wide variety of published, copyright information.

eBooks can help your research by enabling you to bookmark chapters, annotate text and use instant searches to find specific words or phrases. Several eBook files would fit on even a small laptop or PDA.

NEW: Save money by eSubscribing: cheap, online access to any eBook for as long as you need it.

Annual subscription packages

We now offer special low-cost bulk subscriptions to packages of eBooks in certain subject areas. These are available to libraries or to individuals.

For more information please contact webmaster.ebooks@tandf.co.uk

We're continually developing the eBook concept, so keep up to date by visiting the website.

www.eBookstore.tandf.co.uk